PRAISE FOR *Queen Bees and Wannabes*

"A useful, how-to manual for parents with step-by-step instructions for what to do in the trickiest situations." — *Newsweek*

"A chilling account of the life our girls navigate in their school lunchrooms and hallways." — *Time*

"Wiseman's straightforward humor, sound advice, and practical approach make this a must-read for anyone involved in the lives of teenage girls." — *Publishers Weekly*

"Invaluable to any adult struggling to help a girl get through her teens." — *Booklist*

"Wiseman is a natural teacher and comedian." — *Houston Chronicle*

"Wiseman talks frankly and often humorously about the 'Girl World.'" — *Kansas City Star*

"Upbeat, interesting, and down-to-earth." — *Slate*

"Wise, humorous, life-affirming advice for parents that is utterly respectful of girls. *Queen Bees and Wannabes* is Mapquest for parents of girls, from fifth grade all the way to young adulthood." — PATRICIA HERSCH, author of *A Tribe Apart: A Journey into the Heart of American Adolescence*

"Wiseman gives parents the insight, compassion, and skill needed to guide girls through the rocky terrain of adolescence. This is such an honest and helpful book; we recommend it highly." — SARA SHANDLER, author of the bestselling *Ophelia Speaks*, and NINA SHANDLER, author of *Ophelia's Mom*

"Laced with humor, insight, and practical suggestions, *Queen Bees and Wannabes* is the one volume that's been missing from the growing shelf of girl-centered publications. Wiseman explains the inner workings of teen culture and teaches parents, educators, and peers how to respond." — WHITNEY RANSOME and MEG MILNE MOULTON, executive directors, National Coalition of Girls' Schools

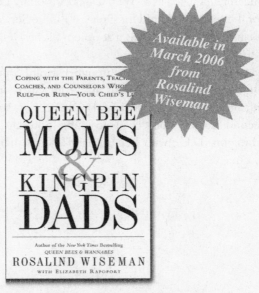

She is an advisory member of the Corporate Alliance to End Partner Violence, and was a liaison to the American Bar Association's Domestic Violence Committee. Ms. Wiseman was a member of the Violence Against Women Act's Subcommittee on Girls and School Violence. She has been recognized as a "Who Cares" Visionary Leader, a national finalist for the Jefferson Award for Greatest Public Service by an Individual 35 Years and Younger, and was a recipient of the Donner Foundation's 21st Century Fellowship.

Ms. Wiseman is certified through Harvard University's "Program for Young Negotiators." She holds an advanced bachelor of arts degree in political science from Occidental College, Los Angeles, California, and a second degree black belt in Tang Soo Do karate. She lives in Washington, D.C., with her husband, James, her son, Elijah, and her dog, Luke.

QUEEN BEES & WANNABES

Helping Your Daughter Survive Cliques,
Gossip, Boyfriends, and Other Realities
of Adolescence

ROSALIND WISEMAN

THREE RIVERS PRESS • NEW YORK

Published by Three Rivers Press, New York, New York.
Member of the Crown Publishing Group, a division of Random House, Inc.
www.randomhouse.com

THREE RIVERS PRESS and the Tugboat design are registered trademarks of Random House, Inc.

Originally published in hardcover by Crown Publishers, a division of Random House, Inc., in 2002.

Printed in the United States of America

Design by Debbie Glasserman

Library of Congress Cataloging-in-Publication Data
Wiseman, Rosalind, 1969–
Queen bees and wannabes: a parent's guide to helping your daughter survive cliques, gossip, boyfriends, and other realities of adolescence / Rosalind Wiseman.—1st ed.
1. Teenage girls.   2. Teenage girls—Psychology.   3. Parent and teenager.
I. Title: Parent's guide to helping your daughter survive
cliques, gossip, boyfriends, and other realities of adolescence.
II. Title.
HQ798.W544   2002
649'.125—dc21   2002002739

ISBN 1-4000-4792-7

20 19 18 17 16 15

First Paperback Edition

*Dedicated to Elijah, Elena, and all my students . . . I expect great things
from each one of you and look forward
to seeing you come into your own.
And
to Zoe—and the woman
you are becoming.*

Acknowledgments

Here it is. Everything I think about everything I've taught for the last ten years. It's all here for everyone to see. So where do I begin . . .

First and foremost I must thank Andy and Becky Adler for their purchase of a battery-operated baby swing. At the tender age of two weeks, I placed my son, Elijah, in this swing in my tiny home office where I wrote as fast as I could between feedings and changings. Ten months later, Elijah could eat this swing for breakfast but the book is done and I have become a multitasking queen.

Even as I sit here, I worry that there is something I have forgotten to include, but this book is my best attempt at explaining my work and the experiences I have had with girls and boys over the last ten years. I had this opportunity because I was privileged to help create the Empower Program organization. Everyone who has worked, interned, and volunteered at the Empower Program contributed to this book. In particular I would like to thank Kasey Sher, Stephanie Olson, Rick Doten, Gwo Ping Yang, Kris Gooding, Farra Trompeter, Jessica Lux, Sydney Campbell, Audrey Chen, Randy Mamiaro, Christine Triollo, Shanterra McBride, Katy Otto, Nigel Okunubi, Antione Jeter, Toni Blackman, Courtney From, Emily Irish, Robin Abb, Dave Thomas, Kim Ward, Sara Trembath, Sara Tolford, Caitlin Finnegan, Kevin Neil, and Catriona Johnson.

For most of my career, I have often felt that I was hitting my head against a wall. But there have been some people who did get it from the beginning and supported me throughout. I want to especially thank Linda Howard, Nathan Isikoff, Patty Abramson, Melanie Lyons, Monica Winsor, Janet Hagberg, Elizabeth Periello Rice, Esta Soler, Raj Vinnakota, Josh Edelman, Callie Irish, Schuyla Goodson-Bell, Lori Robinson, Siligo Middle School and Mark Kelsch, Joan Kuriansky, Sherry Ettleson, Jackson Katz, Miriam Zoll, Amy Richards, Pat Johnson and all the health teachers at Suitland High School, Cathy Channick, Camy Vitullo, Pat King, Marcy Syms, Martha Johns, Linda Collyer, and Mark Anderson. In particular, I'm extremely grateful to Gaylord Neely, who has always seen what I could be and loved me just the way I am. If I have forgotten anyone, it's only because I'm overwhelmed looking back over the years and remembering all the people who let me pursue this idea.

To my friends who have become Empower family and friends of friends who have been roped in, too: Stephanie Adams, Yael Ouzillou, Shara Kaplan, Sujuata Tewani, Maren Leed, and Paige Albiniak.

To Melissa Buckley and Ana Mitric, my high school friends, who have assisted me by recalling our more painful high school moments and allowing me to talk about these moments in my classes. Can you imagine having a close high school friend share your most humiliating high school experiences with teens around the country? Rest assured I do penance by admitting to my students that I lied about Melissa messing around with a boy when we were fourteen. To this day, I haven't apologized enough.

I'm incredibly fortunate to have had my sister, Zoe, edit this book from beginning to end. What a gift it is to have a seventeen-year-old criticize the book twenty-four/seven and begrudgingly give it her approval. I am eagerly looking forward to the day when she tells me I have done a good job. She has recently told me that she thinks "we" will never be done writing on this subject. I would also like to equally thank all the experts who read the drafts and gave me their stories, thoughts, worries, and advice: Sara, Erica, Cloe, Jessey, Victoria, Ani, Remy, Jenny, Molly, Keisha, Anika, Anna, Jessica, Ellen, Lara, Leenie, Zeina, Nikki, Jessa, Morgan, Nini, Nidhi, Samara, Ellie, Max, Erin, Jake, and Alexandra. All the girls past and present from GAB. All of my National Cathedral School sixth-grade wellness classes, but especially the sixth grades of the 1999–2000 and 2000–2001 school year.

My "in-house" editors: Jane Randel, Ellen Silva, and Julie Holter (who has amazing instant recall of junior high). To Lisbeth Fuiscz for helping me with all the books and good discussions. To my father, Steve Wiseman, my most enthusiastic editor and champion.

My official editor, Betsy Rapoport, who comes up with the best subtitles and challenged me to do my best work, and my subofficial editor and the best agent I've ever had, Jim Levine. This has been a true collaboration. I look forward to working with Betsy on another book—between facials and salt rubs—at a fabulous spa of Crown's choosing.

To Ole, Elijah's wonderful babysitter, for maintaining my sanity during Elijah's first year.

To the Bacons, because without Katie's wedding none of this would have ever happened.

To my aunts, Mary, Nancy, and Peggy, for raising me to believe I have something to say—and people may want to hear it.

To my mother, for having the faith that this book would not be a personal exposé of her parenting. Thank you for laughing so hard you couldn't speak when you read the chapter about lying and discovered that I had lied to you constantly.

And of course, I would be remiss in not giving credit to the people who suffered the most as I wrote this book: my husband, James, and my son, Elijah. Some people think it was a little much to write this book while pregnant, on maternity leave, and when I returned to work. At the time, I didn't see what they were talking about. Now, I totally agree. What in the world was I thinking? However, in spite of the challenge, it seems as if we've all survived. Elijah knows who his mother is and he has been very understanding while I worked for his college tuition. In conclusion, I would like to promise him that I will try my best not to be a crazy parent. I can't guarantee it, but I'll do my best. He has two parents who love each other and love him—so he may have a shot.

Contents

Acknowledgments   vii

Introduction   1

1.   Cliques and Popularity   18

2.   Passport from Planet Parent to Girl World: Communication and Reconnaissance   49

3.   The Beauty Pageant: Who Wants to Be Miss Congeniality?   75

4.   Nasty Girls: Teasing, Gossip, and Reputations   111

5.   Power Plays: Group Dynamics and Rites of Passage   151

6.   Boy World: The Judges and the Judged   175

7.   Girls Meets Boy: Crushes, Matchmaking, and the Birth of Fruit Cup Girl   201

8.   Pleasing Boys, Betraying Girls: When Relationships Get More Serious   234

9.   Parties: Sex, Drugs, and Rock 'n' Roll   276

10.   Getting Help   305

Grace Notes: Before You Go   313

Movie List   317

Resources   319

Good Organizations and Their Websites   328

Index   331

QUEEN BEES

& WANNABES

Introduction

"My daughter used to be so wonderful. Now I can barely stand her and she won't tell me anything. I feel totally shut out. How can I find out what's going on?"

"There's a clique in my daughter's grade that's making her life miserable. She doesn't want to go to school anymore. Her own supposed friends are turning on her, and she's too afraid to do anything. What can I do?"

"My daughter has perfect skin and a beautiful body yet she complains constantly that she has acne and is too fat. I raised her to feel good about herself and she's breaking my heart. What should I do?"

"My daughter is eleven and she wants to shave her legs. She follows me around the house begging me. I think it's totally inappropriate but she won't stop talking about it. How do I make her realize she's too young?"

"My daughter printed out an e-mail from her boyfriend and left it on the mail table. It was horribly abusive. Did she leave it out on purpose for me to see? What should I do?"

Welcome to the wonderful world of your daughter's adolescence. Ten seconds ago she was a sweet, confident, world-beating little girl who looked up to you. Now she's changing before your very eyes—she's confused, insecure, often surly, lashing out. On a good day, she's teary and threatening to run away. On a bad day, you're ready to help her pack her suitcase. She's facing the toughest pressures of adolescent life—test-driving her new body, figuring out the social whirl, toughing it out in school—and intuitively you know that even though she's sometimes totally obnoxious, she needs you more than ever. Yet it's the very time when she's pulling away from you.

Why do teenage and preteen girls so often reject their parents and turn to their girlfriends instead—even when those friends often treat them so cruelly?

Every girl I know has been hurt by her girlfriends. One day your daughter comes to school and her friends suddenly decide she no longer belongs. Or she's teased mercilessly for wearing the wrong outfit or having the wrong friend. Maybe she's branded with a reputation she can't shake. Or trapped, feeling she has to conform to what her friends expect from her so she won't be kicked out of the group. No matter what they do to her, she still feels that her friends know her best and want what is best for her. In comparison, she believes that you, previously a reliable source of information, don't have a clue. For parents, being rejected by your daughter is an excruciating experience. Especially when you're immediately replaced by a group of girls with all the tact, sense of fairness, and social graces of a pack of marauding hyenas.

Whatever you feel as your daughter goes through this process, you can be sure that she'll go through her share of humiliating experiences and constant insecurity—that's normal for teens. Most people believe a girl's task is to get through it, grow up, and put those experiences behind her. But your daughter's relationships with other girls have much deeper and farther-reaching implications beyond her turbulent teen years.

Your daughter's friendships with other girls are a double-edged sword—they're key to surviving adolescence, yet they can be the biggest threat to her survival as well. The friendships with the girls in her clique are a template for many relationships she'll have as an adult. Many girls will make it through their teen years precisely because they have the support and care of a few good friends. These are the friendships where a girl truly feels unconditionally accepted and understood—and they can last into adulthood and support her search for adult relationships.

On the other hand, girls can be each other's worst enemies. Girls' friendships in adolescence are often intense, confusing, frustrating, and humiliating, the joy and security of "best friends" shattered by devastating breakups and betrayals. Girls' reactions to the ups and downs of these friendships are as intense as they'll later feel in intimate relationships.

These early relationships can propel girls into making dangerous decisions and shape how they mature into young women. But your daughter is too close to it all to realize the good and bad influence of her friends. She needs guidance from you.

This book will examine cliques, reputations, gossiping, rebellion, bullying, crushes, and boyfriends. It will show you how your daughter is conditioned to remain silent when intimidated by more powerful girls—and the lessons she learns from this experience. It will teach you how to recognize which friends will support her and which could lead her toward situations that threaten her emotional health and sometimes even her physical safety. It'll show you how your daughter's place in her social pecking order can affect whether she'll be a perpetrator, bystander, or victim of violence when she's older. This book will also reveal how these dynamics contribute to the disconnection and struggle between the two of you.

I'll also describe and explain the key rites of passage your daughter is likely to experience: getting an invitation to an exclusive party in sixth grade . . . or getting left off the guest list; her first breakup with a friend; the first time she dresses up for a party in the latest style; and so on. These are all critical milestones for her, but they're rites of passage for you, too. Just as they can be exhilarating or traumatizing for her, they can be equally challenging for you as her parent, and not just in terms of the extent to which they try your patience; mishandling them can threaten your relationship with her. I'll help you navigate them together.

Moreover, this book will show you how constantly changing cultural ideals of femininity impact your daughter's self-esteem, friendships, and social status and can combine to make her more likely to have sex at an early age and be vulnerable to violence at the hands of some men and boys. It will also explain what you can do to help your daughter avoid these pitfalls.

Understanding your teen or preteen daughter's friendships and social life can be difficult and frustrating. Parents often tell me they feel totally shut out from this part of their daughter's life, incapable of exerting any influence.

This book will let you in. It'll show how to help your daughter deal with the nasty things girls do to one another and minimize the negative effects of what's often an invisible war behind girls' friendships.

Before I go any further, let me reassure you that I can help you even if you often feel that you're at war with your daughter.

It's perfectly natural at this stage that she:

- Stops looking to you for answers.
- Doesn't respect your opinion as much as she did before.
- Believes that there's no possible way that you could understand what she's going through.
- Lies and sneaks behind your back.
- Denies she lied and went behind your back—even in the face of undeniable evidence.

On the other hand, it's natural that you:

- Feel rejected when she rolls her eyes at everything you say.
- Have moments when you really don't like her.
- Wonder whose child this is anyway because this person in front of you can't possibly be your sweet wonderful daughter.
- Feel confused when conversations end in fights.
- Feel misunderstood when she feels you're intruding and prying when you ask what's going on in her life.
- Are really worried about the influence of her friends and feel powerless to stop her hanging out with them. (Because, of course, she'll keep the friends you don't like if you expressly forbid her from seeing them.)

THE MOTHER/DAUGHTER MAELSTROM

Moms and daughters seem to have the hardest time with each other during girls' adolescence. Your daughter craves privacy, and you directly threaten her sense of privacy. You feel you have so much to offer her—after all, you've been through the changes she's experiencing—and you think your advice will help. Think of your daughter as a beaver; she's constantly cutting down logs, branches, twigs, anything she can find, dragging them to her den, trying to create a safe haven from the outside world. In her eyes, you're always stomping on it: asking why the logs are there in the first place when you have this nice one that would look so pretty; rearranging the branches; hovering around the entranceway yelling your suggestions and saying that it would look much better if it was just a little more organized. You're not just totally disturbing her peace, you're storming her sacred retreat.

While this privacy war is natural, it creates a big problem. Girls are often so focused on resisting the influence of their parents that they rarely see when their peers are influencing them in the wrong way. Teens often see things in very concrete, either/or ways. You, as the parent, are intrusive and prying, which equals bad; her peers are involved and understanding, which equals good. She pushes you away, making even more space for the bad influences.

FATHERS FEEL IT, TOO

This book isn't only for mothers. Fathers also have struggles with the child who just moments ago was "Daddy's little girl." Still, there are many ways your unique perspective can help your daughter. Just because you were never a girl doesn't mean you can't help your daughter get through all this mess. In fact, it could be a lot worse. You could be the mother. Even if you're raising your daughter on your own, you still probably won't get into the teeth-baring, no-holds-barred battles that mothers and daughters do. I know lots of dads feel rejected and pushed aside when their little girl suddenly turns into a moody teenager. But in reality, this is an opportunity for you to become a genuinely cool dad. I don't mean you let her get away with stuff, side with her against the mom, or drive her wherever she wants. I'm talking about the dad who patiently waits around until she wants to talk, then listens without being judgmental, isn't afraid to look foolish or show his emotions, shares the "boy perspective," and is able to communicate his concerns without coming across as controlling and dogmatic. You're probably dying to warn your daughter off those hormonally crazed ruffians panting at the door; you were one once and you still remember what it felt like. But if you launch in with "what boys really want" and come across as the crazy-control-freak-doesn't-have-a-clue father, you've lost a golden opportunity. Your job is to present your wisdom in a credible manner so she won't blow you off and think your opinions are outdated and irrelevant. Through your relationship with her, you can teach her that her relationships with men must be mutually respectful and caring. This book will help you.

WHAT WORKS FOR DADS . . .

I can't tell my mom anything because she'll freak. But I'll tell my dad. He gives me excellent advice because he has experience from a boy's perspective. I'll be upset because a guy hasn't called me in three days and my dad will tell me that the guy is shy. It's easier to tell my dad because he doesn't get worked up like my mom, even though my mom is cool and she's even a guidance counselor. But he's more funny and light-hearted. Brianna, 16

I like going to my dad because I get a different perspective. Amy, 15

AND WHAT DOESN'T

Sometimes dads do let you get away with things that moms would never let you do. I think it makes problems between moms and dads in their marriage because mom's always the bad guy. Jasmine, 15

What I can't stand is when he says "Come to me anytime" but then he freaks and screams at me. He thinks all these guys are all over me and that I'm going to get pregnant. Bianca, 14

BELIEVE IT OR NOT, YOUR DAUGHTER STILL WANTS YOU IN HER LIFE

When I ask girls privately, even those who struggle the most with their parents, they tell me they want their parents to be proud of them. You may look at her in the middle of an argument when she's screaming that she hates you and think there's no way you can get through to her, but you can and will if you learn to see the world through her eyes.

> *You always want attention from your parents. Especially if you're doing something you aren't sure about.* Sam, 15

> *Parents don't realize that their children look up to them. When I know that deep in my mother and father's heart they really don't agree with what I'm doing, that really hurts.* Eve, 12

> *I want a better relationship with my parents. I know I have to build their trust back, talk to them and listen to them and it will work out fine.* Keisha, 14

> *I know I should listen to my parents, even if they're wrong.* Abby, 16

The danger is that when your daughter opens up enough to let you in, she makes herself vulnerable, and that's when you can really hurt those fragile feelings:

> *My mom and dad won't let me talk about my depression because they think we should keep it in the family. They worry about what everyone else will think. Everyone has problems. Why are we so special that we have to pretend that we're so different?* Amanda, 16

> *When my mom sees me eating chocolate, she sometimes makes comments about watching my weight. But she doesn't need to say anything. I can tell by her expression.* Felicia, 14

My older sister has an eating disorder. Last year the doctors wanted to hospitalize her but my parents thought they could take care of it at home. I overheard them discussing it, and saying that they could tell people she had mono.   Christine, 17

And you can unwittingly make her turn to people you don't want her to rely on:

My family is against me so I have to turn to this boy. [I need to] realize what I have done to myself and wake up.   Jesse, 15

They've told me that I'll never be anything and have compared me to people they don't like or people who have done wrong in the past. I hate that.   Carla, 14

I don't have great friends and I could see them getting me into trouble. But they accept me for who I am and my parents don't.   Jill, 14

DEVELOPING YOUR GIRL BRAIN

Parents tell me that one of the hardest things they have to accept is that as their daughters get older, they have less control over which people they hang out with. They hate admitting that they won't be there when their daughters face the difficult decisions that could impact their health and safety. When your daughter was little, she came crying to you when there was a problem and you swept in like a white knight to solve it. Now, you're lucky if you even have a clue what the problem is, and if you sweep in to save the day instead of teaching your daughter how to handle it, she'll either be angry with you for intruding or believe she can't learn to take care of herself. How can you help her? Start by thinking the way she does.

In this book I will teach you to develop a girl brain. It's like looking at the world through a new pair of glasses. Developing this ability isn't dependent on using the latest slang (and it's impossible to keep up anyway). The key to building your relationship with your daughter is understanding why she's turning away from you and toward her friends, and maintaining a relationship with her anyway. And even though she may be acting as if you aren't an important influence in her life, you are—she just may not want to admit it. If you can learn how to be her safe harbor when she's in trouble, your voice will be in her head along with your values and ethics.

The first step is to understand what your daughter's world—the Girl World—looks like, who has power, who intimidates her, whom she intimidates, where she feels safe, and where she doesn't. Where and when does she feel comfortable and with whom? Who does she go to for advice? What common things can ruin her day or make her feel on top of the world? An even harder task is to assess her. What is she being teased about? Why are other children mean to her? Or even harder to admit, why would she be cruel to others? What would make her lie or sneak behind your back? Get inside her head, and you'll understand where she's coming from.

It helps to remember what it was like to be your daughter's age. Remember your experiences, the role models (both good and bad), and the lessons learned from your family, your school, and your culture. Suspend the worry, the common sense, and the wisdom you have accumulated over the last years. Think back to what you were like and what was important to you back then.

REMEMBERING THE LUNCH TRAY MOMENTS

Let's go back to middle school (are you suppressing an involuntary shudder?). Parents, teachers, and other adults are telling you what to do. They're especially telling you what you can't do. You have a close group of friends, but for some reason one of your best friends comes up to you between classes and tells you that one of your other friends is spreading rumors about you. Your face feels hot; you can feel everyone looking at you. Thoughts race through your head. What did you do? Why is she mad at you? Are your friends going to back you or side with her? All of a sudden, a question drives an icy stake of fear through your heart as you stand there clutching your orange plastic lunch tray in the cafeteria line: Where are you going to sit at lunch?

Can you remember what it was like? Not too pleasant. As adults, we can laugh at how immense and insurmountable problems like those "Lunch Tray Moments" can feel when you're young. But in Girl World they're vital issues, and to dismiss them as trivial is to disrespect your daughter's reality.

Everyone knows that girls are under tremendous pressure to fit in; this is one of the reasons why they suffer from a decrease in self-esteem as they enter adolescence. This decrease is usually attributed to teen magazines, MTV, and other aspects of popular culture that give negative and conflicting messages to girls. While there's some truth in this, it doesn't explain the whole story. Girls have strict social hierarchies based on what our culture tells us about what constitutes ideal femininity. At no time in your daughter's life is it more important to her to fit these elusive girl standards than adolescence. But who is the prime enforcer of these standards? The movies? The teen magazines? Nope, it's the girls themselves. They police each other, conducting surveillance on who's breaking the laws of appearance, clothes, interest in boys, and personality—all of which have a profound influence on the women they become. Your daughter gets daily lessons about what's sexy (read "in") from her friends. She isn't watching MTV or reading quizzes in teen magazines by herself. She processes this information with and through her friends.

We can't just point the finger at the media for the things girls do to each other. We also have to point to ourselves for not challenging the culture that creates these problems, and we must, as must our daughters. Girls will only reach their full potential if they're taught to be the agents of their own social change. As we guide girls through adolescence, we have to acknowledge it, name it, and act to change the effect of Girl World on girls.

SO WHY LISTEN TO ME?

For the last ten years I've been learning from and teaching girls. As the cofounder and president of the Empower Program, I have spent thousands of hours talking to girls between the ages of ten and twenty-one about everything from gossip and cliques to rape and abusive relationships. Our motto is "Violence should not be a rite of passage," but for far too many girls, it is.

Along with Empower's staff educators, we developed a curriculum called "Owning Up"™* that teaches young people between the ages of twelve and twenty-one the skills to understand and proactively address the impact of Girl World (and Boy World, too). Today, through Empower and "Owning Up,"™ we teach over four thousand boys and girls each year in the Washington, D.C., area and reach thousands more through our professional training programs throughout the country. Under the direction of professionals at Mount Sinai Adolescent Hospital and Rutgers University, our program evaluations show significant decreases in verbal and physical aggression in our students after the program's completion. In conjunction with Liz Claiborne, Inc., I have developed educational materials about abusive relationships and created specific tools to help parents reach out to their daughters.

In PTA meetings and with other groups, I talk to parents who feel overwhelmed by the challenges of parenting a teen, whether they're trying to rescue a daughter in an abusive relationship or helping one cope with the tribulations of being passed over for the prom.

I teach girls today in a variety of settings—from weekly health classes to speeches in front of high schools, universities, and youth organizations. Whether I'm teaching in the most exclusive private school or the largest public school, the girls all bring the same concerns and fears. No matter what their income, religion, or ethnicity, they're struggling with the same issues about the pleasures and perils of friendships and how they act as a portal to the larger world.

I'm frequently asked why I started Empower. The easy answer is that I was in an abusive relationship in high school. My "therapy" was self-defense, which I taught, in turn, to high school girls as soon as I graduated from college. While martial arts did start me on a path that ended with my cofounding Empower, it isn't the only reason. When I first developed the "Owning Up"™ curricula, I looked back to my adolescence for initial answers. How did I, a "normal" girl, become vulnerable to violence?

Until fifth grade I'd grown up in a close community inside Washington, D.C., and attended a small public neighborhood elemen-

*"Owning Up" is trademarked and copyrighted by the Empower Program.

tary school. I had many friends of different races, nationalities, and economic backgrounds. I was part of a clique but I was friends with lots of students. The summer after fifth grade my family moved to Pittsburgh, Pennsylvania, and I attended a well-respected, private all-girls school. My experience there was extremely difficult. I had my first miserable tray moment when girls wouldn't let me sit at their tables. The popular girls were catty and mean-spirited. I returned to Washington the next year and enrolled in another private but coed school and the girls were just as bad. Very quickly I lost any remaining sense of self-confidence and became terrified of becoming a social liability. As a result, I became a keen observer of what would keep me in the group and what would get me tossed out.

My experience is hardly unique. Was it so bad that it contributed to my getting into an abusive relationship in high school? I believe it did. I craved validation from other girls; I had looked around and realized that I had to have an insurance policy that would keep my social status secure—and the easiest way to do that was to have the right boyfriend. He was "right" to the outside world, but behind closed doors he was mean and abusive. I had no idea what to do.

I was no one's idea of a likely target for assault and abuse. I was a competitive athlete. I had a supportive and loving family. I didn't abuse alcohol or drugs. So what was going on? There are three answers. One, like so many girls, I was amazingly good at fooling myself. I'd convinced myself that I was smart, could take care of myself, and could handle any situation. I denied that I could get into situations that were over my head, even when I had clear evidence to the contrary (like being abused by my boyfriend). I was so confident, I'd walk into incredibly dangerous situations because I wouldn't admit I was in danger. Two, like a lot of girls, I felt powerless when threatened. I now know that even highly articulate girls become voiceless when faced with the threat of sexual harassment or violence. These are the girls who won't tell someone to leave them alone because they're afraid they'll be labeled as uptight, a bitch, or because they don't want to hurt anyone's feelings. Three, once I was in the relationship, my assumption that having a boyfriend would increase and secure my social status was correct. The relationship made me feel mature, confident, and assured of my place in the social hierarchy of the school.

When I first conducted surveys of the girls I was teaching in Washington, D.C.'s, private schools, 23 percent reported experiencing sexual violence, including abusive relationships. Like me, these girls attended excellent schools and were given every opportunity to be confident young women—yet they were vulnerable to the same kinds of violence. (A national survey published in the *Journal of the American Medical Association* in August 2001 confirmed the same one-in-five figure.)

After hearing so many girls say the same things, I began to wonder: Where did they learn to be silent? Where did they learn to deny the danger staring them in the face? When I asked them, a common theme came out immediately. Our culture teaches girls a very dangerous and confusing code of behavior about what constitutes "appropriate" feminine behavior (i.e., you should be sexy, but not slutty; you should be independent, but you're no one without a boyfriend). We like to blame the media and boys for enforcing this code, but we overlook the girls themselves as the enforcers.

Clearly, girls are safer and happier when they look out for each other. Paradoxically, during their period of greatest vulnerability, girls' competition with and judgment of each other weakens their friendships and effectively isolates all of them. This is what the power of the clique is all about, and why it matters so much to your daughter's safety and self-esteem.

Once I figured this out, I got busy. I created the Empower curriculum to address the connection between girls' friendships and vulnerability. I love what I do. I love the feeling when I first walk into a classroom with a group of girls and tell them that all we're going to talk about is their friendships, enemies, reputations, and popularity. They look at each other in disbelief. There's an immediate buzz in the room—we're going to talk about a juicy secret. Are they really going to get to talk about this stuff? Once we get going, it's hard to stop.

As I enter Girl World, talking with girls in school hallways, cafeterias, and teaching in their schools, Girl Scout troops, athletic teams, and church groups, something becomes clear. In trying to prepare girls for adolescence, adults are failing. We refuse to see what's really going on in their lives. We trivialize and dismiss these experiences as teen drama. Adolescence is a time when social hierarchies are powerfully and painfully reinforced every moment of every day. Girls can be each other's pillars of support and saviors, but they can also do horrible things to each other—and the lessons they learn from one another set all of them up for worse experiences in the future.

Almost as often as I talk to girls, I talk to their parents. I often feel like a translator between girls and parents; an ambassador who shuttles between Girl World and Planet Parent, two fiefdoms with different languages and rules. Why is the communication between these two worlds so lousy? For many parents, the need to deny that their little girl is growing up so fast can make it difficult to listen to what their daughter is really saying. The first hint that their daughter is sexually maturing can fill parents with an anxiety that only widens the communication gap with their daughter—at the very time when the daughter needs guidance the most. The other reason is parents don't like to admit to themselves that their daughters could be mean, exclusive, and catty—or, on the other end of the spectrum, isolated and teased. Parents so often see their daughter's behaviors as a reflection of the success or failure of their parenting that they refuse to look at their daughters for who they really are. On the other hand, girls are renegotiating their relationship with their parents at a time of maximum change and confusion. One moment they can be impossibly distant and sneaky, wanting and demanding to be treated as adults; two seconds later they're clingy and scared, insisting that their parents psychically divine that now they want to be treated like little girls again.

This book will ask you to see the world through your daughter's eyes. It'll ask you to acknowledge and respect the environment she interacts with every day. You may not want to know everything about Girl World, but if you want your daughter to realize her full potential, have a sure sense of herself, and be happy and safe, knowing her world is paramount.

Most chapters will begin with a thorough analysis and description of a different aspect of Girl World. Next, in the "Checking Your Baggage" section, I'll challenge you to answer a few questions about your experiences when you were your daughter's age, because understanding your own biases and preconceptions can show you how they've affected your behavior toward your daughter. Then I'll give you specific, step-by-step strategies to help her.

For further assistance, I've asked girls to take an active role in the development of this book. I've shown multiple drafts of every chapter to girls of different ages, races, cultures, communities, and socioeconomic levels. They've helped me fill in missing perspectives, pushed me to delve more deeply into certain issues, and offered their "political commentary," which you'll find throughout the book. They've anonymously shared personal stories, feelings, and opinions—all to help you know how to reach out to your daughter in the best possible way.

The girls have also taught me about the "landmines" you'll find throughout the book: things parents do and say that are guaranteed eye-rollers and shut the door to effective communication. They usually seem insignificant (for example, don't say "boys," say "guys"), but they can make the difference between your daughter listening to you or tuning out completely because she thinks you're hopelessly out of touch. (Remember how you winced when your parents asked you if something was "groovy" or "far-out"?) As you read this, you may be thinking that pointing out landmines is a lost cause, since anything you do, including breathing or looking in her direction, makes her roll her eyes, but I promise you that you can decrease the number of embarrassing things you do. (For some reason, the way dads sneeze and moms laugh are landmines, but you can't change everything about yourself!)

Don't beat yourself up if you think your relationship with your daughter is terrible. Parenting a teen is really difficult, and the reward is way down the road when she emerges as a cool adult. Allow me to quote my own mother, who said, "When my children were teens, if I liked them for five minutes a day, that was a good day."

So be honest. You don't have to like your daughter all the time. You don't have to like her at adl. (Many parents tell me they've never stopped loving their daughters, but they certainly stopped liking them for a while.) One father I know refers to his increasingly distant daughter as "the exchange student." One mom calls her daughter "TLO," "The Loathesome One," when the girl is out of earshot. You're allowed to wonder why you had kids in the first place. Once you acknowledge these rotten—and believe me, universal—feelings, their power over you tends to decrease and you don't feel so guilty. And when other parents tell you that they're so lucky because "their kids don't drink and do drugs and they always tell them everything," just nod your head and smile, like I do, and know that the girls are pulling a fast one.

BEFORE YOU GET INTO
THE HEART OF THE BOOK

Your task is difficult. Instilling values, respecting your daughter's growing individuality, influencing her to make good decisions, and protecting her while giving her the freedom to make mistakes is hard, hard work. A lot of the time you'll feel as if you're banging your head against a wall.

This book will give you strategies so that your daughter's adolescence is bearable for both of you. It will teach you to talk to your daughter in a way that doesn't make her groan and roll her eyes when you speak. She may even walk away from your conversation admitting to herself (not to you, never to you) that you know what you're talking about.

You can help your daughter develop a strong sense of self. You can teach her personal responsibility, confidence in her abilities, and empathy toward others. You want her to be an authentic person able to realize her full individual potential while being connected to her loved ones and community.

You can build a strong, healthy relationship with your daughter as long as you take a long-term view, focus on the overall goal, and challenge yourself to be as honest as you can.

I also promise to answer the biggest questions of all: Should I read her diary? and When do I know she's lying to me?

JUST BETWEEN YOU AND ME

This book may be painful to read. If I hit a nerve, I have only one request. Take a moment to reflect. Ask yourself why what you read bothered you so much. Did it call up memories of your own experience as a victim, bystander, or perpetrator? Did it give you a sinking feeling that your daughter is a target or evildoer? Is it hard to face the fact that your daughter is thinking and acting in ever more adult ways? Acknowledge the pain you feel, but don't let it stop you from learning all you can about your daughter's world. Everything in this book comes from what girls have told me over the last ten years I've been teaching, and from girls' comments as they have read drafts of this book. I'm not accusing girls of being bad people, judging parents as incapable, or predicting which daughters will be failures as adults. I'm reaching out to you, as parents, educators, and role models, to show you what I think girls are up against as they struggle to become healthy young women who will make our communities better.

Now, let's start by looking at the place responsible for so much of our girls' horrible behavior toward each other: cliques.

Cliques and Popularity

Mrs. Clarke, a well meaning but clueless fifth-grade PE teacher, tells the girls to get into a circle for a game. Mrs. Clarke wonders why it takes the girls so long to get into a simple circle. The reason, which she fails to see, is right in front of her. Who will hold hands with whom? As the girls vie for the various positions that will display their social status of the day, Mrs. Clarke gets impatient and yells at the girls to get it together—now! And then a horrible thing happens. Carla, the most popular girl in the grade, happens to be standing next to Cynthia, the class loser. Will the impossible happen? Will Carla allow Cynthia to hold her hand? As their hands touch, Carla grazes Cynthia's fingers and then jumps away as if she's touched a dead fish. The other girls giggle while Cynthia also pretends it's funny.

. . .

Yes, we're exclusive, but it's just popularity. I'm the queen but I'm not mean. People exclude themselves. Nobody else has the power to do that. I'm perfect and I'm not in denial.   Anonymous Queen Bee, 12

We want them to belong to someone and if they don't, it hurts.
Mary, mother of Ani, 13

Why does Carla react this way? Why does Cynthia feel that the only thing she can do is laugh it off? Why is the teacher so clueless about what's happening with the girls? This chapter answers these questions.

No matter how good a parent you are, how popular your daughter is, or how great her friends are, she'll run into problems with popularity and cliques. For better or worse, it's the experiences she has in the clique that will teach her volumes about friendship, support, understanding, power, and privilege. On a daily basis, she'll learn what kind of girl she has to be in order to be accepted by her group, and this will influence everything from her choice of boyfriends to the classes she takes, her after-school activities, her clothes, her hairstyles, the people she talks to, the people she doesn't talk to, her beliefs and values, and her overall sense of self.

The common definition of a clique is an exclusive group of girls who are close friends. I see it a little differently. I see them as a platoon of soldiers who have banded together to navigate the perils and insecurities of adolescence. There's a chain of command and they operate as one in their interactions with their environment. Group cohesion is based on unquestioned loyalty to the leaders and an us-versus-the-world mentality.

Cliques reinforce your daughter's bonds with her friends. They also break apart or at least weaken the bond between a daughter and her parents. This is painful for you, but it's dangerous for your daughter, because the clique teaches her to turn to and exclusively depend on the members of her clique when she's in trouble, and not to ask for help from you (or another adult). This chapter will help you analyze cliques so you can better understand what your daughter is going through, identify her position in the clique, and know how to talk to her about it so she can get the help she needs.

Cliques are worst in sixth, seventh, and eighth grade. Your daughter will also have a difficult time whenever she's new to a school or when she's in the youngest grade of a school, because she's challenging the already existing social hierarchy. People want to know where she fits. When I tell women what I do for a living, most immediately want to share with me the terrible things they experienced when they were that age; even if it was thirty years ago, they can remember the names of the horrible girls who were mean to them. If your daughter is in these grades, know that she's dealing with the worst of it right now. But even if she's in high school, knowing what she learned from cliques when she was younger is absolutely critical to understanding her perspective, behavior, and choices now.

Before I go any further, I want to make clear that I don't think there's anything wrong per se with cliques. They're natural. Girls tend to have a group of girlfriends with whom they feel close, and often these friendships are great. They share secrets, can be themselves, hang out and act silly, and usually think that they will be supported no matter what. But something in the way girls group together also sows the seeds for the cruel competition for popularity and social status.

Girls are often their own and other girls' worst enemies, and for some the rivalry defines their adolescence. I have watched time after time as a sweet, intelligent girl plots another girl's humiliating downfall. It's hard to admit, especially when the evildoer is your own child or one of her close friends.

LANDMINE!

**Girls can't stand the word *cliques* and will be immediately
defensive if you use this word to describe their group of friends.
They assume you're accusing them of being exclusive.
Don't read this chapter and immediately ask your daughter
what clique she's in!**

POPULARITY

For some girls, popularity is magical. Popularity conveys an illusory sense of power. Some girls think that if they can achieve it, all their problems will disappear. Some become obsessed and measure the popularity barometer daily, then issue constant weather reports. Others dismiss it, thinking the whole thing is ridiculous. Some are angry and deny they care, although they really do. Some feel so out of it they give up.

One of the funniest things about teaching girls about cliques and popularity is their paranoia. If they even have a clue as to what I'm there to talk about, most are convinced they're being unfairly singled out for being particularly exclusive and mean, and that the teachers have called me in to set them straight. For the record, this has never happened. Teachers know there are some classes that are more "cliquey" than others, but they're used to it. I'm brought into a school not to target a particular group of girls, but because popularity issues are so common yet teachers, counselors, and principals don't know what to do about them.

So imagine you're invisible and walk with me into a classroom where I'm going to discuss cliques and popularity. This is what you'll see: thirty girls grouped together in clumps of usually four or five. They're sitting on chairs, sitting on each other, doing each other's hair, reading, or sitting by themselves. Some are even studying. I start the class by asking the girls to close their eyes and answer by a show of hands how many of them have had a friend gossip about them, backstab them, or be exclusive. All hands immediately shoot up. I ask the girls to keep their hands up and open their eyes. They laugh. Then I have them close their eyes again and ask them to answer by a show of hands how many of them have gossiped, backstabbed, or been exclusive about a friend. Much more slowly, some bending from the elbow instead of extending their hand, all the hands go up. I tell them to keep their hands up and open their eyes. They laugh again, but nervously.

After five minutes or so, without exception, the following occurs: A girl, usually generically pretty and surrounded by four or five girls, will raise her hand defiantly and say, "Ms. Wiseman, the girls in this grade are not exclusive and we don't have cliques. People hang out with the people they want to. We just all have our own friends." As she's speaking, there are many expressions of disbelief and eye-rolling from the other girls in the room. It's truly hard for me not to laugh out loud. Without exception, three things will be true about this girl: first, she'll always be one of the meanest, most exclusive girls in the room; second, she honestly believes what she's saying; and third, her parents will be in total denial about how mean she is. It's enough to make your head spin, unless the same thing has happened over and over again. So how do we get the girls to tell the truth? There's only one way: anonymity.

I tell the girls to take out a piece of paper, sit wherever they want around the room *except* next to their friends, and anonymously tell me if they think the girls in their grade are in exclusive cliques. As you watch them find a place to write, the power of cliques is evident. The girls can't wait to write, but most want to hide as they scribble away. Especially if the girls are younger, they sit in closets, under their desks, under the teacher's desk, and even in lockers (if they're small enough).

When they're done, they fold the paper in any way they want. I usually get papers condensed into the smallest balls imaginable or folded into the smallest squares. Sometimes I even get origami. Some girls hand me the paper unfolded and defiantly tell me they don't care who knows what they wrote. I put all the answers in a box and take it with me to the front of the room.

Everyone sits in a circle. The air is filled with expectation. Before I begin, I remind the girls to "own up" to their own behavior and not focus on figuring out who wrote what. I read aloud most of the responses (girls can write "for your eyes only" if they don't want their answer to be read out loud). Even now, I must watch for wandering eyes, since some girls will try to recognize handwriting through the back of the paper (even though I have a clipboard for this very reason). They can't help themselves. When they realize I won't let them see the paper, they give each other meaningful stares as they telepathically communicate the presumed identity of each author.

Not surprisingly, the girl who initially raised her hand and declared that there are no cliques holds the minority opinion. Here are the responses from a typical sixth-grade class.

From the bottom of the social totem pole:

I'm uncool. Let's face it. There are many cliques among the "cool."
                                                                Emily, 11

In this grade there are cliques and I hate it. Popular people diss people all the time. I know I'm part of a clique, but my clique was formed of the girls that were excluded and shunned. We like each other for who we are, and not by our hair, looks, clothes, or popularity. These girls are my real friends, no matter what happens.   Michelle, 12

From the middle:

I guess, for want of a friend, girls are willing to hurt anyone and don't care what stands in their way.   Kiana, 12

There are cliques and even exclusive clubs. There are about three or four cliques and some are nice. The rest are exclusive and mean. Sometimes I feel like I have to conform and be boy-crazy.
                                                                Kim, 12

And from the top:

> *There are cliques in this class and everybody is popular in their own group. The cliques are intertwined. I think the popular people are really nice. There is gossip but no backstabbing.*   Paige, 13

> *I think there are cliques, but we aren't mean to each other mostly. But there are occasional breakouts of trouble.*   Carrie, 12

Can you picture "occasional breakouts of trouble"? A classic popular girl understatement. What it usually means is that one girl has completely humiliated another. Why were the girls so reluctant to admit the gossiping and exclusivity out loud? What was silencing the girls from telling the truth? The power of cliques silences them because those in positions of power won't take responsibility for their actions, and those not in positions of power fear the consequences of speaking out in public. So when girls do talk about it, they only talk with their friends and in private places like school bathrooms, their bedrooms, or on the phone. The only girls who aren't afraid to speak out in public are those who are so out of the social pecking order that they have nothing to lose by saying what they really think.

Popular girls, like any other group of privileged people, often don't recognize their privilege. They know little about people outside of their group and are reluctant to admit what they do to put other girls down. In contrast, the girls on the outside usually know a lot about what's going on with the popular girls.

But once the silence is broken, the truth comes out. Girls want to talk about what's really going on between them. They just have to be in an environment where they can speak their truth.

Good Popularity vs. Evil Popularity

I'm not saying it's inherently bad to be popular, but sometimes girls have had to help me realize that I may make it sound as if it is. A few years ago I was teaching a group of sixth graders about popularity when an adorable girl in pigtails politely raised her hand and asked me, "Ms. Wiseman, why do you think all popular people are bad?"

Nothing like a twelve-year-old to reveal your issues! Of course she was right—there are popular girls whom people really like. So I came up with the following definitions for good popularity and bad popularity (girls like to call it "evil popularity"). The good kind is when a girl is genuinely liked because she's nice to people. Simple but true. When your daughter is popular like this, if you could spy on her when she's with other girls, you would be proud to say she's yours.

But when I talk about popularity with students, they want to talk about good popularity for only about thirty seconds. They are more interested in knowing why the definition of good popularity doesn't describe the popular girls they know. Very quickly, the questions start to fly: Why are popular girls so mean? Why is everyone so afraid of them? No one likes the most popular girl, so why does she have the most friends? They're describing the other kind of popularity. The evil kind. In the girls' words:

"She's the meanest to everyone."
"People live in fear of her."
"She has all the power and she'll crush you."

Who is the personification of evil popularity? I bet you're way ahead of me.

THE QUEEN BEE AND HER COURT

We need to give girls credit for the sophistication of their social structures. Our best politicians and diplomats couldn't do better than a teen girl does in understanding the social intrigue and political landscape that lead to power. Cliques are sophisticated, complex, and multilayered, and every girl has a role within them. However, positions in cliques aren't static. Especially from the sixth to eighth grade, a girl can lose her position to another girl, and she can move up and down the social totem pole. Also, your daughter doesn't have to be in the "popular" group to have these roles within her group of friends. Because girls' social hierarchies are complicated and overwhelming in their detail, I'm going to take you through a general breakdown of the different positions in the clique. However, when you talk to your daughter about cliques, encourage her to come up with her own names and create roles she thinks I've missed. If you can answer yes to the majority of items for each role, you've identified your daughter. So, here are the different roles that your daughter and her friends might play:

Queen Bee
Sidekick
Banker
Floater
Torn Bystander
Pleaser/Wannabe/Messenger
Target

The Queen Bee

For the girl whose popularity is based on fear and control, think of a combination of the Queen of Hearts in *Alice in Wonderland* and Barbie. I call her the Queen Bee. Through a combination of charisma, force, money, looks, will, and manipulation, this girl reigns supreme over the other girls and weakens their friendships with others, thereby strengthening her own power and influence. Indeed, she appears omnipotent. Never underestimate her power over other girls (and boys as well). She can and will silence her peers with a look. If your daughter's the Queen Bee and you could spy on her, you would (or should) be mortified by how she treats other girls.

Your Daughter Is a Queen Bee If . . .

- Her friends do what she wants to do.
- She isn't intimidated by any other girl in her class.
- Her complaints about other girls are limited to the lame things they did or said.
- When she's young, you have to convince her to invite everyone to her birthday party. When she does invite everyone you want, she ignores and excludes some of her guests. (When she's older, you lose your privilege to tell her who she can invite.)

- She can persuade her peers to do just about anything she wants.
- She can argue anyone down, including friends, peers, teachers, and parents.
- She's charming to adults, a female Eddie Haskell.
- She can make another girl feel "anointed" by declaring her a special friend.
- She's affectionate, but often that affection is deployed to demonstrate her rejection of another girl. For example, she sees two girls in her group, one she's pleased with and one she isn't. When she sees them, she'll throw her arms around one and insist that they sit together and barely say anything to the other.
- She won't (or is very reluctant to) take responsibility when she hurts someone's feelings.
- If she thinks she's been wronged she feels she has the right to seek revenge. She has an eye-for-an-eye worldview.

She thinks she's better than everyone else. She's in control, intimidating, smart, caring, and has the power to make others feel good or bad. She'll make stuff up about people and everyone will believe her.   Anne, 15

Who was the Queen Bee in your junior and/or high school? (If you were the Queen Bee, it's okay to admit it.) Remember how much power she had? Keep in mind that Queen Bees are good at slipping under adults' radar (including parents, teachers, and myself). Some of the nicest girls in my classes, who speak the most eloquently about how terrible they feel when girls are mean to each other, turn out to be the most cruel.

We're like an army!   Amanda, 13

Most Queen Bees aren't willing to recognize the cruelty of their actions. They believe their behavior is justified because of something done to them first. Justifications usually begin with, "For no reason, this girl got really upset about not being in the group. I mean we told her nicely and she just wasn't getting the hint. We tried to be nice but she just wasn't listening." When a Queen Bee does this, she's completely bypassing what she did and defining right and wrong by whether the individual was loyal (i.e., not challenging her authority).

If that sinking feeling in your stomach is because you just realized your daughter is a Queen Bee, congratulate yourself. Honesty is the first step to parenting an adolescent successfully.

What Does She Gain by Being a Queen Bee?

She feels power and control over her environment. She's the center of attention and people pay homage to her.

What Does She Lose by Being a Queen Bee?

A real sense of self. She's so busy maintaining her image that she loses herself in the process. She can be incredibly cynical about her friendships with both boys and girls ("They're only sucking up to me because I'm popular; they don't really like me."). She's vulnerable to having intimate relationships where she believes her image is dependent on the relationship. She may easily feel that she can't admit to anyone when she's in over her head because her reputation dictates that she always has everything and everyone in control.

LANDMINE!

If you think your daughter has one of these roles, don't use the words *Queen Bee* or *Wannabe* when talking with her; she'll immediately become defensive. Just keep them in your mind as you're talking with her.

The Sidekick

She's the lieutenant or second in command, the girl who's closest to the Queen Bee and will back her no matter what because her power depends on the confidence she gets from the Queen Bee. All girls in a clique tend to dress similarly (see Chapter 3), but the Sidekick wears the most identical clothes and shares the mannerisms and overall style closest to the Queen Bee. Together they appear to other girls as an impenetrable force. They commonly bully and silence other girls to forward their own agenda. These girls are usually the first to focus on boys and are often attracted to older boys. This is particularly true in seventh and eighth grade (and their behavior is even worse if they're physically mature and going to high school parties, but that's another chapter). The difference between the two is if you separate the Sidekick from the Queen Bee, the Sidekick can alter her behavior for the better, while the Queen Bee would be more likely to find another Sidekick and begin again.

Your Daughter Is a Sidekick If . . .

- She has a best friend (the Queen Bee) who tells her what to do, think, dress, etc.
- The best friend is your daughter's authority figure, not you.
- She feels like it's the two of them and everyone else is a Wannabe (see below).
- You think her best friend pushes her around.

She notices everything about the Queen Bee. She will do everything the Queen Bee says and wants to be her. She lies for the Queen Bee but she isn't as pretty as the Queen Bee.   Madeline, 14

What Does She Gain by Being a Sidekick?

Power over other girls that she wouldn't have without the Queen Bee. She also gains a close friend (whom you may not like) who makes her feel popular and included.

What Does She Lose by Being a Sidekick?

The right to express her personal opinions. If she sticks around the Queen Bee too long, she may forget she even has her own opinion.

The Banker

Information about each other is currency in Girl World. The Banker creates chaos everywhere she goes by banking information about girls in her social sphere and dispensing it at strategic intervals for her own benefit. For instance, if a girl has said something negative about another girl, the Banker will casually mention it to someone in conversation because she knows it's going to cause a conflict and strengthen her status as someone in the know. She can get girls to trust her because when she pumps them for information it doesn't seem like gossip; instead, she does it in an innocent, I'm-trying-to-be-your-friend way.

> *Her power lies in getting girls to confide in her. Once they figure out she can't be trusted, it's too late because she already has information on them, and in order to keep her from revealing things, girls will be nice to her.*   Leigh, 17

The Banker is almost as powerful as the Queen Bee, but it's easy to mistake her for the Messenger (see below). She's usually quiet and withdrawn in front of adults and can be physically immature in comparison to her friends. This is the girl who sneaks under adult radar all the time because she seems so cute and harmless.

Your Daughter Is a Banker If . . .

- She is extremely secretive.
- She thinks in complex, strategic ways.
- She seems to be friends with everyone; some girls even treat her like a pet.
- She's rarely the subject of fights.
- She's rarely excluded from the group.

What Does She Gain by Being a Banker?

Power and security. The Banker is very confusing to other girls because she seems harmless and yet everyone is afraid of her.

What Does She Lose by Being a Banker?

Once other girls figure out what she's doing, they don't trust her. With her utilitarian mind-set, she can forget to look to other girls as a trusted resource.

> The girls can't oust the Banker from the clique because she has information on everyone and could make or break reputations based on the information she knows.   Charlotte, 15

The Floater

You can usually spot this girl because she doesn't associate with only one clique. She has friends in different groups and can move freely among them. She usually has protective characteristics that shield her from other girls' cruelty—for example, she's beautiful but not too beautiful, nice, not terribly sophisticated, and avoids conflicts. She's more likely to have higher self-esteem because she doesn't base her self-worth on how well she's accepted by one group. Because she has influence over other girls but doesn't use it to make them feel bad, I call her the Floater. Girls want to be the Floater because she has confidence, people genuinely like her, and she's nice to everyone. She has the respect of other girls because she doesn't rule by meanness. When backed into a corner, the Floater is one of the few girls who will actually stand up to the Queen Bee. While Floaters have some power, they don't have the same influence and impact as Queen Bees. Why? Because Floaters don't gain anything by sowing seeds of discontent and insecurity among the other girls; Queen Bees do.

> I have always felt that many potential Floaters are either swallowed up by the popular crowd or choose not to identify with popular people at all and instead create their own groups. In every girl there is a Floater who wants to get out.   Joanna, 17

> I don't think there are real Floaters. Maybe I'm just bitter, but most of the time they are too good to be true.   Liza, 17

Your Daughter Is a Floater If . . .

- She doesn't want to exclude people; you aren't always having fights with her about spending time with people she considers "losers."
- Her friends are comfortable around her and don't seem intimidated; she's not "winning" all the conversations.
- She's not exclusively tied to one group of friends; she may have a jock group she hangs with, then the kids in the band, then her friends in the neighborhood.
- She can bring another person into a group on her own with some success.

What Does She Gain by Being a Floater?

Her peers like her for who she is as a person. She'll be less likely to sacrifice herself to gain and keep social status.

What Does She Lose by Being a Floater?

Nothing!! Count yourself truly blessed that she's your daughter.

If you're thinking this is your daughter, wait. It isn't that I don't believe you, but please read all the roles before making your final decision. We all want to believe the best about the people we love, but sometimes our love blinds us to reality. I've met countless parents who truly believe their daughters are Floaters, and they're not. It should go without saying that just because your daughter isn't a Floater doesn't mean she won't become an amazing young woman and/or that you haven't done a good job raising her. But if you insist on seeing her in a way that she isn't, you won't be able to be as good a parent as she needs you to be.

The Torn Bystander

She's constantly conflicted between doing the right thing and her allegiance to the clique. As a result, she's the one most likely to be caught in the middle of a conflict between two girls or two groups of girls. She'll often rationalize or apologize for the Queen Bee and Sidekick's behavior, but she knows it's wrong. She often feels more uncomfortable around boys, but can be very easily influenced by the clique to do what it wants (for example, getting together with a boy they decide is right for her). The status she gets from the group is very important, and the thought of standing up to the more powerful girls in the clique is terrifying. She's honest enough with herself (and maybe with you as well) to know that she doesn't like what the Queen Bee does but feels powerless to stop it.

Your Daughter Is a Torn Bystander If . . .

- She's always finding herself in situations where she has to choose between friends.
- She tries to accommodate everyone.
- She's not good at saying no to her friends.
- She wants everyone "to get along."
- She can't imagine standing up to anyone she has a conflict with; she goes along to get along.

> *She's confused and insecure because her reputation is over if she doesn't stick with the Queen Bee, but she can be really cool when she's alone.*   Anne, 13

What Does She Gain by Being a Torn Bystander?

By associating herself with more powerful girls, she has access to popularity, high social status, and boys.

What Does She Lose by Being a Torn Bystander?

She has to sacrifice a great deal. She may not try new things or she may stop doing things she's interested in (plays, band, "geeky" clubs, etc.) because her friends make fun of her. She may dumb herself down to get along with others. This doesn't mean her grades will suffer, although they could. Lots of girls hide their academic accomplishments from their peers for this reason. ("I know I totally failed that test.") It more likely means that she presents herself as less intelligent than she is. This is merely irritating when she's a teen, but literally stupid when she's an adult in a job interview.

The Pleaser/Wannabe/Messenger

Almost all girls are pleasers and wannabes; some are just more obvious than others. This is one of the more fascinating roles. She can be in the clique or on the perimeter trying to get in. She will do anything to be in the good graces of the Queen Bee and the Sidekick. She'll enthusiastically back them up no matter what. She'll mimic their clothes, style, and anything else she thinks will increase her position in the group. She's a careful observer, especially of the girls in power. She's motivated above all else to please the person who's standing above her on the social totem pole. She can easily get herself into messy conflicts with other people because she'll change her mind depending on who she's interacting with.

As a Pleaser/Wannabe/Messenger her security in the clique is precarious and depends on her doing the Queen Bee's "dirty work," such as spreading gossip about a Target (see below). While the Banker gathers information to further her own causes, the Pleaser/Wannabe/Messenger does it to service the Queen Bee and get in her good graces and feel important. But she can easily be dropped and ridiculed if she's seen as trying too hard to fit in. (One of the worst accusations you can make of a teen is to say she's trying too hard. In Girl World, all actions must appear effortless.) The Queen Bee and Sidekick enjoy the convenience of making her their servant, but they love talking behind her back. ("Can you believe what a suck-up she is? That's so pathetic.")

When there's a fight between two girls or two groups of girls, she often serves as a go-between. Her status immediately rises when she's in active duty as a Messenger. It's also the most powerful position she can attain, which means she has a self-interest in creating and maintaining conflicts between girls so she doesn't get laid off.

Your Daughter Is a Pleaser/Wannabe/Messenger If . . .

- Other girls' opinions and wants are more important than her own.
- Her opinions on dress, style, friends, and "in" celebrities constantly change.

- She can't tell the difference between what she wants and what the group wants.
- She's desperate to have the "right" look (clothes, hair, etc.).
- She'll stop doing things she likes because she fears the clique's disapproval.
- She's always in the middle of a conflict.
- She feels better about herself when the other girls are coming to her for help, advice, or when she's doing their dirty work.
- She loves to gossip—the phone and e-mail are her lifeline.

What Does She Gain by Being a Pleaser?

The feeling that she belongs; she's in the middle of the action and has power over girls.

What Does She Lose by Being a Pleaser?

Personal authenticity—she hasn't figured out who she is or what she values. She's constantly anticipating what people want from her and doesn't ask herself what she wants in return. She feels insecure about her friendships—do girls really like her, or do they only value her for the gossip she trades in? She has trouble developing personal boundaries and the ability to communicate them to others.

> *She's insecure and you can't trust her.*   Carrie, 14

The Target

She's the victim, set up by the other girls to be humiliated, made fun of, excluded. Targets are assumed to be out of the clique, one of the class "losers." While this is sometimes true, it's not always the case. Just because a girl is in the clique doesn't mean she can't be targeted by the other members. Often the social hierarchy of the clique is maintained precisely by having someone clearly at the bottom of the group's totem pole. Girls outside the clique tend to become Targets because they've challenged the clique or because their style of dress, behavior, and such are outside the norms acceptable to the clique. Girls inside the clique tend to become Targets if they've challenged someone higher on the social totem pole (i.e., the Queen Bee, Sidekick, or Banker) and need to be taken down a peg.

Your Daughter Is a Target If . . .

- She feels helpless to stop the girls' behavior.
- She feels she has no allies. No one will back her up.
- She feels isolated.
- She can mask her hurt by rejecting people first, saying she doesn't like anyone.

This role can be harder to figure out than you would think, and your daughter may be too embarrassed to tell you. She might admit she feels excluded, or she might just withdraw from you and "not want to talk about it."

> *Targets don't want to tell their parents because they don't want their parents to think they're a loser or a nobody.*   Jennifer, 16

What Does She Gain by Being a Target?

This may seem like an odd question, but being a Target can have some hidden benefits. There's nothing like being targeted to teach your daughter about empathy and understanding for people who are bullied and/or discriminated against. Being a Target can also give her objectivity. She can see the costs of fitting in and decide she's better off outside the clique because at least she can be true to herself and/or find good friends who like her for who she is, not for her social standing. Remember the girl who wrote that she was in the loser clique but at least she knew her friends were true friends? A lot of girls don't have that security.

What Does She Lose by Being a Target?

She feels totally helpless in the face of other girls' cruelty. She feels ashamed of being rejected by the others girls because of who she is. She'll be tempted to change herself in order to fit in. She feels vulnerable and unable to affect the outcome of her situation. She could become so anxious that she can't concentrate on schoolwork.

I didn't understand why I was so unhappy in sixth grade. I couldn't have told my parents that girls were being mean to me.   Erin, 17

Girls will almost always withdraw instead of telling a parent.
                                                              Claire, 14

If a girl's stuck in a degrading clique, it's the same as when she's later in a bad relationship. She doesn't expect to be treated any better.
                                                              Ellen, 15

1. Often there will be two Queen Bees in a grade who will fight for power over an entire school year.

2. Girls can switch roles. Wannabes can become Targets. Bankers can become Queen Bees. Switching usually happens at the beginning of the school year, when a new student arrives, or when physical development separates the girls into little girls and young women.

3. It's not only the superior, or alpha, clique that has this hierarchy. Other cliques can have them, too.

TREACHEROUS WATERS

OK, now you know the different roles girls play in cliques. The next questions are: How were these roles created in the first place? Who and what determine these positions and power plays? Why are girls able to get away with treating each other so badly?

It isn't really that big a secret. As girls become teens, the world becomes a much bigger, scarier place. Many girls go from a small elementary school to a much larger, more impersonal institutional school.

THE RULES OF THE CLIQUE: A SNAPSHOT

My group has rules and punishments about everything. There are seven of us and there can only be seven. I mean, we have kicked people out for breaking the rules and only then can we add someone.

We have rules about what we wear. You can only wear your hair up (like in a ponytail) once a week. You can't wear a tank top two days in a row. You can only wear jeans on Friday and that's also the only time you can wear sneakers. If you break any of these rules, you can't sit with us at lunch. Monday is the most important day because you want to look your best—it sets the tone for the rest of the week. So wearing something like sweats on a Monday is like going to church and screaming "I hate Jesus!" when you walk in the door. Friday is downtime. When we hang out that night, we wear sweats, watch movies, and talk about what bothered us during the week.

If you want to invite someone to lunch [from outside the group], you have to formally invite them and the group has to vote on it. We do this because it's like buying a shirt without your friends telling you whether you look good in it or not. You may like someone, but you could be wrong. If three or more people in the group really like her, we offer the girl an extended invitation—for a whole week. That's a trial period—it's like getting a dog at the pound and trying her out before you get her a license and call her "Fluffy."

Gabrielle, 15

In elementary school, students are usually based in one room, with one teacher. The principal sees them on a daily basis and parents are often active in the school's activities, going on field trips, bringing food for bake sales, and volunteering in after-school programs. By the end of fifth or sixth grade, girls are beginning to prepare to leave this safe, comfy haven of elementary school. They alternatively look forward to and dread moving on to middle school or junior high.

Then comes the first day at the middle school or junior high—and everything changes. Adults, in our profound wisdom, place them in a setting where they're overwhelmed by the number of students, and they become nameless faces with ID security cards. If you ever want to remember what it feels like, go to your daughter's school and hang out in the hall when the bell rings right before a lunch period (you probably have lots of times to choose from since most schools have so many students that they need multiple lunch periods, which means some students eat their midday meal at ten A.M.). When the bell rings, walk from one end of the hall to the other. It's hard enough simply navigating through this noisy throng. Now imagine navigating the same hallway and caring what each person thinks of you as you walk by.

We put our girls in this strange new environment at exactly the same time that they're obsessively microanalyzing social cues, rules, and regulations and therefore are at their most insecure. Don't underestimate how difficult and frightening this is for girls, and give your daughter credit for getting out of bed in the morning.

Trapped in the Life Raft

Imagine you and your daughter on a cruise ship. The cruise director's job is to make sure your daughter is reasonably happy and entertained. There are scheduled activities and if she hurts herself, someone will be there to get her back on her feet. She knows most of the people on the ship and everything is familiar. But just as lemmings communicate with each other when it's time to start hurling themselves off cliffs and into the sea, girls start telling each other the ship is stupid and boring and it's time to get off. As you watch helplessly, she leaves behind everything that is safe and secure, gets into a life raft with people who have little in common with her except their age, and drifts away.

Once in the raft she may ask herself, how did I get here? Why did I go? But when she looks around, sees that the ship is impossibly far away, the waves are too big, and there are a limited number of supplies, she quickly realizes that her survival depends on bonding with the other girls in that life raft. But your daughter isn't stupid. This realization is quickly followed by another one: She's trapped.

I know this is a dramatic metaphor to demonstrate girls' fear. But it shows how trapped many girls feel, forced to be a certain way in order to be accepted by their peers. They perceive that their only choices are to be trapped in the life raft or thrown into the water. There really is no choice. You stay, hope things get better, and try to survive until you're rescued. To girls, the life raft of the clique can truly feel like a matter of life and death.

When I'm teaching the girls in class, I get them to talk about these feelings by giving them the following exercise: Describe the characteristics and appearance of the girl everyone wants to be, the girl with high social status (i.e., one of the leaders in the life raft); now describe the characteristics and appearance of the girl who has low social status, who's likely to drown. Next, we put the characteristics of high social status within a box and place the characteristics of low social status outside the box (off the raft), as demonstrated in the "Act Like a Woman" box.*

Shy	Pretty	Happy	Too Opinionated
	Confident	Money	and cause-
Fat	Hangs out with	Thin	oriented
	right guys	In control	
Acne	Nice on the	Popular	Gay
	outside	Athletic	

The box shows what girls think they need in order to stay in the life raft and what characteristics will get them thrown out. I visualize most of the girls I teach as squeezing into this raft and hanging on for dear life. They'll tolerate almost anything to stay in—and there's always the threat of being cast out.

A few footnotes from the girls: Being athletic is acceptable only if the girl has a thin, "feminine" body—a large, "masculine" build is unacceptable, which is why many excellent female athletes worry about getting bulky if they lift weights. Sexual promiscuity is more acceptable (meaning she won't be called a slut) if a girl is popular. A girl with few friends who is low in the social hierarchy will get a reputation as a slut for the same behavior that doesn't cost a popular girl anything, and very few girls will associate with her.

*Paul Kivel, *Boys Will Be Men: Raising Our Sons for Courage, Caring, and Community.* (Canada: New Society Publishers, 1999).

Are there some girls who are comfortable swimming in the waters? Are there girls who would rather drown than be in the raft? Sure, and sometimes these girls are stronger for the struggle. But in many ways, every girl has to deal with the life raft, because her society's social pecking order is based on this metaphor. At the very least, even if she doesn't care, her peers do, and they're judging her accordingly. So no matter where your daughter is—sitting securely, teetering on the rails, bobbing in the waters with a life preserver, swimming strongly, treading water, or drowning—know why she bonds so tightly with her friends and why being cast out can be so frightening and paralyzing. Her fear also makes it more difficult to ask for help. From her perspective, that cruise ship is very far away; you probably couldn't get to her even if you tried.

But how do people get thrown out of the life raft? Look at the words outside the box. These are weapons. For example, imagine your daughter is in the popular group. One of the girls in her group teases another girl for being overweight. Your daughter may feel bad, but what would happen if she stood up to the teaser? Any challenge to the powers that be is seen as an act of disloyalty; she might be thrown out. Even the threat of being thrown out is enough to silence most girls.

Cliques are self-reinforcing. As soon as you define your role and group, you perceive others as outsiders, it's harder to put yourself in their shoes, and therefore it's easier to be cruel to them or watch and do nothing. It doesn't matter if we're talking about social hierarchies, racism, sexism, homophobia, or any "ism," this is the way people assert their power, which really translates into discrimination and bigotry.

You've probably raised your daughter to stand up for people who are victimized. But you're a long way away on the cruise ship, and heeding your advice—and perhaps her conscience—won't put her back on board with you. See why your daughter is so tempted to "do the wrong thing" even when she knows better?

HOW SCHOOL LOOKS TO YOUR DAUGHTER

Some of us remember middle school and high school only too well. Others might need to jog their memory to recall what the hallways looked like. I asked a few girls in my Empower classes to draw maps of their schools. You might ask your daughter to do the same. No matter what the details of her drawing, you'll discover the lay of the land your daughter traverses everyday. And, if your daughter is willing to share her map with you, how does it compare to your high school experience?

CHECKING YOUR BAGGAGE

- Where did you fit in middle school?
- Where did you fit in high school?
- What did you get from being a part of this group?
- Did you ever want to leave the clique but felt like you couldn't?
- Were you ever tormented by someone in a clique?

My daughter has always been incredibly private. She won't share information with me. I have no idea what clique she's in or if she's even in one.
                                                                  Nancy

My mother said nothing to me my whole life. I would come home and she would come home from work and shut the door. With my kids, I want them to tell me everything.
                                                                  Mandy

I went to the same school as my daughter does now and there are the same cliques as there were then. Athletes, popular girls. I was an athlete but I was heavy, so I was never popular.
                                                                  Alex

HER CLIQUES AND YOU

Accept the following:

You'll often have to rely on thirdhand information. You won't be around when she gets into trouble. Your influence is limited to what you can do before and after. The only people guaranteed to be around her when she does get into trouble are her peers. Think of it this way: Where does your daughter hang out with her friends? How often do you hang out in these places? Would you even want to if you could? Teens have access to each other in ways no adult does. This means that she'll have to stand up for herself with your support but not your physical presence.

If you want to really understand what your daughter's world looks like, ask her to draw a map of her school that shows who hangs out where. I asked two sixteen-year-old girls to do this exercise, an Indian-American girl from the east coast and a junior

(a) *Available for flirting, but there's a few jerks among them... a few dorks too.*

(b) *Gauntlet #1 - the guys are checking you out, esp. if you're someone that they semi-know.*

(c) *Oh Lord - Bitches, Incorporated. These are the real drama queens.*

(d) *Gauntlet #2 - the real test. These are the older guys, the ones everybody wants, the ones that judge your looks right as you walk by instead of waiting till you're past*

(e) *Uh oh! physics teacher - didn't turn in my last problem set.*

(f) *These are the cute little girls who want to be part of the older group - annoying, but cute.*

from the southwest. I flinched when I saw their artwork. Their worlds are harsh, judgmental places—but they're typical of what many girls tell me their school experience is like.

KEY:

Indians

Model United Nations Boys

Choir Girls

Popular Girls

Popular Guys

Jocks

Cheerleaders

(1) Group of Junior Girls

(2) Group of Sophomore Girls

(3) Animé Lovers

(4) Asians

(5) Techies/Drama People

(6) Bio Study Group

(7) Model United Nations Girls

Stairs

Doors

GYM II

rooms

(c)

(j)

(f)

(2)

WeiGHt Rooms

rooms

GYM I

AUDITORIUM LOBBY

(3)

AUDITORIUM

MUSIC WiNG

(5) (i)

Main office

(g) The library - a haven for the _real_ geeks, the ones who don't have real friends.

(h) The Asians are always friendly, even if they are, obviously, exclusive.

(i) Although the Drama people are friendly, they're very unsubtle when they hit on you.

(j) Gross! Sweaty, smelly... this is where you know the athletes have been.

(k) _So_ ditzy - but sweet.

TECH ED. BUILDING

Preppies & Skaters

Preppies (It's shady over here.)

"sex tree"

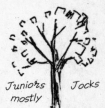

Juniors mostly   Jocks

People make out over here.

LOCKER BAY
(Mature Freshman & Sophomores)

preppy tree

senior locker bay

Drugs here, too.

COVERED TABLES

Hispanics	Football & "Easy" Girls	Populars	Populars
Arabs	Football & "Easy" Girls	Populars	Populars
Blacks	Wrestlers	Sophomore Girls That Judge	Freshman Girls That Judge

ACADEMIC BUILDING

worst strip of walking as far as judging is concerned

Girls' Bathroom

Boys' Bathroom

Girls' Smoke-out Bathroom

Girls' Bathroom

Boys' Drug-dealing Bathroom

More Hacky-Sack Kids

VENDING MACHINES

office

ROTC
kids

Asians

GOTHICS/
GAYS/LESBIANS TREE

BOYS' GYM

LOCKER BAY
(Freshmen
& Juniors)

Pot Smokers here

BENCH

Nerdy Freshmen
(ones who
don't "belong")

AUDITORIUM

Hacky-Sack Playing Kids

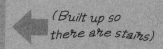

(Built up so
there are stairs)

Fat Girls
& Scrawny Boys

IF YOU GO   INSTEAD OF
WALKING BY THE WEIRD KIDS BY
THE AUDITORIUM, YOU GET
JUDGED AND CALLED NAMES.

Un-Popular Party Kids & Ecstasy
& Acid Users (mostly juniors)

Cafeteria

ENTERING/EXITING - YOU GET
JUDGED AND YOU, NATURALLY,
COMPARE YOURSELF TO THEM.

Popular Girls -
Judgers Anorexic

More
Goths

SMOKING
BATHROOMS

Preps

Preppies

B-Ball Boys

B-Ball Juniors

YPHONES

Attitude Girls

Wannabe populars

Immature Boys

Preppy Girl Judges

Sex Table

Drug-dealer Table

You have to get out of denial. Your daughter will make poor choices, behave in cruel and unethical ways, and/or be on the receiving end of both. If you want to raise a girl who survives adolescence (I mean this literally) and develops into a responsible, ethical woman, you have to accept this reality.

Remember the life raft. When she's having a problem with friends, when she dreads going to school because she's having a fight with another girl, remember the life raft and how terrifying it can be to swim in an ocean with predators all around and no rescue in sight.

Talking to Your Daughter About Cliques

It can be really hard to talk to your daughter about her role and experiences in the clique. As a general rule, unless she brings it up, don't begin the conversation by asking about her personal experiences. Instead, start the conversation by asking her opinion. Ask her to read this chapter and tell you what she thinks, or summarize it for her if reading it feels like homework to her. What rings true for her and what doesn't? If she tells you that there's nothing in the chapter that applies to her experience, don't let that be the end of your conversation. Ask her what does. What you're looking for is a starting place. You might also watch a TV show or movie together, and help her figure out what the girls' roles are in the clique.

Approach your daughter as an observer of other girls. Then, when she's opened up to you about what she sees, you can ask what she thinks her role is. Most likely she'll start talking about herself as she talks to you about her friends. You can use the definitions I use in this book, but be ready to discard them if she's reactive. Let her define her experience for you. As I said earlier, it's great if she comes up with her own names for roles in the clique. Some good questions to ask are:

- What do people gain and lose from their role?
- Why does she think that person is in that role?
- How does it impact her to watch these things happen with her friends?
- How does she feel when it happens to her?

In the chapters that follow, I'll give you more specific advice on how to help your daughter, depending on the situation and where she stands on the social totem pole. For now, I'll describe your key task as a parent depending on your daughter's general position in the clique: from a powerful position, in the middle, or the target.

Position of Power (Queen Bee, Sidekick, Banker)

If she operating from a power position, it'll be hard for her to admit when she's in the wrong, and she's unlikely to show empathy for other girls. Always emphasize taking responsibility for her actions and not blaming others.

If your daughter is in a position of power, she'll likely have an eye-for-an-eye outlook on life. If you try to talk to her, she'll either put up fierce resistance or be as smooth as silk. Don't be fooled by the smooth approach. She's only doing that because she's smart enough to know that placating you will get you off her back faster.

Caught in the Middle (Floater, Torn Bystander, Pleaser/Wannabe/Messenger)

Don't create a situation where she feels that she has to choose between you and the person described above because that girl is cooler than you are. Tell her you know she's in a difficult position, but encourage her to take responsibility, because her torn feelings look like two-faced behavior to other girls.

Ask her, "Who's making the decisions in your life?" She doesn't like when you make decisions for her, so she shouldn't like it when the Queen Bee makes decisions for her. But remember, no matter how close you are, you can't provide the social validation she gets from her friends, or convince her that she doesn't need it in the first place. The key to success in this conversation is to make your daughter understand that, by following the clique, she's not in control of what she wants. Don't blame her for not being able to stand up for herself. Give her credit for talking about it openly. Practice with her or have her write down what she wants to communicate to the more powerful girls.

Target

If you identify your daughter in this role or if she ever has an experience where she's a Target, let her talk about it at her own pace. These situations can be very humiliating, so give her space but make sure she knows you are available to talk to anytime. If she tells you she's a Target, don't freak out and threaten to call the school or other parents unless she asks for your help. If she really doesn't want to talk to you, respect her feelings. (In the next chapter I'll talk more about the importance of finding an ally for your daughter in those cases where she's not comfortable talking to you. In Chapter 4, I'll discuss how to help your daughter stand up to those in power in the clique.)

No Matter What . . .

Whatever position she's in, always affirm your daughter in some way. Tell her that you recognize that these situations are really difficult and it's equally hard to know what to do. Most adults struggle with these same issues, and they don't handle them well either. If you think a story about when you were a teenager will be something she can relate to, tell her. But don't tell her what to do. Instead, describe the behavior you respect. Work with her as she comes up with a plan that describes specifically what she wants to happen differently, and how she can make that happen. (Tell her she can always blame you if her friends come down on her.) Your daughter will feel better just knowing you understand life in Girl World.

Passport from Planet Parent to Girl World

Communication and Reconnaissance

The longer I teach girls and speak to their parents, the more I become convinced that Girl World and Planet Parent are in different universes. Parents tell me that what they most want is a passport that will admit them to Girl World and the ability to translate the foreign language and understand the customs they find once they get there. But you don't want to be a casual tourist, you want to really get inside the culture. In this chapter I'll give you some general strategies to help you communicate more effectively with your daughter and translate what she's saying. (In later chapters I'll show how to apply those strategies more specifically.) I'll also show you how to get the information you need to tour Girl World without reading your daughter's diary or snooping through her e-mail.

But before I stamp your passport, I'm going to challenge you to evaluate your parenting style and how that impacts your daughter. If you don't have an effective parenting style, you can't be an effective communicator.

WHAT'S YOUR PARENTING STYLE?

In my work with parents I see a variety of parenting styles and philosophies. Most of them are based on love, but some are also driven by fear and denial. Look over the styles below. Yours is probably a combination of styles, but see which ones resonate with you the most. You can also ask your daughter what she thinks.

The Lock-Her-in-a-Closet Parent

This parent believes it's possible to control a daughter's movements and choose her friends and boyfriends. This parent also believes that telling her to "just say no" to drugs, alcohol, and sex will work. (It won't.) I can't tell you how many times I've run into these parents only to find out that their daughters are doing all of the above—they're just really good at hiding it. Even if you could lock your daughter away until she's eighteen, you're only prolonging the inevitable. When she comes out she'll want to experience things on her own without any guidance from you. If this is your parenting philosophy, you're teaching your daughter to sneak behind your back and get herself into serious trouble without giving her the skills to get out or the resources to help herself.

The Best Friend Parent

Best friends? Some of you may laugh at this because you count as a good day one in which you and your daughter are on speaking terms. But there are others of you out there. I know because I've met you at PTA meetings and parent coffees. You come up to me and assure me that your daughter would never do anything you don't approve of because she tells you everything and you're best friends. Don't be hurt, but I doubt it. Never assume that your daughter isn't doing something solely because you don't approve of it or because you believe she tells you everything. I can virtually guarantee you're in denial. In any case, your daughter doesn't want you to be her best friend; she wants you to be her mother or father. Your connection with her is profound and unique.

Sometimes parents really are their daughter's best friend. However, most often this ends abruptly sometime in early adolescence. These parents can feel terribly rejected. A few parents manage to think of their daughter as their best friend through high school, but I've never seen this work out well. The daughter feels torn between resenting the overinvolved parents and feeling guilty about rejecting them. Or she's so dependent on the parents that she never learns to form her own independent relationships. In the first case, the daughter is forced to take extreme measures to separate from the parents. In the second case, she never grows up.

The Hip Parent

This parent will do anything to be liked by the daughter and her friends. This is the parent who buys beer for parties during high school, often justifying this behavior (usually after a party has gotten out of hand and other parents are furious) by believing that if the kids are going to drink, they may as well do it under their own roof. On its face, it seems like a good point—teens *are* going to drink, and it *is* better to have them in a safe place than driving around looking for parties. But by buying the beer, the hip parent is condoning the abuse of alcohol and its use as a social crutch.

I've never seen a child who respected the Hip or Best Friend parent. Both types are easily manipulated and disrespected by their children, especially in front of others. So while it may feel good in the short term, it isn't responsible parenting. And forget discipline. Once you go down this road, it's almost impossible to set guidelines and rules that your daughter will take seriously. Your child wants and needs you to be a parent, not a friend with the ID.

Pushover Parent

The only girls who don't wish they had this kind of parent are the girls who actually do. Daughters of pushover parents are primarily left to make their own mistakes with no guidance and no parental consequences. Teens want rules and boundaries. They may rebel, but deep down they know that rules and boundaries make them feel safe, that there's order to the world and that someone's looking out for them.

> *What's the difference between the two? I would say that the Pushover lets you change the rules whenever you want and the Hip Parent has rules but they are really cool, like "No beer in the bedroom."*
>
> Becca, 16

Benign Neglect Parent

This parent wants to do the right thing but is simply too exhausted and distracted by work and other obligations to create the structured environment a daughter needs. The biggest problem is inconsistency—the par-

ent initiates rules but then they're forgotten because the parent is distracted or just too tired to enforce discipline. When the daughter breaks
a rule, she can take advantage of the parent's guilt and insecurity to
morph the conversation from the daughter's behavior to the parent's bad
parenting.

No-Excuses Parent

This parent has some wonderful qualities, demanding the best from a
child and holding her to a high standard of accountability and personal
responsibility. Through their words and deeds, No-Excuses Parents show
their daughter that she should always get up no matter how many times
she's pushed down. These parents usually raise girls who would make
any parent proud: girls who get good grades, are respectful to others,
and so on. There's only one problem with this kind of parenting: Since
the daughter has been taught that she should take care of whatever
problem faces her, she can be reluctant to ask for help. If she's in over
her head, she can easily feel ashamed that she isn't strong enough to
overcome her problems on her own. Shame is a powerful feeling. It can
make girls feel so bad that they've let the family down that they inter-
nalize their feelings and become self-destructive and/or disconnect from
the family.

Private Parent

This close relative of the No-Excuses Parent believes that family problems should stay within the family. Daughters raised in this style get the
message that imperfection isn't human, it's wrong—or why else the
secrecy? They grow up afraid to reach out for help. While privacy is
important (especially to a teen!), it shouldn't come at the expense of getting family members the resources they need.

No-Privacy Parent

On the other end of the spectrum, and more publicly embarrassing, is the
no-privacy parent. This parent believes that anyone, often unsuspecting

strangers or unlucky dinner guests, should be included in family disputes, even if—or especially if—they include the revelation of embarrassing and humiliating information about individual family members. Because teens are often sensitive about sharing any personal information beyond their name, most parents could be innocently accused of this parenting style, but there's a difference between giving factual information and telling your new best friend about the gory details of the last fight you had with your daughter. Girls with this parent will go to great lengths to create privacy—usually by sneaking behind their parents' backs.

Don't-Ask, Don't-Tell Parent

Through an unspoken agreement, the daughter doesn't tell the parent what's going on and the parent doesn't ask. When parents feel unprepared and/or don't have the support they need, they often feel that ignorance is bliss. This makes for superficial conversations at the dinner table, but in the meantime, the daughter can be foundering.

Overbearing Parent

This parent's love, anxiety, and fear combine either to overwhelm and incapacitate the daughter or drive her away. She often feels suffocated and fights back by becoming defiant.

These parents often suffer from the not-my-daughter mentality. I'm not saying that your daughter is immediately guilty when she's accused of bad behavior. What I'm saying is that our society suffers greatly because people aren't being held accountable for their behavior and they lack a moral compass that directs them to behave honorably. An effective parenting style and philosophy is the key to raising individuals who'll feel a social responsibility to improve their communities.

Who are the winners in my parent pageant?

The Worried Parent

Oh, wait, that's every parent! Those furrows in your brow and gray hairs are there for good reason.

The Loving Hard-Ass Parent

Of course, this is my favorite parent. Parents with this philosophy know there may be things their daughter hides from them, but they don't take it as a personal insult or an indication that their relationship with their daughter is weak. When they make mistakes they own up to their behavior and right the wrong, and they encourage their daughter to do the same. They demonstrate that you can learn from mistakes and be better for it. They love their daughter unconditionally but hold her accountable for decisions and behavior that go against the family's values and ethics. When they're told that their daughter may have done something wrong, they listen and don't blame other people for their daughter's behavior. At the same time, they never make her feel ashamed of who she is.

> *I hate to say it, but my parents really are pretty cool! And all the other parents I can think of that are cool are really very similar to mine. They're laid-back, but not oblivious or completely separate from my life. They trust me. They genuinely like me and like spending time with me. They know what goes on in my life, but they can take a hint when it's time for them to leave me alone. Of course there are the occasional fights or disagreements, but in the end, I think they only help make our family life stronger.*   Julie, 16

I urge every parent to become a Loving Hard-Ass Parent.

THE APPLE DOESN'T FALL FAR FROM THE TREE

Just as I challenge girls to own up to what they do that contributes to their being their own worst enemies, I'm also challenging you to own up to what you do that contributes to girls' social hierarchies. Girls can be just as intimidated and hurt by parents who compete in popularity through their daughters.

> *My daughter goes to an all-girls high school. They have a formal dance every year and there's a group of mothers who organize the dance from the food to the decorations. All the mothers were invited*

to a lunch at one of these mothers' homes; we were told to bring pic-
tures of our daughters. I got there and they were all sitting around,
talking about their daughters and exchanging photographs. Just as I
was about to pull my pictures out, I looked at the other mothers' pic-
tures and it hit me. They were all the same pictures of their girls from
the dance. All the girls were in the same clique, their mothers were a
clique, and my daughter and I weren't included. Here I was, a Harvard
lawyer, board president of national organizations, and I felt so small.
I quietly put my pictures back in my purse and left. I was so mad.
Those women deliberately excluded anyone who wasn't part of their
daughters' cliques! When I got home, I talked to my daughter about
it and she couldn't believe I was surprised.   Gina

My eight-year-old daughter had just started at a new school when the
mother of a Queen Bee approached me. She wanted to invite my
daughter to her daughter's birthday party, but she told me to keep it
quiet because the two other new girls hadn't been invited. For a
moment I was elated that my daughter had made the cut, but then I
realized both my daughter and I were being co-opted by the clique. I
was so torn. I wanted my daughter to be included, but at what price?
                                                              Frank

So ask yourself some very difficult questions: You're your daughter's best
role model; are you talking about other people in a way that you're proud
of? What is she learning from you? When you run up against people who
push your buttons, how do you react? Do you want your daughter acting
the same way? Are there girls you want your daughter to be friends with
(or not) because of social status?

When I speak to parents, I ask them to consider their parenting style
and their duty to be a good role model to their daughters. I also ask them
to create a Parental Bill of Rights that spells out their rights and responsibilities in relation to their daughter. Ask yourself the following questions:

Your Parental Bill of Rights

- What do you need in your relationship with your daughter? *I have
  the right to get the information I need to keep my daughter safe.*

- What are your responsibilities to your daughter? *I'm responsible for helping her become an independent adult through being a good role model and holding her accountable for her actions.*
- Under what circumstances would you ask someone for help with a problem you're having with your daughter? *When I believe it's too uncomfortable for my daughter or the issues she's tackling are making me so crazy that my input will only make the problem worse.*
- Does your daughter know your answers to these questions? *I'm not sure, but I should find out.*

Your daughter also needs a Bill of Rights with you. Ask her the following questions:

Your Daughter's Bill of Rights with You

- What do you need in your relationship with your parent(s)?
- What are your responsibilities to your parent(s)?
- Under what circumstances would you ask someone for help with a problem you are having with your parent(s)?

I want to come to them with problems and get advice and sympathy—not anger or controlling behavior. My responsibility is to keep them informed of where I am, what I'm doing, never lie, uphold their values, and try my best.   Toya, 16

OPENING UP THE LINES OF COMMUNICATION:
TEETH-PULLING 101

I know, I know. You just want to visit Girl World and talk to your daughter about what's going on in her life. Why does she respond by disclosing nothing more than name, rank, and serial number to the evil interrogator? I believe there's nothing better you can do for your daughter than continue to be a loving, engaged part of her life. I also know how hard it is to have a meaningful conversation with a teenage girl if you don't approach it right.

Before you even think of engaging your daughter in an in-depth conversation, know that there are a few certainties that make your task more difficult:

- If you press her to answer more completely than "fine" and "okay" when you ask her how school is, she'll initially see your interest as an invasion of privacy and a waste of time.
- If you tell her you want to "talk" to her, she'll sigh, roll her eyes, and assume you're blaming her for something.

I have some suggestions to get around these common hurdles. First, appreciate that those monosyllables and grunts in response to the daily question of how things are going at school are normal. Asking your daughter a general question like "How was school today?" is too difficult (there was that horrible math test, then Carla didn't say hi to her, then the buttons on her shirt popped open in front of the boys . . .). Instead, ask her specific questions. For example, "What happened in English class today?" or "How did health go?" is less overwhelming.

When you ask her about her life ("So, what's new?"), she might assume you know something bad or that she's in trouble and immediately go into defensive mode. Once she's defensive, you'll never get anything out of her.

> *Maybe starting with "You're not in trouble. I just want to know what's up with you" would work better.*   Katherine, 17

If you, a newly minted Loving Hard-Ass Parent, don't want every conversation short-circuited, you need to make better communication with your daughter a priority. Look for opportunities to bond when you have no other agenda but to check with your daughter just to see that she's okay. Make the most of your time together when you're making dinner, watching TV, driving around on errands. But don't limit yourself to spontaneous opportunities for sporadic conversations. I strongly recommend that you create more focused time just to connect.

At least once every couple of weeks, take your daughter out to a coffee shop or some other place she likes to go where the two of you can sit down and talk, away from other siblings and distractions for both of you. Take her to school one day and leave early so you can stop for bagels and juice. Avoid going to a place where either one of you may run into someone you know. At any point, but especially in the beginning, refrain from making any comments about what she's wearing, homework she's supposed to be doing, or the room she's supposed to be cleaning. Don't talk about schedules, upcoming events, or things you need to get information about. Just as important, watch out for those landmine remarks like, "You should wear your hair pulled back like that more often. You're so pretty when you can see your face." (In Girl World, that's code for, "I don't like the way your hair looks the rest of the time.")

Get your daughter her favorite drink and don't make faces when she orders something you think is disgusting and/or unhealthy. (That's another talk.) Sit down at a table she chooses, get comfortable, and start: "I'm so glad we're doing this. I know we're both so busy but I really want to check in with you. Even if you think this is boring, I want you to know that whatever's going on in your life is important to me, yet I also respect your privacy. So I thought we could spend some time together and you can tell me what you feel comfortable with. So what's up with . . . "

Don't be afraid of silence. Sit with your daughter until she's ready to talk. If she just sits there for a while and it looks like that's the way it'll stay, you can say, "There's no rush, it's more important to me that you're comfortable."

If you want a backup in case she won't talk, bring or allow your daughter to buy a couple of magazines that she wants to read (again, don't comment on her choice of reading material) and bring a book or magazine for yourself and just sit together and read. Often, the first step to talking is feeling comfortable sharing space with someone.

You'll get answers if you set up a comfortable environment and listen respectfully. Even if she complains later to her friends, believe me, she appreciates your effort. If, however, you've never done something like this before, expect her to say something during this talk that sets your teeth on edge. She's your daughter, she's a teen, and she's an expert on you and what gets under your skin. She's an expert button pusher.

If she reacts to your overture by being obnoxious, take a deep breath and remember your goal for the conversation: to connect. For example, she might say disdainfully, "Why do you care all of a sudden? Are you feeling guilty because you're never around? Don't think you can be parent for a day and I'll spill my guts, 'cause that's not happening." At this moment, you may wonder why you bothered and whose child this is anyway. But underneath the obnoxious tone she's telling you something.

Beyond the problems she may be having with her friends, she wants you around more. This is just the way she feels most comfortable telling you. She's hurt and it's always easier to lash out; although that doesn't excuse her delivery. She also may have reason to distrust you and before you go any further, it's critical to acknowledge her feelings. Instead of shutting down and fighting with her, ask, "Why would you say something like that? I really want to know." Then listen.

LISTENING: THE HARD PART

Now we get to the listening part. This can be very hard for parents! Most parents ask leading questions so they can "share" their opinion. This won't work on your daughter. You might as well pay for the coffee and go home.

> *Don't sigh, roll your eyes, or click your teeth. These are all very annoying when you're talking to your Martian parents!*   Alexa, 13

Be honest with yourself about your agenda and goals. Are you keeping an open mind and trying to get general information from your daughter, or are you out to confirm your preconceived opinions? Let's suppose you don't like one of her friends and you want to know more about what your daughter does with this girl after school.

MOTHER: *So what's up with Kathy? You seem to be spending a lot of time with her.*

DAUGHTER: (silence for five seconds)

MOTHER: *Does she do well in school? Does she hang out with anyone I know? Do I know her parents?*

In this scenario you need to admit that your goal isn't finding out what's up with your daughter. Instead, your agenda is to communicate your anxiety and worry that Kathy isn't a good influence. You weren't trying to connect, you were leading the conversation to confirm your own suspicions. Girls see through this easily and will shut down. Anyone would. Let go of your agenda and let your daughter take the lead. Try to be as quiet as possible, and keep your responses nonjudgmental ("I'd like to hear more about that"; "I'm not sure I understand what you're saying, could you run it by me again?")

Mark these get-togethers in your calendar; they're unbreakable dates. You want to establish a pattern that says you're there just for her, you don't want to get involved only when there's a problem, and that you're capable of having a conversation that doesn't revolve around your role as Enforcer. The younger your daughter is when you start these one-on-one conversations, the more she'll see that you're someone she can turn to when she needs support.

Unfortunately, you can't depend on your daughter coming to you when she's upset. The older she gets, the less she'll want to involve you in her problems (often because she considers you one of the main sources). At twelve, she may come crying to you when a girl has been mean to her, but at fifteen, she'll more likely keep it inside or talk to her friends. Even when she can't bring herself to approach you and say, "Mom, I really need to talk to you," she may broadcast signals that she wants your help. Here are some signs to watch for:

- She hangs around where you are but doesn't necessarily say anything.
- She says she doesn't feel well and wants to stay home with you, but there doesn't seem to be anything physically wrong.
- You're about to drive somewhere on an errand and she volunteers to go with you. In the words of Joanna, sixteen, "I like this strategy because she has to focus on driving and can't freak out about what you're saying."
- She asks you to watch a television show with her.
- She slips a very casual reference to her problem into the conversation.
- She tries to get other people out of the house except you.

If your daughter wants to talk to you but also couches it as "no big deal," don't believe her. If she actually wants to talk to you, she's already telling you that she thinks it's a big deal. Anytime your teen daughter wants to talk, drop everything and pay attention. You're ready to talk when she's ready to talk.

In any conversation like this with your daughter, there are two goals: The first is having a productive conversation with her. This means that through the process of your conversation, you want to affirm her and show that you're a good resource and a nonjudgmental listener. The second is helping her develop realistic strategies to confront her problem effectively. You'll never accomplish the second goal without the first. Later in the book I'll walk you through when you need to contact others for additional help (see Resources).

There are some general rules to keep in mind when talking to your daughter:

- **Affirm your daughter's feelings.** ("That must have been really embarrassing," "That's awful," "You must feel really sad," "I would have wanted to spit nails if that happened to me.") Don't be a Truth Cop, intent on verifying the accuracy of everything she tells you right away. The facts will come out over time, but your daughter's emotional truth is what it is, and you should affirm that.

- **Don't use the slang your daughter uses.** There's nothing more ridiculous to a teen than an adult who tries to be hip by using teen slang. Slang changes so fast that it's impossible to keep up anyway. Nevertheless, some parents think that if they use it, they'll relate to their daughter better. Not true. It only looks like you're trying too hard—and there's nothing worse to a teen. If she uses a word you don't understand, ask her to explain it to you. She may laugh at how clueless you are, but it demonstrates that you respect and are interested in what she has to say and how she describes her world.

- **Share your own experiences/stories from when you were her age, especially the ones where you made mistakes and learned from them.** As a general rule, it's better to avoid telling stories about your adult experiences because you need to maintain boundaries with her. The purpose of this storytelling is to empathize—"I know what you've been through, because something similar happened to me"—not to preach.

- **Don't just do something, stand there.** In other words, don't try to fix all of her problems. Resist making everything all right by solving her problems. You want to empower her so she has the skills to get through her problems with your support and guidance. Sometimes your daughter just wants to voice her concerns about something and isn't looking to fix it right away. If she does want to take action, ask her, "What ideas do you have for fixing this?" "Do you want to sound any of them out with me?" Only after you've worked through her ideas might you suggest, "I think I may have some other ideas that could work, too. Do you want to hear them?"

- **Give her ownership of what she does (good and bad) and let her make mistakes.** Even if her solution seems half-baked to you, the fact that it's her idea means that she's working toward independence. Encouraging that is more important than making sure she tries the best (i.e., your) solution.

- **Remember to accept silence.** You are her parent. This means that when you discuss difficult or uncomfortable topics with your daughter, she may not respond right away. Don't think you always need to fill the silence. You can ask her about it after a while by saying, "You just got really quiet when we talked about 'X'; why is that?"

- **Don't make fun of her.** In your daughter's most dramatic moments, you may be tempted to make fun of her. Let's be honest; it can be challenging to take her seriously. But as a general rule, as tempting as it is, keep the joking comments to yourself and just be supportive and ask questions.

- **Even if you have a great relationship with your daughter, it's a good idea to have an ally, someone who shares your values and whom your daughter feels she can go to for help and advice if you hit a communications barrier.** Perhaps she wants to talk about a sexual experience but doesn't feel she can go to you; make sure she has someone like a trusted relative (perhaps an older sibling, aunt, or uncle), a member of the clergy, or a guidance counselor she can talk with. You both should agree on who that person would be. The rule has to be that anything she discusses with her ally remains confidential, unless it involves harm to herself or others. You might build a relationship with the parent of her best friend and have a deal that your daughter will talk with her best friend's mom, and her best friend will talk with you.

After your conversation, or anytime she's feeling bad, affirm her and tell her you love her. Do something for her that will make her feel special and taken care of. Buy her flowers or a smelly candle. Let her talk extra-long on the phone or watch a movie. If she enjoys them, let her take a bath without her brothers or sisters bothering her.

HOW TO GET THROUGH HER REALLY BORING STORIES

I admit it. Sometimes girls tell such boring stories that I'm screaming inside my head for them to get to the point. Even at the end of the story, the point can remain elusive. But the most important thing is to get a girl talking. When she describes a particular situation, it's easy to get lost in the vocabulary and minutia ("and then she said that, which I could not *believe,* so I said . . . and then I was like *so mad* . . . "). It's also okay to admit to yourself that you're incredibly bored listening to what you consider is unbelievably trivial. When you feel your eyes start to glaze over, focus on the goal: You want her to feel that she can talk to you and you won't be judging the things she says. Help her figure out the skills and strategies to learn from the problem she's describing. Ask her what she wants out of the situation and what the obstacles are in making that happen. While these are opportunities to instill your ethics and values into the process she's going through to figure it all out, keep the focus on listening and reflecting.

Sometimes when I tell my parents stories, I specifically don't want *their advice. All I want them to do is listen.* Keisha, 16

In addition to having regular conversations with your daughter, you also need other information sources. It's not that you shouldn't trust your daughter. It's just foolish to depend on her to tell you the whole truth all the time.

YOUR LITTLE ANGEL IS A LIAR AND A SNEAK

Almost all teenagers lie. I'm not saying "all," because I'm allowing for the possibility that there's a teen who doesn't. When my mother reminisces about my adolescence, it always begins with, "You give birth to this wonderful kid and you can never imagine in your wildest dreams that this person that you love so much would lie to you. And then they do. All the time." Needless to say, I lied to my mother all the time. Even when I didn't need to. I lied about everything: where I was going, who I was going with, why I wanted to go in the first place. I lied when there was no reason to lie. I just didn't want her to know anything about what was going on in my life. Not all girls are as bad as I was, but I've yet to meet a girl who was always honest with her parents. Don't take it personally if your daughter lies to you. It's part of the process of her becoming independent from you, of figuring out what you are and aren't entitled to know about her—and of figuring out what she can get away with.

What Makes a Good Liar?

- She bases every lie on a grain of truth. This truthlet can be used later if she's caught and she'll hang on to it for dear life. This is why a girl can be so self-righteous when she's caught.
- She gives you so many details that you get confused.
- She approaches you when you're distracted and/or tired.
- She gets friends to back up the story. (You can undermine this strategy by developing close relationships with the parents of your daughter's friends, as I'll describe shortly.)
- She truly believes what she's saying.
- She's angry with you for something else so she feels justified in lying.

My mom recently got divorced and I was really upset about it. So I thought it was totally okay for me to tell her I was sleeping at my girlfriend's house when I was really at my boyfriend's house.

         Molly, 15

How Can You Tell When She's Lying?

Some parents believe they have the magic power to look their daughter in the eye and the truth will come spilling out. Maybe. If you're really good, your daughter may crumble under the stern, unflinching parental lie detector. But a good liar can pass this test easily. A good liar is cool and collected and continues to hold her ground no matter what. She has an excellent memory and can recall sequential, minute details, for example, "We went to Alicia's house at eight, then we got something to eat and we happened to run into John and Mike and we didn't know that they had alcohol in the trunk of their car until we got pulled over."

So here's how you figure it out.

- Trust your gut—if it sounds funny, it is.
- When she tells you her plans, stop what you're doing and pay very close attention to what she says she's doing, where, when, and with whom. Write it down and keep a copy of your school directory or other lists handy (see below) to double-check parents' numbers.

If your daughter tells you she's going to be at a friend's house, there's a very good chance she is—for about five minutes. Just enough time to go into her friend's house, check out what her friend is wearing, borrow some clothes, grab something to eat, and then they're out the door to their real destination: a party, a boyfriend's house, or some other place you'd rather she not go. Some girls will try to weasel their way out of trouble by telling their parents they're sleeping over at a friend's house. Technically, she isn't lying, because eventually she planned to end up back at the house where she said she'd be. How was she supposed to know the party she went to was so far away, she got stuck there, and the party got so out of control that another parent called you at three in the morning?

If you suspect something like this could be afloat, here's what you do. Of course, confirm the sleepover with the friend's parent. But if you forget or tried to and didn't get in touch in time, here are some backup strategies: Call the friend's house. If your daughter is pulling a fast one on you, she'll have a friend cover for her. When you call, the cover will say your daughter is in the bathroom (or some other reason why she can't come to the phone right now). The cover will assure you that your daughter will call you back in a few minutes. You know what happens when you get off the phone; you may have done it yourself. The cover frantically calls your daughter where she really is (a boy's house perhaps?) and tells her to call you. Your daughter will then call you pretending she's where she's supposed to be. (Caller ID makes it harder for your daughter to disguise where she's calling from.) Tell your daughter that you happen to be in the neighborhood and are going to drop by the friend's house in a few minutes. This may be completely implausible but it won't matter. She'll go into teen panic mode and it should become clear that you caught her.

If She Says "You Don't Trust Me!"

You don't nor should you!   Fran, 17

What's the difference between lying and sneaking? Think of lying as untruthful words and sneaking as untruthful actions.

What Makes a Good Sneak?

- She takes advantage of your exhaustion, distractibility, and denial that she would sneak behind your back in the first place.
- She has strategic backup plans. If the first plan to sneak out of the house doesn't work, she always has an alternative.
- She's patient and intelligent. She can think three steps ahead to get what she wants.

Let's say you've told your daughter that she can't go to a party because she's not old enough. If your daughter easily accepts your decision and it's clearly contrary to what she wants, she could be placating you and planning to sneak behind your back. Don't take it personally. She isn't sneaking against you. She just thinks that what she wants is way more important than anything you have to say.

> *You know what would be funny? Put a tracking device on your daughter so you could compare where she tells you she's going and where she actually goes.*   Zoe, 17

If you don't trust your daughter, admit it. But be very clear about why before you talk to her. If she really can be trusted, but you're having a hard time with her growing independence, you have to own up to that. She has to earn your distrust by her actions, not because of your own baggage or because you think teens are inherently untrustworthy.

It's a painful fact of life that your daughter is probably going to lie and sneak. But to be a good parent, you're still going to need to know what's going on in her life. You need to lay a pipeline for a reliable flow of information from credible sources. You need reconnaissance strategies.

RECONNAISSANCE STRATEGIES

1. Become friendly with the parents of your daughter's friends. Get together with your daughter's friends and their parents once a month. You can have a potluck dinner or meet for an early dinner out, drinks, or coffee. Knowing that her parents and her friends' parents are meeting on a regular basis may make your daughter slightly paranoid, which is exactly what you want. Your daughter needs to feel that the adults in her life have an active interest in her and care about what she does. Once you've established your group, have the parents' phone numbers readily available at all times. Keep a copy of the phone list at work, in your bedroom, and in the kitchen.

2. Keep a copy of the school directory in a secret place. Girls hide their school directories and school lists so it'll be harder for you to contact other parents or school personnel. Make a copy of your daughter's school directory as soon as it comes in the mail (if it gets sent home with your daughter, either hound your daughter to see it, or call the school and ask for one to be sent to you in your name, perhaps at your work address) and put it somewhere she doesn't know about. For example, label a folder "Taxes 1998" and keep it there. Keep your copy at work if she's really good at finding your hiding places. However, most public schools don't have these directories, so try to pull together as comprehensive a phone list as possible from the sports team roster, Girl Scout troop list, church group, and so on.

3. Whenever possible, get her friends' 411. Get as complete a list as possible of your daughter's friends' cell phones, pagers, or beeper numbers and keep them in a secret place. If your daughter has a cell phone, you may feel reassured that you can reach her and vice versa when necessary. But cell phones also make reconnaissance much more difficult. It's common for girls to give their parents their friend's cell numbers and lie about where they're supposed to be. So keep these numbers handy for comparison.

> *Everyone has a cell phone nowadays. It's simple to say you're going to someone's house and then give your parents an alternate number of one of your friend's phones; I've made my friends change their answering machines. I'm* brilliant!   Becca, 16

OOPS, I DID IT AGAIN: SHOULD YOU READ YOUR DAUGHTER'S DIARY OR E-MAIL?

When parents tell me that they "accidentally" found their daughter's diaries when they were cleaning their rooms or just happened to run across their daughter's private e-mail, I have to laugh. They sound just like their daughters when they're caught doing something they weren't supposed to do. And just as you don't believe her when she gives you a ridiculously lame excuse, she doesn't believe you either. Believe me, you don't have to read her diary or go through her e-mails to find out what's going on with her. She'll tell you what you need to know if you follow the strategies in this chapter.

   The only time I can possibly see a reason for reading a diary or e-mail is if your daughter has totally shut down, you have followed the communication strategies in this book, you're getting nowhere, and you're really worried she's doing something dangerous to her health.

> *I say things in my diary that I don't mean all the time. It's not like you'll write when you walked the dog, did your homework, and went to bed. You write in your journal when you're very happy, very miserable, or very angry.*   Paloma, 16

WHAT TO DO IF YOU CATCH YOUR DAUGHTER LYING

The reconnaissance has paid off, and you've caught your daughter lying. The only thing more difficult than talking to your daughter when she's upset is when she's done something wrong. Girls are amazingly good at dodging and evading. When they're caught and they know they're going to get in trouble, they'll obsess on their evasion tactics. You, too, should be similarly focused, but in a more positive direction.

Here's the trick: Information is power. Never let your anger get the best of you, because then you'll be more likely to divulge what you know. Approach your daughter with the strategy that you really want her opinion about what happened. Get her defenses down. By doing this, you demonstrate that you respect her perspective (note that I didn't say agree), but you're also getting as much information as possible without letting on what you know. Any girl worth her weight will know when she's in trouble; the key is to first figure out how much her parents actually know. There may well be things you don't know. Her goal is to keep it that way.

Write down what your daughter is saying as she's saying it. I know this sounds over the top, but you'll notice any contradictions in her story much more quickly. You'll also have a record so she can't deny you said something you're sure you said or vice versa. Girls take advantage of how tired and distracted parents are. So it'll make her nervous and she may accuse you of not trusting her. If you don't trust her, remember, it's okay to admit it. Or at the least, don't lie and tell her you do when you don't. Just tell her you want to make sure you get her side of the story.

Never Confront Her in Front of Her Friends!

Either wait until later, or ask her to join you in the kitchen. Saving face is very important to your daughter. If you confront her in front of her friends, you'll embarrass her and she'll lash out—most likely at you. Think of it this way. She knows you'll always be her parent, so there's more freedom in how she can treat you. That's a downside to being a parent who'll always be there; your daughter takes your relationship for granted. Her friends are different. She constantly has to prove herself to them. One way she can do this is if she shows how independent she is by talking back to you.

You're not giving in to her or letting her get away with something if you wait until she's alone. In fact, waiting is a punishment unto itself. Remember when you got in trouble? Often the worst part is when you know you're caught and waiting for the ax to fall.

If you do have good reason not to trust her, tell her why. Describe the specific actions that led to your suspicions, explain how you feel, and what she can do to gain back your trust. Remember, your daughter may give you incremental information. Give her the space to do it. Whether she's in trouble with you or she's had a bad experience that she wants to share with you, she'll probably parcel out the story in chapters, if not sentences.

Having the Conversation

You found out an hour ago that your daughter has lied to you about where she went last night. She told you she was at a friend's house, but she went out with her friend and some boys. You found out when a mother called you, thinking her daughter was sleeping over at your house. You've taken some time to calm down and plan your strategy.

YOU: *I want to talk about what happened last night. Tell me what you think happened.*

YD: *How should I know? I don't even care, because I'm just going to be punished anyway.*

YOU: *Well, what do you think I think happened?*

YD: *You think I lied to you; which I didn't by the way, because I was supposed to be sleeping over at Maggie's house and I went out instead. But you didn't tell me that I couldn't go out with them and I was going to sleep over at Maggie's house.*

YOU: *You did lie to me because you told me information to mislead me about where you would be. Do you agree or not?*

YD: *I didn't lie!*

YOU: *I don't think you're answering my question: Did you give me information to mislead me because you didn't want me to know what you were doing?*

YD: *Whatever (which means, if you say it that way, I guess you're right).*

YOU: *Well, first I want to know why.*

YD: *Because you'd get mad and I was obviously right because you're freaking out over nothing.*

YOU: *I'm freaking out for two reasons. First, you intentionally misled me. Two, by misleading me and Maggie's parents, no adult knew where you were. I know that was the point, but the reality is when you make decisions like that, if you get in a situation you want to get out of, it may get considerably harder if no one knows where you are.*

YD: *So what's my punishment?*

YOU: *You lied because you wanted me out of your face. Ironically, the consequence is that I'm now going to be much more in your face. Your lying forces me to act like a controlling parent and treat you like a child. You can't use the phone and e-mail for one week. And you will have to build back the trust you have lost. I'm not sure how long that'll take, but I do know that it'll be a process over time.*

If She's Sneaking Out of the House

Don't get bogged down in the details so that you're arguing about whether she sneaked out on Thursday or Friday. The important thing is that if she's sneaking out, you have to address the issues of dishonesty and safety.

YOU: *I know you're sneaking out of the house. I don't want to argue about it, but I want you to know that I know it. I could lock you in the room every night and treat you like a child and a prisoner in your own home, but I don't think that would be an effective way of dealing with this problem, because I'll become the enemy and you'll sneak out whenever you get the chance. I assume you don't want to be treated like a child, yet you're forcing me to treat you like one. If you continue to sneak out then I'll worry about you until I know you're safe, and I won't trust you. Then we have a relationship of mutual distrust and you see the house as a prison. So what do you want to do about this?*

If she doesn't back down and have a reasonable conversation with you after you've said this then take away something concrete or a privilege that you do have control over. Remind her that the reason why you are treating her like a child is because her actions leave you no alternative.

What Is the Worst Punishment You Can Give Her?

In talking to girls for this book, it's very clear what they consider the worst punishment. Time and time again, they all say the same thing. The worst punishment is losing your respect and disappointing you and taking away their ability to communicate with their peers. Countless girls have told me a variation on the quotes below:

> *I have deep respect for my dad and I talk to him about a lot. The worst punishment he could give me without saying it is to lose his respect and trust in me.*   Jane, 16

> *I hate when I get into trouble because my mother cuts off my phone privileges. I don't know anything that's going on!*   Claire, 14

> *Dads are more forgiving, especially if you cry and they think, "Oh well, I did the same thing when I was her age". . . . Moms know you better . . . and when she finds out, she really has something on you. Dads don't want to know what's going on.*   Courtney, 14

But tangible punishments are also important! Anytime you take away her ability to communicate with her peers, it's a serious punishment. E-mail, phone, grounding so she can't go out—all hurt where it matters most.

YOUR DAUGHTER WILL TAKE YOU SERIOUSLY IF . . .

For any of this to work, you must practice what you preach. You can do nothing worse to undermine your authority than be hypocritical. Your daughter can smell it on you a mile away. Don't lay down your values, expect her to follow them, and then act differently yourself. If you gossip about other people (especially other children she knows), don't expect her to do anything different. If you lie or sneak around, expect her to do the same. If you make a mistake and don't own up to it, don't expect her to hold herself accountable. If you're defensive and refuse to apologize, she'll be self-righteous. It doesn't mean you can't make mistakes and admit that to her (in fact, that in itself can be a great bonding moment for both of you). Being a credible role model depends on you consistently demonstrating the core values you believe in and want her to practice.

You Aren't a Failure

Many parents I work with tell me they feel like a failure when their daughter struggles so much. The only way you can fail is if you don't try, you disconnect, you don't hold her accountable for her behavior, or you don't teach her to value empathy, thoughtfulness, and critical thinking. Be kind to yourself. Parenting is often overwhelming, and very few of us are taught to develop effective coping skills.

> *It's so hard for us [parents] to be reflective. It's too painful to be aware of our choices—what we've given up and what they've embraced. When I look at my own daughter, I often feel like a failure. I feel responsible and guilty that I can't fix her pain, I can't fix society overnight, and I can't find her the help she needs.*   Kara

> *There's so much shame when your daughter has problems. Other parents talk about their kids' activities and school. It's so hard to discuss what's going on because I feel different and that everyone else is perfect. Part of me knows better and part of me wonders . . .*   Michaela

> *I went to a couple of parent meetings and talked about the problems my daughter was having with other girls. All I got was stony silence or people being nice in a patronizing way by expressing sympathy at best, but never suggesting that what I or my daughter are going through has ever happened to them or their daughters. Never did I hear "I know what you mean—this happened to my daughter." So I felt like a freak, and didn't trust what other parents would say about her, so I shut my mouth.*   Susan

> *Why are parents so anxious to convince other parents that their child is perfect and isn't going through the usual teen angst?*   Belle

Know that you're not alone. If you reach out, you will find a community of parents that can band together for support and sharing.

ALWAYS REMEMBER

Parenting isn't a popularity contest. You don't need to be your daughter's best friend. You need to be her parent by setting limits and holding her accountable when those limits are broken. Even if she says she hates your interference and accuses you of violating her privacy, rest assured her hatred is temporary. If you continue to be a Loving Hard-Ass Parent, no matter how much of a pain in the ass she is now, she'll apologize later, thank you, and raise her own kids well.

Now we're ready to go back to Girl World and take a closer look at how girls enforce the rules on a daily basis. It's the way girls get tossed out of the raft—the Beauty Pageant.

The Beauty Pageant

Who Wants to Be Miss Congeniality?

Your thirteen-year-old daughter has just been invited to a party, and she's convinced you she needs new shoes. Your selective memory kicks into gear and you temporarily forget about the last time you attempted a shopping expedition with her. Off to the mall you go. As soon as you walk in, you're bombarded by monitors flashing videos, neon signs proclaiming the brands your daughter covets, and perky store assistants barely older than your daughter. You begin to feel exhausted, defeated, and slightly paranoid that the whole situation is conspiring against you. Which, of course, is true.

Then it happens. She sees the pair that she *must* have. You groan. They look ridiculous, they're too expensive, the heels are too high (she'll break her ankle), and they're too sexy for a girl her age. You hold up a pair you like: "What about these?" Your daughter sighs, then begs, then barters ("Just let me get these shoes and I'll do the dishes for the next month!"), then launches into an outright self-righteous tantrum to the strains of "You're *so* mean!"

I have seen girls in this situation who have thrown the alternative shoes across the store, leaving the perky assistants to crawl under displays for them. (Yes, you can take a moment and give yourself credit for not having one of these girls as your daughter, but I'm sure you have seen them and been silently smug.)

I was totally justified! Those shoes were so cool!

Okay, on the face of it, this is a ridiculous fight over shoes, but why is this situation so contentious? First, it's hard to see your daughter grow up.

Those shoes could easily symbolize your daughter's developing sexuality and you could understandably and correctly think she's growing up too fast. No matter how hip and cool you think you are, when your child starts wanting to be sexy and grown-up, it can be very upsetting. It's possible that you're overreacting ever so slightly to a pair of shoes. Meaning that she thinks you're freaking out.

But those shoes are equally meaningful to her. Why is she acting like it'll be the end of the world if she doesn't get them? Until recently you may have believed your daughter was a reasonable person. What's motivating her to act like this? What may be hard to remember in situations like this is that those shoes could be the ticket to social acceptance.

Remember, it's *never* just about the shoes.

It's about style and beauty and image, and how they impact your daughter's relationship with the clique. How does this affect your daughter's place in the social hierarchy? Is there anything you can do to stop your daughter from wearing cropped tops, tight hip-hugging pants, or shoes that make her six inches taller? When she wakes up in the morning and feels too ugly to walk out the door, do her friends make her feel better or will they make her feel worse? How do race and class impact your daughter's definition of beauty? These are the questions this chapter will answer.

Ironically, when I first started teaching, it was easy to overlook beauty's impact on girls because it's as ubiquitous and invisible as the air they breathe. Beauty and style are so important to the Girl World that it wouldn't exist without it. When you look at your daughter, you see a beautiful girl. But she probably can't look past that too-big nose, or that pimple on her chin; they're a constant source of humiliation. Girls have told me for years that they struggle to survive in a painful world where the value of self-worth is too often tied to an impossible standard of beauty. The following sums up how they see the world.

WHAT YOU MUST KNOW

- Most girls are obsessed about their looks. If they aren't, they've found another way to express themselves through a talent or skill that builds their self-esteem.

- If there's something about their physical appearance that they do like, girls will never admit it because they're afraid other girls will accuse them of being vain.
- If there's something about their physical appearance they don't like, they're obsessed by it.
- Girls need constant reassurance from each other that they fit in and look good.
- Girls are constantly comparing themselves to each other.
- Girls know they're manipulated by the media to hold themselves to an impossible standard of beauty, but that doesn't stop them from holding themselves to it anyway.
- When a girl has a friend who's starving herself, she's often torn between worry and envy, because thin equals good (this can change depending on race and culture, but the dominant culture dictates thin equals good).
- Being beautiful doesn't guarantee popularity, but it limits how low down the pecking order you go.
- The way a girl decides to "mark" herself—from piercing a nose, lip, or dyeing her hair to wearing GAP or BCBG—identifies how she sees herself and to what group she belongs. Her markers reveal her place in the social hierarchy.

Adolescence is a beauty pageant. Even if your daughter doesn't want to be a contestant, others will look at her as if she is. In Girl World, everyone is automatically entered. How does a girl win? By being the best at appropriating our culture's definition of femininity. However, a girl can win by losing if being in the running means she has to sacrifice her individual identity.

As a parent, you may be appalled that your daughter is being so heavily judged by her looks, especially if you're raising her to value her inner worth much more than her external appearance. The best way to help her is to appreciate that everyone is in the pageant, regardless of whether they want to be or not. Like the Miss America pageant, there are many individual competitions leading up to the crown; your daughter will have to compete in all of them.

It is impossible to win the contest . . . but I think a lot of girls perceive others to be the winner, but in actuality those girls are just as competitive and unsure of themselves as everyone else.   Isabel, 17

FEMININITY: THE RULES OF THE PAGEANT

Your daughter doesn't need special classes to learn how to be a girl in our society. From the moment she wakes up until she goes to bed, a girl learns with constant reinforcement how she's supposed to behave. What she wears, how she cuts her hair, says hello, and shakes hands all reflect how our culture expects femininity to be expressed.

Trying to get it right overwhelms girls. They're afraid to make mistakes and often aren't even sure what those mistakes are. Frequently they feel as if they not only have to be perfect but achieve that perfection effortlessly. That's why teen magazines are so important to girls; they tell them two things: what the "right look" is and how to know if they've got it wrong (witness the infamous "Glamour Don't"). The most popular features of those magazines are the letters girls send in to confess their worst, most humiliating moments, because girls desperately want to be reassured that there are other girls struggling with all this mess—just like they are.

Girls are bombarded with the Victoria's Secret definition of femininity, which means having hips and curves (but only in the right places), being hairless and clean, and smelling good. This kind of femininity is powerful and simultaneously elusive. This is what girls are chasing.

The ingredients to win aren't based on looks alone. It's about coming to terms with how others perceive you as a whole package. Your appearance is merely the wrapping. Like any present, if you're "wrapped" well, people will think the gift is more valuable.   Zoe, 17

Despite several waves of feminism, the image of the shrieking girl driven up onto a chair by a mouse or bug until a boy comes along to save the day is alive and kicking. Ask them, and most girls will tell you they think this scene is pathetic. But your daughter has probably seen girls behave in exactly this way. She may have even been the one shrieking. Why? Because although we have told girls that they're as smart and as competent as boys, they still get conscious and unconscious messages that they need a man to validate their self-worth and that, to get the man in the first place, they have to present themselves in a nonthreatening (read feminine) manner.

Of course, definitions of femininity have become progressively more complicated. Look at soccer star Mia Hamm or tennis champions Venus and Serena Williams. Women who are strong, aggressive, and competitive athletes are now "allowed" to be considered feminine. But look deeper. On the field, Mia Hamm acts in stereotypically masculine ways. She's intense, fearless, and on the attack. But once she's off the field (as her shampoo advertisements show), she becomes the pretty girl with the beautiful bouncing hair. Off the tennis court and in the Avon and Reebok commercials, the Williams sisters' amazing muscles are downplayed behind soft clothes and makeup. Girls get the lesson that "masculine" behavior is acceptable only in specified arenas. To get social validation, girls must still be soft, pretty, and nonthreatening.

In any case, whether or not it's now acceptable for girls to have muscles is a red herring. What messes girls' heads up is chasing an ideal. It doesn't matter if that ideal is a Victoria Secret model or the Williams sisters—both have extreme body types that are difficult, if not impossible, to achieve. All of this means that we still haven't gotten beyond girls valuing their place in society by how closely their body comes to society's current ideal image of femininity. Nor is chasing ideals limited to the beauty magazines. In response to the teen magazines, well-meaning adults have written countless books and other magazines that popularize yet another impossible ideal—the girl with high self-esteem who isn't allowed to admit she likes *Seventeen* magazine or ever feels fat.

> *Beauty makes you a different person. You can be insecure and still be confident. You evolve into a different person. It's a lot easier to change everything about you. People will say [about themselves] I look better today, but that doesn't mean they think they're hot.*
>
> Lupe, 17

HERE SHE COMES . . . MISS AMERICA

Every school has one. The golden girl who bears aloft the holy grail of beauty. When she's around, boys lose their power of speech. When she leaves, she's all they talk about. Girls are intimidated or envious of her and think her life is perfect. But listen to what one of these icons has to say:

> I take [the Owning Up empowerment] class every year because I forget. I forget that I'm worthwhile, that I can tell my boyfriend what I want in our relationship. I forget that I am beautiful. There's so much around me telling me that I am not. I come here to remember.
>
> Faith, 16

I'm sure it wouldn't surprise you that this girl typifies the classic definition of beauty: tall, thin, blond, and beautiful. If this girl—the one everyone wants to be like, the one no one thinks has any problems, including feeling ugly and fat—thinks this, imagine what other girls feel?

Your daughter, like every girl, has moments when she has similar feelings. When I ask girls, "In an average day, how many times do you think about your weight and/or your appearance, and what percentage of those comments are negative versus positive?," they laugh at me for thinking they ever have positive comments! For some, these moments of insecurity are just that—moments when they feel good or bad, secure or insecure. But for far too many others, these moments dictate an entire self-concept. It's all interconnected—the value a girl places on beauty as a basis for her self-esteem, the value she places on the social pecking order, and the choice, quality, and dynamics of her friendships.

That girls are insecure about their looks is hardly news. But as a parent, you have to be smart about how beauty and fashion play their part in your daughter's life. When I ask girls what a stereotypical "beautiful" woman looks like, they answer the same way, regardless of race or ethnicity: She has to be thin, with long hair, good teeth, and big breasts. Whatever your daughter looks like, she doesn't think she looks like that. Your daughter knows that the girls in the magazines are airbrushed and probably have fake boobs, but it doesn't stop her from comparing herself to them and feeling inadequate. Girls *know* that if Barbie were life-size, her body would be so out of proportion that she wouldn't be able to walk. Girls *know* that magazines, TV, and movies are in the business of making girls feel insecure so they'll buy their products. They *know* companies are advertising in all three so that girls will buy their products. Yet in spite of their awareness and sophistication, they still get sucked in.

Girls are also constantly comparing themselves to each other and rarely do they feel they measure up. I teach countless girls who are beautiful by anyone's standards, yet they're absolutely convinced that their flaws are all anyone sees, because they're comparing themselves to the girls they see in *Seventeen*, *YM*, and *Cosmopolitan*. So when your daughter tells you how incredibly ugly she is, how fat her thighs are, or how big her nose is, you have to realize that she believes it—no matter what you tell her to the contrary.

> *I have never met a person who thinks she's pretty. You sit and pick apart every flaw. The combined list of how you don't measure up really adds up.*
>
> Joni, 15

THE EVENING GOWN COMPETITION: WHY MARKERS MATTER IN YOUR DAUGHTER'S TRIBE

The pursuit and attainment of the elusive standard of beauty is one of the most critical components of girls' power structure. Girls are keenly aware of these dynamics and, unfortunately, very few of them feel there's anything they can do to stop them. Ironically, it isn't so much about the individual girl's look that will get her into the clique but her willingness to conform to *their* look that grants acceptance. If your daughter conforms, they'll support her. If she rebels and strays from their norm, she'll be ostracized with one sentence: "*What* are you *wearing?*"

The Queen Bee doesn't necessarily create the look, but she's both a conduit of information on the look from the media to the rest of her clique and its ultimate arbiter and enforcer. She'll strictly adhere to the rules and quickly correct any girls who stray outside the set definition of cool. The fear of censure is so strong that it can largely dictate who gets into the "higher" cliques and encourages all girls to be Wannabes. The result is that the girls in these cliques all start to look the same.

> *It's not that they're all beautiful, but those girls all look alike. They seem like they're all sisters. They have the same body structure and*

*they're all petite. They all walk together, laugh together, and have
older boyfriends.*　　　　　　　　　　　　　　　　　　　　Lynn, 16

That's what markers are all about. A marker is the signifier of your tribe, such as clothes, hairstyle, what sports you play, what clubs you belong to, what partying you do, how well you do in school, how much money you have. A girl's "look" is the most significant way she communicates to her peers where she belongs. It's no different from stripes on a zebra or even tags (identifying markers) for a gang. Some markers have broader significance: the brand of jeans you wear, the way you tie your shoelaces, whether you pierce your navel, whether you shave your underarms and legs. Markers for a particular clique might be more specific; the lacrosse team clique (usually the older or more athletically inclined girls plus one or two anointed freshmen) might all wear a particular scrunchie.

Unfortunately, when parents have difficulty with their daughters' appearance, it's often because they don't know, and therefore don't see how, their daughters' markers are a wealth of information and thus the key to knowing how and when to reach out to her.

The dominant, or alpha, clique (the stereotypical one we know from bad movies about high school) absorbs and reflects media images with little interpretation; they're the girls who look like clones of the latest pop stars. The beta cliques create their look in response to or in opposition to the alpha clique.

Markers matter because they affirm to the girls in the clique that they belong in the social hierarchy; they get the attention of others (especially boys), and they announce to the world who's in and who's not. The girls who adhere to the Queen Bees' dictates most closely have more power and influence over the girls in their own clique as well as those outside it.

THE SWIMSUIT COMPETITION: WHO GETS BOOBS FIRST

Breasts are one of the most obvious signifiers of femininity. Do you remember the girl who developed breasts first in your circle of friends? Were you that person? Remember the taunting from boys and comments from other girls? Like the first daffodil of spring, this girl signals that puberty has officially begun. Many boys are transfixed by the changes her body is going through, and the other girls can be simultaneously anxious, intrigued, and envious. She's a lightning rod for all the other children to bounce their preadolescent anxiety and excitement off of. And if you're a twelve-year-old girl in full bloom, the chance of handling this situation well is from slim to none.

This dynamic can be even more confusing if and when a girl notices the power of her sexuality. All of a sudden, this girl is getting lots of attention and is gaining popularity because she has a part of the girl ideal. She can be conflicted between wanting and liking the attention and disturbed by what it means. She likes being objectified because she's getting attention, but is it the kind of attention she wants? Yes and no.

> When I was younger, girls were worse than the boys about my boobs getting bigger. I remember in sixth grade I went to a pool party. There was only one other girl who was developing like me. I had been running around—it never occurred to me then to be self-conscious—but she had purposefully stayed in the pool to hide. I liked developing because I was coming into myself and sometimes I don't want my body to be commented on.
> Olivia, 16

> When I was in fifth grade, one girl developed DD breasts. Her breasts were the topic of everyone's conversation. It got her a lot of attention. Maybe it was a front, but she seemed to like it. Girls were so envious and called her a slut because boys flirted with her. When I had a birthday party, we all made fun of her by putting towels down our shirts and pretending to flirt with invisible boys. But I guess she would never know if a boy liked her for her.
> Simone, 17

> A boy asked me if I would wear shoes if I didn't have any feet. I said no. Then he asked, so then why do you wear a bra?
> Marcy, 16

Simone's claim of making fun of an early-blooming friend is self-deceptive. In fact, Simone and her friends were emulating her and trying on what it would feel like to have the power and ability to flirt with boys. Breasts give you the right to flirt.

One of the ironic results of feminism is that some girls are comfortable being objectified and don't feel subjugated if they are. It's the Madonna philosophy that flaunting their sexuality doesn't come at the expense of their personal power but is in fact a source of power. Most early bloomers, however, don't know how to handle this. They see that their best chance to escape girls' condemnation is to continually put themselves down, hide their bodies, and never admit liking the attention they're getting because of their breasts. If popularity is the prize, think of attention as the tiara. Everyone wants it, but there are codified rules for how you handle yourself when you take your victory walk. Olivia, who developed early, felt the brunt of her friends' envy.

> Once I got up to do a presentation in front of the class and one of my friends whispered to another friend "Olivia's thighs are so fat." I could totally hear her.   Olivia, 16

Breasts are power. Olivia's friends were taking away her power by making her feel insecure about another part of her body. She felt horribly self-conscious and wondered "Why are my friends saying such means things? Do I pretend that I don't hear them and let them get away with this? Do I confront them? Do other people hear them? Do they think the same thing? Do I have fat thighs?" Hard to concentrate on your work when something like this is going on.

When you see your daughter at dinner one evening and ask her how her presentation went, she might give you an unenthusiastic "fine." You might be thinking she didn't prepare well enough; she might be thinking she barely survived walking through a bed of burning coals.

The Competition No One Wins

> I have struggled my whole life with my weight. Two years ago I was much heavier and people made fun of me. I would cry every day after school.   Anne, 15

> I don't have a big butt. People compare me to a white girl. I'm teased a lot for being too skinny. I wanted to hang out with people who would accept me for not being so curvy.   Aliesha, 17

I could fill this book with the feelings girls have about their weight. Whether girls worry about being too thin or having curves in "all the right places," it's a given that whatever they weigh is never good enough. Cliques reinforce the paranoia girls feel that they're all losing the battle against each other. Behind every girl's concern when her friend starves herself is the simultaneous worry that "If she thinks she's fat, then I'm obese!" Her internal voice whispers, "Am I worried about her, or am I really envious that she has enough control that she can starve her body into submission?"

I recently received the following from a tenth-grade girl who has a friend who is anorexic.

> We used to be a lot closer, but she just seems to have pushed everyone who's concerned out of her life. But even if we don't end up being great friends like we used to, I just want her to stop feeling like she has to control every ounce of food that passes (or doesn't) through her body. I want her to feel happy with her life and with who she is, and I don't want her to carry this disease with her to college where I fear she'll be lost forever.
>
> Of course I want to get her help, but I'm not really in any position to do that, and since she is still in stage number one, denial, then getting her help would be like trying to tell a brick wall to move. I hate to look at her because she should be in a National Geographic of poor, starving children in Rwanda. I'm much more aware of eating disorders than I ever was. I can tell when the people around me aren't eating. The effect of her disease is my paranoia. My conversations with other people seem to at one time or another revolve around eating disorders and how many people we know who have one.
>
> Laurie, 15

AND THE WINNER FOR MISS CONGENIALITY IS . . .

A select few claim the tiara of beauty, but most girls vie for acceptance by angling for Miss Congeniality. The winner of this award is the girl who humbly dismisses her beauty by insisting that she's fat or unattractive, and "you're so pretty." This award is highly coveted because it acts as insurance to protect the winner from the cruelty of other girls.

Girls know they'll pay a price for their supposed vanity; as much as they crave the attention of being considered attractive, it's safer not to be the reigning beauty queen.

Rule Number One of the Girl World: When you're with your friends, always put yourself down, especially in comparison with them (which you're always doing), and compliment them. (When you're not with them, you can say what you think.) Picture what happens when one girl tells another girl how great she looks. Does the recipient of the compliment thank her? Rarely. Instead, the response is usually some variation of "Oh no, I look so fat and horrible. I can't believe you would say that. You look so much better than me." Girls must degrade themselves after being complimented in order not to appear vain.

Rule Number Two of the Girl World: Leap to your friends' defense when they put themselves down; they'll leap to yours when you put yourself down. So you say you're fat? "Omigod, you look so good!" Girls literally compete with each other about who's the fattest ("You're so much thinner than me, compared to you I'm such a cow"). (Behind your back, the best you can hope for is that your closest allies say nothing when the Queen Bee or someone else slams you; worst case, they join in.) One girl told me that when she was in seventh grade, hanging out in the girls' room with her friend, the friend asked her, "Do you think we're pretty, average, or ugly?" The girl immediately gave the Correct Answer: "You're pretty. I'm average." The friend responded, "I think we're both average." This violation of the code of Girl World is sheer genius. The friend is able to put down her friend while getting immunity by simultaneously putting herself down. Her friend can't get mad at her, even though she'd clearly said something mean.

When I ask girls what they like most about their body, they always mention asexual parts such as teeth, hair, or eyes. They *never* say they love their abs, legs, butt, or breasts, because Girl World forbids giving yourself high marks for the "sexy" parts. Admit any positive attribute about yourself and the other girls will accuse you of "being all that" or "being stuck up." They'll have the right to do whatever's necessary to tear you down. So when I tell the girls they can't choose hair, teeth, or eyes as their favorite attribute, they literally squirm and look for the nearest exit! It's hard to know if a girl's saying that she's fat or otherwise unattractive ("I'm such a pig") because she actually feels she is or if she's saying it in order to put herself down to protect herself. The danger is that the two ideas will intermingle and wreak havoc on her self-esteem.

In order to get along with other girls and deal with our culture's preoccupation with beauty, girls have a high tightrope to walk across with no net. The definition of femininity is complicated, and it's easy to make mistakes. If they have a fleeting moment of feeling "I look good!" it's guaranteed to be taken away by a flip through a magazine or a snide comment.

CROSSING OVER AND CROSSING OUT

I talk properly and I don't classify myself as part of black culture. People call me white-washed and a sell-out. When I was younger I tried being black more. Now I look back on that and think that wasn't me. But at the same time, when I look at the magazines, there's nothing for me. All the makeup and hair products are for white girls. I look at the black magazines for images, but it's still hard.   Aliesha, 18

One of the things I always felt growing up as someone of mixed racial heritage was that I didn't fit in anywhere. On the one hand, I was presented with the white image of beauty as the blue-eyed, blond-haired, tall, skinny, big-breasted All-American girl. On the other hand was the Asian image of beauty as petite, slender, long dark hair, exotic features, and pale skin, actresses like Lucy Liu, Ming Na Wen, and the women in Crouching Tiger, Hidden Dragon. *The only thing I had in common with any of those images was that I was fair-skinned, otherwise I never felt like I measured up. For people of mixed backgrounds, you kind of fall through the cracks when you look at fashion magazines. It's also true that Asian women try to look more white. My mother, for instance, puts tape on her eyelids to make them look rounder. One of my Korean friends once told me I was lucky that I had pale skin because when she went to Korea, people told her she looked like a "country girl" because she's naturally tan. There are also operations that some girls get to make their eyes look more "white," and some girls get nose jobs to make their noses look more "white." This doesn't occur only in the States either; in Korea, plastic surgery is a huge industry. It's because they also get Western fashion magazines there and are presented with the Caucasian standard of beauty and will get nose jobs, fix their eyes, and get operations on their jaws to make their faces look less round, less Asian and more white. When you look at women like Jennifer Lopez and Beyonce Knowles, who both have blond highlights and look like white women with tans, you realize that racism still plays itself out in what we are presented with as "beautiful."*   Ellie, 21

It goes without saying that talking about racism and classism is uncomfortable. We live in a society where people are so frightened of talking about differences that well-meaning people are often tongue-tied when race is brought up, and everyone defines themselves as middle class even if they own two houses and send their children to private schools. I have definitely struggled with this in my own teaching. It has silenced me in the classroom.

Girls suffer because of racist standards of beauty. When I bring this up with the girls I teach, the white Queen Bees and their court usually become self-righteous. They're angry with me; am I accusing *them* of racism? The girls of color usually look at me with amazement; are we really going to talk about this? The more diverse schools already get it; the more sheltered schools panic. I'm not an expert on these issues, but this is what the girls have told me. It's hard to talk about, but all parents need to know how this impacts their daughter.

No matter what race your daughter is, you can't talk about our culture's definition of beauty and femininity without also understanding how racism interacts with both and directly influences your daughter. If everyone thinks the tall, skinny blonde with the perky little nose is so beautiful, how are you supposed to feel if you're an African-American girl with kinky hair, curves, and a fuller nose? Even with the popularity of hip-hop, beauty is still largely defined by "white." Think of the most popular African-American models and actresses. Can you think of any who have really dark skin, kinky hair, and large hips? They all look like variations of Halle Berry. While we have a few African-American models that girls of all races think are beautiful, holding them up as proof that our definition of beauty is less racist than it used to be doesn't hold water. For all the media coverage of her famed derriere, Jennifer Lopez only became really popular after she shrank her butt by working out. Halle Berry, with her extremely light skin, thin body, and straight hair, is no proof that our culture is race-blind; she's only showing that the easiest way to be black and beautiful is to look white. Many black girls I work with have told me that when they pledge black sororities, they're held to the "paper bag" test—meaning if their skin is darker than the color of the bag, they don't get in.

> *I hate when people say you're pretty for a dark-skinned girl.*
>
> Monica, 16

And it's not just African-American girls who are unconsciously taught that lighter skin is better.

> *The Indian standard of beauty is long hair, light skin, graceful, big doe eyes, and curves, but only in the right places. My culture has always thought that the paler a girl's skin is the more beautiful she is. The prejudice still exists now, even among the girls in my group. My mother is always telling me not to be in the sun to preserve my relatively pale skin. My friends talk about other Indian girls, deriding them because they're dark.*
>
> *I used to hang out with a clique of all Indian girls, but we were full of contradictions. We say that we have friends in other groups, but we don't. You had to pretend that you belonged to many different cliques, but the reality was that you could only belong to the group to be accepted by the group. We were trying to be white girls, and yet we were saying that we were proud of being Indian and our heritage. How much whiter could you possibly try to be? Wearing an Indian anklet (especially because Indian clothes and jewelry are trendy right now) is cool, but discussing the partition of India and Pakistan isn't.*
>
> *The Indian clique was exclusive, but the only way I can be proud of my heritage is not to be part of the Indian clique. Part of this is selfish because, like all girls, I want to be more special than everyone else, and I couldn't be in that group. Nevertheless, life in that group*

was a whole lot of pretending. The ones who take the most authentic pride aren't part of their cultural group. One of my closest friends is Japanese and she thinks the same thing.   Nidhi, 16

Growing up and going to school in a town with a large minority population, I thought I was ugly because I didn't look like any of my friends. It didn't help that I was a late bloomer and was an extremely awkward adolescent. I had a sudden growth spurt and it took me a while to figure out what to do with arms and legs (clumsy is an understatement). I had straight hair where most of my friends had dark curly hair, I was tall, pale, skinny, and flat-chested, where most of my friends were shorter than I was, had curvy figures, and brown or black skin. Even if girls were my height or taller, they still had curves where I didn't. The prettiest and most popular girls in my school looked nothing like me and this made me feel ugly in comparison. It was a reversal of wanting to fit the blond, blue-eyed ideal, I wanted to look less white and like more of a minority. It was actually a double-bind because by white standards I wasn't beautiful either, because I wasn't blond, blue-eyed, with a big chest. Even so, I rejected the blond image of beauty in favor of wanting to look like more of a minority because I wanted to be accepted in school and be pretty by those standards.   Ellie, 21

Acting White

Even in the most diverse schools, black students often have a hallway and lunch tables that they occupy year after year. If a black student doesn't want to hang out there and maintains friends in other groups, does she still fit in with her black clique? Not usually. In fact, these girls tell me they often get grief for trying to be white. In schools with racial and economic diversity, there's often a dramatic separation of students based on class. The wealthier students of color are often torn: Where do they sit in the hallway or cafeteria? Where is their loyalty?

It's a classic conundrum. Middle-class black girls tell me that if they act and talk like poorer black girls, they're accused of acting "ghetto." They're put down if they don't personify white culture. But when they interact with poorer black girls, they're accused of selling out if they "talk white" as if they're better than anyone else.

> *People all believe that since I am black, I can't live in the suburbs and talk like I do. They all expect me to talk like I come from a bad neighborhood. It gets really frustrating because people are surprised when they see that I'm smart and have a good home life.* Nia, 18

Some of the worst racism can come from within (like the paper-bag test), and it's exceedingly difficult and painful to talk about. When you add poverty to that, it just gets more difficult, but it explains even more why markers for girls are so critical to their sense of self. In many of the poorer schools where I teach, there's always a clique of black girls who have their hair and clothes in the latest styles and nails done. The Queen Bees have the best hair and nails. The girls spend tremendous amounts of money to maintain their markers because doing so solidifies their status in the clique, which bolsters their sense of self in a tough world.

> *White girls have all those problems with eating and being skinny. They're all anorexic. Black girls don't worry about that. We want more curves. We worry about our hair and skin color.* Jada, 14

I was coteaching a high school class on race and beauty at a Washington, D.C., school where the student body is entirely African-American. The students talked about how skinny white girls were and how they didn't have "those" issues. But as we discussed what issues they did have, my African-American colleague said, "I come from California, and no one in this room would be considered light-skinned." You could have heard a pin drop, then hostility radiated from the back row, where the Queen Bees sat—all girls who had straightened their hair, had the best clothes and nails, and the most "white" features. As I watched their conversation unfold, I noticed that I had pressed myself into a wall as if to make myself invisible because the emotion in the room was so tense— we were traveling to forbidden territory. But girls have to go there because if we don't challenge this kind of internalized racism, girls will keep attacking each other's sense of self.

Bad Hair

Many women who aren't black have no idea how important the issue of "good" and "bad" hair is in the black community. The only thing that comes close (and it really doesn't, because there isn't the same history behind it) is weight. My experience as a white woman is that you rarely hear anything about it. Let's be honest, if you're reading this and aren't black . . . Did you know that perming "white hair" curls it, but perming "black hair" straightens it? That those beautiful long braids black women wear are made from hair extensions, cost hundreds of dollars, take up to ten hours to complete, and are braided so tight that women often get terrible headaches? Or a girl is told she has "good hair" if it's like white hair and bad hair if it's kinky?

Shanterra, my colleague, is a young black woman from Dallas, Texas. She's from a close family, is an active church member, and attended Southern Methodist University, where she studied opera. She and I were teaching a class of sixth-grade girls. She told them that when she dreadlocked her hair, she had to explain and justify her decision not only to family and friends but many other people as well. (Members of her community thought "locking" your hair was bad, since racism had influenced them to believe that white, "soft" hair is better.) She was asked if she was Rastafarian, and people made comments that implied her hair was dirty.

As Shanterra told the sixth-grade girls about her experience, they were spellbound. The black and Latina girls in the class looked at her as if she was revealing a deep, dark secret. The white girls looked at her as if she had just pulled a rabbit out of a hat. She asked if any of the girls wanted to talk about similar experiences; here are only a few of their responses:

I have to sit for an hour every morning while my mother yanks my hair. It makes me cry because it hurts so much.
I hate having to do my hair! I wish it were softer!
Sometimes the perms can really burn your skin.
You get your hair braided and they braid it so tight I get a really bad headache.
People always say nappy hair is bad and I have nappy hair and there isn't a thing I can do about. It makes me feel bad.

The white girls in the room were shocked. They had no idea their friends were going through this.

Regardless of your daughter's race, class, religion, or ethnicity, it's important for her to realize the connection between cultural definitions of beauty and racism. These definitions push girls to want to be what they aren't. Wealthy girls will wear clothes with rips in them and buy from consignment stores precisely because they don't have to. Poorer girls will spend vast sums of money on the "right" jeans and shoes so they can present the image that they can afford it. Many non-African-American girls will emulate the stereotypes of the "ghetto" image (white students acting "black" are often called "wiggers") while some girls of color strive to look like "little white girls." Girls accept these words without analyzing the significance behind them. Just as words like "bitch" and "slut" reflect sexism, so do words like "wigger" and "acting ghetto" reflect our culture's racism.

Every culture has its own beauty issues. Often other cultures try to imitate whites. Often they defy it. Either way, every culture's ideas of beauty are in some way related, or a reaction to a white standard.

Iris, 16

Acting Black

While black girls are struggling with accusations of acting "ghetto" or "white," other girls are ironically dealing with the opposite. Julie and Ana are tenth graders in a large public suburban high school. Their mannerisms and speech so closely mimic the stereotypes of urban black culture that if you closed your eyes and listened to them, you would swear they were black. In fact, they're first generation Korean. So what's the attraction?

One of the principle characteristics of the black stereotype is that you look powerful and in control—someone people respect and fear. Several studies have reported that African-American girls have higher levels of self-esteem than their Latina and Caucasian counterparts. Is this really true, or are they just talking a good game? If the studies were true, wouldn't African-American girls experience less violence than Latina and

Caucasian girls? Wouldn't they be less likely to get themselves into unsafe situations because they would have better defined personal boundaries and be confident enough to communicate their boundaries to others? Studies show that these girls are just as vulnerable to violence.

African-American girls in my Empower classes often tell me that they're taught by their mothers, aunts, and grandmothers to be on guard. Be tough. Don't let anyone see you vulnerable and weak. These girls talk a good game. When you feel that you have little backing you up, you have to look like you're strong because if you don't, you become prey. You can't admit you're out of control, because admitting that would mean that the world is a very frightening place and you can't stop bad things from happening to you and/or the people you love.

Because the world (especially school) can be a very scary place, I see that children of all races and ethnicities are impressed with this attitude; they naturally want to emulate the power and intimidation that appears to go with it. Even girls from privileged backgrounds put up this front. But it crumbles easihy when you're trying to gain acceptance into a group or gain and keep the attention of someone you're attracted to. Far too many girls from a range of backgrounds feel that they constantly have to watch their back. They learn to play a good game of looking tough; sometimes they're so busy maintaining the facade that they convince themselves they can handle anything and they'll walk right in to danger.

No matter in which category your daughter falls, the Beauty Pageant is a ruthless competition. Even if she wins, she may lose, because she may have to sacrifice so much of herself to carry the scepter. You can't pull her out of the pageant, but you can teach her to walk across the stage with grace and dignity, believing in her inherent self-worth.

CHECKING YOUR BAGGAGE

In my experience, mothers' conflicts with their own issues of weight and appearance can be impenetrable blocks that stop them from helping their daughters. There's no way you're going to help your daughter unless you deal with your own baggage about this. (I've found that dads have their own baggage about girls' weight and appearance, but they don't seem to internalaze the issue the way women do.)

- How do you feel about your own weight and appearance? How often do you talk about your weight? Every week? Every day? Does your scale decide whether it's a good day or a bad day?
- Does your daughter know how you feel about yourself?
- What does she think about that?
- What have you said to your daughter about how she looks?

Think back to when you were a teen.

- What part of your body or appearance were you most self-conscious about?
- Did you ever look at certain people in your grade and think they were perfect? If you talked to them, were you intimidated?
- What did you fight with your parents about? Did your parents like your music, clothes, or friends?
- What were your markers when you were a teen? Why did you choose them?
- Think about your standards of beauty—are they "white" standards?

WHAT YOU CAN DO TO HELP

You need to be on the watch for things that will make your daughter a target. Don't wait till she comes home sobbing, because before then months of humiliation could have already occurred. Zoe, 17

There's a lot you can do to help your daughter deal with the incredible pressures she feels from both our cultural ideals and prejudices about beauty and the peer group she faces every day. I'll take you step by step through the Beauty Pageant and offer tips on handling the most common flashpoints, where parents misread what their daughters tell them and intervene in counterproductive ways, undermining the very relationships they want to have. My goal is to help you strike a balance between understanding your daughter's preoccupation with style and beauty and nurturing her to appreciate her intrinsic beauty and individuality.

BEATING THE EVENING GOWN COMPETITION: CEASE-FIRE IN THE CLOTHING WARS

Because it's so easy to see your daughter's behavior and appearance as a reflection of yourself, it's excruciating when she presents herself in a way that makes you want to scream or hide. Think about the clothes and hairstyles your daughter wears from day to day. What message do you think she's trying to send you? What message is she sending to her peers? What should you do if she dyes her hair purple, pierces her lip, or refuses to shave her legs at age sixteen—or wants to shave them at age eleven?

Get over it! Unless she feels that she isn't getting enough attention from you, the way she dresses and does her hair usually has nothing to do with you until the moment you freak out about it and get into a huge fight. The markers girls choose are the quintessential battles between teens and their parents. Many parents see these displays as a sign of disrespect toward them. They're not. Your children want your affirmation. They want you to be proud of them and the choices they make. They want to be accepted by you for who they are, bad clothes and strange makeup included.

If you don't accept her, she'll think you're squashing her, which will make her feel rejected at the precise time in her life when creating and exploring her sense of self through her image is her greatest priority. When you tell her that her tongue piercing is distracting (and you're a little worried about the dental bills), you may believe you're only looking out for her best interests, but she can't hear what you're saying. Instead, she hears that you don't accept who she is. That's why she fights you so hard. She feels as if she's fighting for her soul, that you're denying the person she is. In addition, if you freak out, you'll convince her that the only people who unconditionally accept her are her clique.

I admit that I cringe looking at the piercings I see on some girls. If you fight her, you lose the best way to understand how she sees her social position. And you'll have to eavesdrop on her, rifle through her closet, or read her journal to find out what you need to know. Remember, piercings, purple hair, and trendy clothes are markers your daughter chooses to signify how she wants to display herself to the world. Let's say your daughter is dressed in the latest goth style: she's wearing all black, her makeup is dead white, and her eyes are heavily rimmed with black. No doubt about it, she's frightening. Your first impulse is to say "Go upstairs right now and change into clothes that don't scare people." Instead, put aside your feelings about what it's going to look like to the neighbors. Find out what this means to your daughter. You've got to seriously watch your tone here. Ask her in as friendly and truly curious a way as possible, "Tell me more about your makeup. Why do you like it? What does it stand for?" If your daughter is defensive, say, "I really want to know; why is this important to you? If it's important to you, it's important to me." If your daughter responds that she's doing it to challenge the system, say, "Okay, I can respect that, but I'm not going to lie to you and say it's not hard for me to take you to church on Sunday. But I totally accept that this is your choice to make." It's okay to admit that you don't like your daughter's choices, but it's important to affirm them anyway.

I'm aware that many parents will pose the "slippery slope" argument; if you "let" her choose her hairstyle, makeup, and clothes, what power will you have to forbid her to do drugs or have sex? Guess what? You don't have that power anyway. What you do have is the ability to instill in her the values that enable her to make decisions well. Remember your Bill of Rights. If they include honesty, respect (for self and others), and accountability and your daughter knows this and has internalized them, that's your best defense. The question to ask yourself is: If I asked my daughter what my Bill of Rights is, would she know the answer? She needs to understand your rights and expectations.

A Personal Story

In deference to my own mother, I promised I would keep my family's involvement in this book to a minimum, but the following is one of my favorite stories about my father and sister.

My parents have three children. My brother, Zack, and I are four years apart; Zoe was born when I was fifteen. You would think that all those years of previous parenting would have given my parents a leg up. Unfortunately, parental amnesia struck. When my sister was fourteen, my father and I were sitting in the living room reading the newspaper on a Saturday afternoon when she came downstairs ready to go out in a dress nearly as transparent as Saran Wrap. My father took one look at this dress and freaked out. He commanded her to go upstairs and change into something more appropriate right away. After only a few minutes of fighting with him, my sister conceded and stomped upstairs to change. My father looked at me triumphantly; here was a demonstration of clear parental authority in action. A few minutes later, my sister walked downstairs wearing a T-shirt and pants, kissed my dad, picked up a bag, and walked out the door. I said to my father, "Do you actually think she isn't going to change back into that dress the second she's out of your sight?" He replied, "She wouldn't." Then he realized that she would never, one, concede so easily or, two, go out in jeans and a T-shirt to meet friends. He ran out the door and caught my sister changing back into the dress.

If your daughter wants to dye her hair green, the reason why doesn't change if you forbid her. So let her. In a few years, she'll have only herself to blame when she winces at pictures of herself because her skin looks sallow next to that green hair, and she has a nasty, sullen expression on her face. You, on the other hand, then and now look like the cool, collected parent.

If you fight her on this, you'll lose your credibility when it comes to talking about things that really count: making responsible choices about alcohol, drugs, and sex. You'll prolong the period of rebellion. Your daughter will be so busy fighting you that she won't admit to herself that

DAD ALERT!

Girls have been known to take advantage of their father's lack of awareness concerning girl's clothing. If you ever take your daughter shopping, keep this in mind at all times and don't let your guard down.

One day my dad took me shopping. Pretty soon he got that glazed look in his eye. There was this dress that I really wanted, but I knew he would think it was way too short. So I brought it over with a bunch of other clothes and when I held it up, I folded it over and told him it was a skirt and he believed me!   Kelly, 16 she's making stupid decisions. Sometimes the cliché is true: Pick your battles.

What should you do if your daughter wants to wear something so sexy that it really goes against your core values?

Dressing sexily is about wanting to be mature. Condemning your daughter's newest mini-skirt will only serve to make it more attractive. You can't simply put your foot down. You have to find some kind of middle ground. Recognize that this is merely a phase.

Cherise, 16

You're not going to be able to duck this battle, but the younger she is, the more control you have and the more she'll listen to you. If you set consistent standards early on and explain them clearly when she's eleven or twelve, she'll see you as a more reasonable person. Many parents feel that explaining the reason for a rule to their daughter is a sign of weakness. I couldn't disagree more. She'll see it as a sign of respect. She'll know what does and doesn't make you proud, and that'll mean something to her. It's your insurance that when she's older and can do what she wants, buy what she wants, and wear what she wants, she'll make better choices.

For now, you're sitting in the living room on a Friday night. Your daughter walks down the stairs and quickly darts past the living room—but not quick enough. You can see that she's wearing a really short skirt, knee-high boots, and a shirt held up by two strings. You want to go ballistic. This is how you have the conversation.

- Mental preparation: Take a deep breath and let go of any anxiety and/or anger. Even if you've already told your daughter how you feel about this style of clothes, remember she isn't wearing them out of disrespect for you.
- Check to see if she has any friends with her. If she does, ask to speak with her privately, but don't say it that way. (That's just as bad as if you talked to her in front of her friends, because "privately" means she's in trouble.) Instead, say something like, "Hey, can you come into the kitchen for a minute? I need to ask you something." Keep your tone casual!

- Check in with her about her plans. Keep the conversation casual, but get the information you need. Then say:

PARENT: *You probably don't want to hear this, but I want to tell you how I feel about the way you're dressed. [Wait until she stops rolling her eyes.] I know I can't really stop you from dressing the way you want. I know that if I forbid you from wearing what you're wearing right now, that you could change as soon as you leave the house. But I love you and want you to be aware and educated so you can take care of yourself.*

The way you're dressed makes me nervous because you look older and sexy, which I know is the point. I'm concerned that people are going to treat you as if you're older and you'll feel pressured to maintain that image. I'm worried that people won't see you for who you are and only see you as an object to be manipulated. Because right now you're fitting a stereotype of a girl who's trying to look older than she is and people often want to take advantage of a girl like that. So while I know I can't stop you, I want you to be aware of what you're projecting to others. I want you to be proud and confident when you walk into a room. So my question to you is this: If you walk into a room dressed the way you are right now, will you be confident enough to be yourself or will you feel that your actions have to match what you're wearing?

DO YOU THINK I'M SEXY? HALLOWEEN IMMUNITY

Have you noticed that girls will use any excuse to dress up in sexy costumes? Halloween is the most obvious example, but girls will do it whenever they feel they can get away with it. And I don't mean get away with it with you, I mean with their peers. These situations are cease-fires in girls' battles with each other where they get to dress as sexy as possible with less fear of recrimination ("Did you see the way she was dressed? What a slut!"). It's the freedom to be a "bad" girl.

It's complete immunity!   Steph, 13

I love Halloween! You can be a devil, angel, or a French maid. It's an excuse to be sexy without worrying about what anyone else is saying.

Lynn, 16

We had celebrity day and everyone used it as an excuse to wear short skirts, low-cut shirts, and high socks, and no one could say anything about it because you can dress up however you want without people calling you a whore.

Nia, 18

So when your daughter dresses up as a belly dancer or the latest sexy rock star, with what you consider to be totally inappropriate clothes (and it doesn't have to be something so dramatic as a whole costume, it could just be a pair of shoes), before you react to her, know her motivation. Like it or not, she's test-driving her power. You have to be able to say to your daughter, "When you wear X, you have to know that people will think of you in a sexual way. There might be some guys out there who don't respect women and will see this as a justification for coming on to you. There are people who will look at you as a target. Be clear about what your boundaries are and what you do and do not want to do with someone." If you've communicated how you feel in a clear, respectful way and allow her to experiment (even if you think it's a mistake), your words will be in her head when she needs them most. (I'll discuss this issue in more depth in Chapter 9.)

THE VANILLA GAP GIRL

You might be just as confused by how to deal with a daughter who is a conformist. You've raised her to be a strong, independent, interesting person. Instead, she slavishly grooms and dresses to look exactly like her friends. She's never happier than when she's going through the racks at The GAP or Abercrombie & Fitch. Is she going to walk in lockstep with her fellow Heathers for the rest of her life?

Not unless you freak out and make it a pitched battle over her identity. If the way she chooses to look now seems boring and superficial to you, trying to make her more "individual" is literally telling her she's not okay as she is, and that's just going to make her invest more heavily in conformity.

OUTLAPPING THE SWIMSUIT COMPETITION

Don't wait for your daughter to come to you. Know with absolute certainty that some time in fifth or sixth grade (depending on the maturity of her class), she'll be comparing her physical development against that of her peers. It doesn't matter if she has big breasts or is completely flat, talk to her about it. Sit down and say: "I want to talk to you about something that's totally normal for someone in your grade [notice I didn't say "normal for your age" because that is a parent thing to say]. I'm not sure if this has happened already, but I'm sure people are physically developing at different rates in your class. Some girls may need to wear a bra and some don't. That's totally normal. But it's also normal for girls to be teased because of it and that isn't okay. Have you ever seen anything like that happen?"

If the answer is no, then end the conversation by assuring her: "Well, I'm glad it hasn't happened, but if it ever does and you want to talk about it or anything else, I'd be happy to talk to you about it." If the answer is yes, listen and keep asking questions about how she feels. Brainstorm with her about what she can do and say to make herself feel better. If she's an early developer and you tell her that other girls are jealous, explain why. But advise her not to accuse her tormentors of jealousy because that will make them even angrier and more vindictive. Start by telling your daughter she's beautiful, that bodies come in all shapes and sizes, and that they're all beautiful. Make sure she has access to the books, zines, and websites that reassure her that what she's going through is normal. It's great to hear it from you, but she needs to hear from her peers that she's not the only one. If possible, find someone your daughter thinks is cool and stylish (remember, this is your daughter's choice, not yours) and have that woman share with her the similar insecurities she had when she was your daughter's age.

It's critical to teach your daughter to be proud of her body as she goes through puberty, but you also need to give her the space to think it's mortifying. She needs you or someone you trust to talk through how puberty impacts her interactions with other people, friends included. Girls need to talk about how physical development makes them feel about themselves and their peers and place it into the context of their lives—not just what happens when you get your period. If this doesn't happen, puberty becomes yet another weapon girls can use to humiliate each other or another way to feel ashamed of their bodies.

> *Girls are often too embarrassed to ask questions, so buy one of those books that explain* everything. *Give a list of websites and books as a way to help. It's also important for teenagers to know that what they're going through is normal, that it happens to everyone (no matter how embarrassing).*
> Chelsea, 18

MORE THAN ONE STANDARD OF BEAUTY

Go through the pages of a fashion or celebrity magazine with your daughter and talk about the homogenized images of beauty you'll find there. Talk about how these impossible standards tyrannize girls, particularly girls of color. This probably won't be news to your daughter, but it's important to get her to articulate it. What does it take out of her to try to measure up? Now talk about how looks matter to her group of friends. What kind of pressure does she feel to uphold the standards of the clique? What happens when she breaks the rules? Your goal here is to increase her awareness of how media images and her friends influence her feelings about her attractiveness and self-esteem. As you'll do in so many other situations regarding her relationship with friends, ask her, "Who's making the decisions about how you look and feel about yourself?"

DEALING WITH WEIGHT: "I'M SUCH A COW!"

You're getting new jeans for your daughter. Sometime over the last year she's developed hips. You have brought no less than twenty different styles and sizes into the changing room for her to try on and she hates all of them. After what seems like hours, she opens the dressing room door and she's near tears. She says to you, "I hate how I look, I am *so fat.*"

Again, this is an area that can really push moms' buttons, although dads certainly aren't immune to their own challenges with this issue. If you're still wrestling with your own issues about weight, these situations

LANDMINE!

Let your daughter have privacy when she's trying on clothes. Don't go into the dressing room with her and under no circumstances open the door without her express consent! Moms have an uncanny ability to open the dressing room door just when their daughters are in only bras and underwear.

can be lightning rods between you and your daughter. For her sake, get yourself together about it so you can be an effective role model.

If you think your daughter is overweight, the first thing to do is stop and check your baggage again. Is she truly too heavy, or are you projecting your own issues onto her?

> *I obsess on my weight and so does my daughter. She hasn't worn a bathing suit in three years and we have a pool.*
>
> Anne, mother of Diane, 16

Could you be panicking when there's no reason? Do you "need" her to be thin to satisfy your standards of beauty? Are you judging her as weak-willed or lazy if she's chubbier than you'd like?

I can't tell you how many heartbreaking discussions I've had with girls whose parents have given them the most toxic—and sometimes unintentional—messages about how "fat" they are. For example, a mom of one of the girls I work with came home from the office and found her daughter eating a chocolate bar. She asked, "Should you really be eating that?" Her daughter heard this simple question as code for "You're fat and you need to lose weight." Other messages are more frank and damaging: "You really need to drop a few pounds." "You'd be so pretty if you just lost weight." "Don't you want to look your best?"

If your daughter really is pigging out on candy and other junk food all the time, and she's genuinely overweight, you do need to address that. Keep the focus on good health, not weight: "I'm concerned that you're eating too much junk food. You look fine, but you'll feel better and your body will work better if you eat healthier food. We need to work together to find healthy things you like to eat. A little bit of junk food is fine, but not if it crowds out the food your body needs." This is a tough battle; girls often hear "eat healthy food" as code for "you're fat."

If weight issues are an ongoing struggle for you, it's best to admit that to your daughter up front. Acknowledge the powerful influence of the media. Even the most emancipated women can't escape the impact of all those messages our culture sends us about what we have to be. Discuss the issue with your daughter. For younger girls, eleven or twelve, look through magazines together and ask your daughter to create a collage of what she considers healthy images of women. Then ask her to do another collage of all the unhealthy images you find in the women's magazines. Help her analyze what's right and wrong with these images. For an older daughter, read Naomi Wolf's *The Beauty Myth* or watch the video *Killing Us Softly*. Then talk to her about the messages she gets about body weight from her friends and the clique. Are these messages that make her feel good about herself? What kind of pressure is she feeling from the group to change how she looks to fit someone else's standard?

The message your daughter needs to hear from you is that you love her just as she is, that she's beautiful. At the same time, you know that the clique will censor her if she steps outside the boundaries of acceptable weight. This is a terrible conundrum for parents. If you help her diet to lose weight, it's sending the message that she isn't okay as she is, even if your genuine intent is to help her be more healthy. If you tell her to forget what the group thinks, you risk her losing the support of her peers, and that's very hard to deal with.

COULD YOUR DAUGHTER HAVE AN EATING DISORDER?

If you suspect your daughter has an eating disorder, either anorexia (she's become painfully thin or is headed that way) or bulimia (she binges and purges), it's essential to see a qualified therapist who specializes in treating these problems. I've listed books and other resources in the resources section of the book. We all have a stereotype of the little girl lost, starving herself to please her perfectionistic, controlling parents. I can tell you that I've worked with many girls whose parents were truly loving and support-

WHAT WORKS—WHAT THE GIRLS TELL ME

- "Offer to go the gym with her so you can do it together."
- "Tell her she's beautiful so at least she knows you care."
- "Help her not stress out about being heavy. Give her 'alone time.' 'My mom lights candles and puts on music so I can relax and it really helps.' "
- "Encourage her to be the person she wants to be and challenge the system."

WHAT DOESN'T WORK
(FAIRLY OBVIOUS BUT PEOPLE DO IT ANYWAY)

- "Don't say she's fat when you're fat."
- "Don't say 'You're so lazy. You don't do anything. You sit on your butt all day.' You don't get home until late; how do you know what she's doing all day?"
- "Don't keep saying 'You're beautiful' all the time; it's just as bad as not saying anything."
- "Don't point out her flaws; it makes her even more self-conscious."

ive and didn't conform to this stereotype at all. Don't waste time blaming yourself for your daughter's eating disorder. Get professional help right away.

THE BATTLE OF BODY HAIR

Shaving, waxing, lasers, plucking, bleaching—body hair has always been a huge issue for girls because it's one of the defining characteristics of femininity, and it's a major aspect of the Swimsuit Competition. Girls have told me that shaving is mandatory for white girls, but a lot of black girls don't shave and don't feel bad about it. The black girls who will feel the pressure to shave are usually in schools of higher socioeconomic levels and surrounded by "white" culture. Most girls will get slammed inside and outside of the clique if they have hairy legs and armpits. If you're surprised by this, ask your daughter the following: What's worse to be in your school: A girl who's "out" as a lesbian but shaves and wears trendy clothes or a straight girl who doesn't shave?

I have had countless moms ask me when was the appropriate time to let their daughter shave their legs. The way they tell it, their prepubescent daughters follow them around the house begging, arguing, bartering for the chance to shave. But what if it's your daughter who doesn't want to shave her legs—ever? What if she takes a stand against traditional girl markers? In sixth grade, parents fight with their daughters about growing up too fast. By eleventh grade, parents can be just as uncomfortable when the opposite happens.

> When I was in fourth grade, I noticed that my mom had no hair on her legs. In sixth grade, my two best friends shaved and pressured me to shave, too. Other girls in my clique said it was OK that I didn't shave because I didn't have dark hair. But by seventh grade everyone shaved except maybe five or six girls. In seventh and eighth grade I lived in fear of someone finding out that I didn't shave. I don't shave because I'm going to feel uncomfortable about myself in high school no matter what. I did have a friend tell me that it was dirty and gay. Girls have sometimes come up to me and said, "You're so brave. I couldn't stand the pressure and the talking behind my back."
>
> My mom tells me that she doesn't have the courage [to not shave] but she totally supports me. If she hadn't, I wouldn't have the courage to be myself. The best thing is that my mom has also always said that if I wanted to shave, I could.   Olivia, 17

Olivia is deliberately choosing markers that effectively separate her from many of her peers and open her up to teasing. She's forming her identity apart from her peers. Her mom has also done a great job. Even though she shaves and is amazed that her daughter doesn't, she has let her daughter choose her marker and supports her for it. Her daughter feels affirmed and knows that her mother stands behind her, even though they may make different decisions about the same thing.

BACK TO THE MALL: DEFINING YOUR "SHOE MOMENTS"

When we last left you, you were grinding your teeth at the mall while your daughter pitched a fit because you wouldn't buy her the shoes she wanted. In response to her increasingly intolerable whining, you ask, "What about those other adorable shoes I bought you last month?" Now you know: A Queen Bee probably made a snide comment about them. *(Never to her face! We may whisper when she walks down the hall . . .)* Those shoes could have become a source of misery and humiliation for her, but she never told you.

So when do you give in and help your daughter fit into the clique and please the Queen Bee, and when do you encourage her to go for it and stand on her own? I'm not saying that you should give in every time she "has" to have something. Far from it. The girl who threw the shoes across the store should be severely punished. *(I was severely punished. I didn't get the shoes!)* What I'm saying is that before you say no, remember the desperation you felt when you were her age and trying to fit in. Remember the pressures she's under in the Beauty Pageant. If you can empathize, it'll be a lot easier for you to come across to her as a reasonably sympathetic person and come up with a mutually agreeable solution where both sides compromise. You want flats; she wants four-inch platforms—you compromise on two-inch heels. You want black; she wants sparkles—she gets something with some decoration. You just shelled out for last month's shoes and don't want to pay a penny more; she has to have this pair—you go halfsies, or she agrees to do extra chores to pay for them, or it comes out of an agreed-upon clothing budget, beyond which every dime comes out of her own pocket.

Remember, it's never just about the shoes. In fact, it's these "shoe moments" that really determine how fast your daughter will grow up. If you don't listen to her, she'll probably figure out a way to get the shoes anyway, hide them from you, and change into them as soon as she's out of your sight. A precedent is being established. She goes to you for help. You say no. She feels that you "just don't get it." She does it anyway but sneaks behind your back. When she's thirteen, it's shoes; when she's fifteen, it's a seventeen-year-old boyfriend. So whether she grows up too fast is in large part determined by how you establish yourself as someone who listens and respects her problems and works with her to come up with mutually acceptable solutions.

Most of us struggle with Beauty Pageant issues throughout our lives. If you can admit and reflect on how the pageant impacts you and your daughter, it takes some of its power away.

> *I often talk to my daughter about the challenge of being* in *the culture but not* of *the culture. Pop culture is fine to know, but it doesn't substitute for character and individuality.*
>
> Carolyn

What Is Beauty Anyway?

*Beauty is the look of happiness on a young child's face when she finds
    her doll*
Beauty is the sound of laughter
Beauty is the smell of a new-blown rose
Beauty is the taste of an exotic food, delicious and beckoning
Beauty is the feeling of love
Beauty can change
It isn't fixed
It is in the eye of the beholder
Beauty is who you are
Beauty is art
Beauty can be the face of a lady, seen by a lover
Or a well-run sewer system, seen by a worker
Or even the purr of a cat, heard by a lonely woman
Beauty can be anything to anyone
*It can be the sound of music, ringing in the ears from a soprano's
    melodious note*
Or the beat of a rap star
Beauty is who you are
It is what you believe
It raises you above the world
It is something even greater
It is the dream of Martin Luther King, Jr.
It is the Declaration of Independence, declaring equality

It is the Emancipation Proclamation
It is the sound of prayer
Beauty is something smaller, too
A little girl on the playground, watching a crowd taunting her
But standing firm as a rock, solid and strong
It is a smile
A squeeze of the hand to say "It's all right"
Beauty is who you are
When you don't let them push you down
But say, "I am me, I can see the beauty of the world
I am the beholder
I am beautiful"

ALEXANDRA PETRI, 14

Nasty Girls

Teasing, Gossiping, and Reputations

Angie and Monica are on the same soccer team. A week ago, Angie began dating Monica's old boyfriend. Monica was talking to three other girls when Angie walked onto the practice field, but the group fell silent as Angie approached. The next day during school, Angie walked by Monica and two other girls and she overheard them saying she was fat, ugly, and a slut. This went on for a week and by then Angie was desperate for it to end. The next time it happened, Angie confronted Monica in front of the other girls.

ANGIE: *Could you stop talking about me? What did I ever do to you anyway?*

MONICA: *What are you talking about?*

ANGIE: *I can hear you telling people you think I'm fat and a slut. What's your problem?*

MONICA: *Look, you're blowing this out of proportion, but I can tone it down for you if you want.*

ANGIE: *Why are you even saying these things about me?*

MONICA: *We're just joking around. I wouldn't take it seriously.*

ANGIE: *Well, whether you're joking around or not, it still hurts.*

MONICA: *Well, I guess we can tone it down a little . . . if that would make you feel better.*

ANGIE: *Look, why are you doing this? Why are you being such a bitch?*

MONICA: *I'd be very careful if I were you unless you can back up what you say. . . .*

Can you blame Angie if she gave up and slugged Monica? Could you blame Angie's parents for thinking Monica was evil, and blaming Monica's parents for raising this monster? What should you do if you're Angie's parent? What should you do if you're Monica's parent?

WHAT YOU MUST KNOW

- 99.99 percent of girls gossip, including your daughter.
- The longer and more adamantly you deny this fact, the worse of a gossip she'll be.
- While we're on the subject, the worse gossip you are, the worse your daughter will be (and you thought she didn't listen to you!).
- Girls will almost always blame their behavior on something or someone else. Let's say your daughter is accused of spreading a rumor. Instead of admitting her guilt, she'll demand to know who exposed her as the information source, as if the snitch were the person who's really at fault—conveniently forgetting that she was the one who gossiped.
- If she's over twelve, your daughter has almost certainly been called a slut and/or bitch by other girls. And she has almost certainly called other girls a slut and/or bitch (that you have never heard these words out of your daughter's mouth is immaterial).

In this chapter we'll look at how teasing, gossiping, and reputations impact your daughter's sense of self, social competency, friendships, and how she talks to you (or not) about them. We'll break down the different ways of handling gossip and teasing whether the target is inside or outside the clique. I'll give you more strategies so you'll know which battles to fight for her and which ones you should let her fight on her own. But I'll also challenge you to take action when your daughter is the one who starts the rumors. Most girls who are gossiped about, gossip themselves. It's more than probable that your daughter has been cruel to someone else. It's up to you to teach her differently.

I know it's hard to imagine your daughter being unkind or downright nasty to other girls, especially if she's never shown this kind of ugliness around the house. Don't be in denial.

> *If you can't assess your daughter honestly, there's no way you'll ever help her. Parents can't imagine why anyone wouldn't like their daughter. Parents won't admit that their daughters could do evil things like spread really mean rumors about someone else. If you can't recognize this, you won't be able to help her.* Zoe, 17

When your daughter walks down the hall to her history class, what's she more likely talking to her friends about: the upcoming class or the latest gossip? Teasing and gossip swirl around your daughter's head every day and they're the lifeblood of cliques and popularity. While your daughter may feel that they provide the forum for bonding with her friends, teasing and gossip can also act as powerful weapons to pit girls against each other.

Your goal is to make sure your daughter learns to take responsibility when teasing and gossiping get out of hand, meaning they're used to tear someone down to solidify someone else's place in the "Act Like a Woman" box. This is an ambitious goal to say the least, because it often means your daughter will have to go against her friends and risk her place on the status totem pole; she may not be willing to think that standing up for someone else is worth that price. Or she may know in her gut that what's happening is wrong, but can't really put her finger on it—or feels powerless to stop it.

Let's go back to the Empower classroom. I'm talking to a group of ninth-grade girls. I ask them to tell me what they like about their friendships with other girls. These are their responses. You can:

Be yourself
Tell her anything
Trust her
Depend on her support
Be silly
Hang out

Share clothes
Tell secrets

But, as you now know, these same friendships aren't always so supportive. Just as the girls want to talk about "good" popularity for thirty seconds and focus on "evil" popularity instead, they would much rather get to my next question: "So, what are the things you don't like so much about your friendships with girls?" These are their responses. She can:

Talk behind your back
Gossip about you
Be two-faced
Be jealous
Be competitive
Be critical
Be judgmental
Tell your secrets
Be a tag-along
Take your man
Make you choose friends
Betray you
Be fickle

As the girls call out their answers, they laugh and crawl over each other to complete the list of mean things they do to each other. The amazing thing is that no matter the girls' race, geographic location, class, or religion, I always get the same answers.

Take a closer look at the "negative" list; a theme should become clear. They're all about competition, about looks, style, friends, popularity, and boys—things girls think they need to secure a place in the life raft.

Are you surprised that the girls didn't include grades and athletics as areas of competition? Some girls do. About a third of the girls I teach include grades and athletics on the list—"she helps me study" versus "she thinks she's smarter than me because she gets better grades" or "she's my favorite teammate" versus "she's always trying to outscore me." Girls tend to consider these attributes as part of the overall package you need in order to to be successful. Simultaneously, they know they can't be too overt about their academic or athletic accomplishments or people will accuse them of being stuck up. I'm not saying that people won't respect a girl if she's a great athlete or student, but neither grades nor athletics by themselves maintain or increase her social position.

Are you incredibly frustrated by the girls' antifeminist, regressive answers? Did you think to yourself, "After all this hard work for women's equality, are girls going backwards?" I don't think so; we just have farther to go. Girls demand more of each other and themselves than they do of boys. In my experience, they do believe that they're as intelligent and competent as boys. But when you're a teen, this "fact" is not as immediately important as "What do people think of me?," "Am I accepted?," or "Did I do anything to humiliate myself today?"

TEASING

Okay, I admit it. I was teased. A lot. You may have read the clique chapter and wondered what clique I was in. Fair question. Since I study cliques for a living, most people assume I had terrible experiences with cliques. I had a bad time, but no worse than what most girls go through.

In seventh and eighth grade I was part of a powerful clique, but I was at the bottom of the totem pole within that clique. From the outside, I looked like I was popular. From the inside, I felt anything but—my position was incredibly precarious. The girls in my clique teased me all the time. I put up with it because I lived in terror that at any minute I'd be expelled from my group. I was so intimidated by them that years later, after I'd graduated from college and was living in San Francisco, I saw the Queen Bee from my old clique in the grocery store and without hesitation ran out of the store. I was mortified that I ran away—after all, I was supposed to be over things that happened to me in seventh grade—yet my feet had a life of their own.

Almost everyone has been on both sides of teasing. So how serious is it? Like all things with girls, teasing is multifaceted. Just as I define popularity in two ways, I have different definitions of teasing. If you're going to be credible to your daughter, you must distinguish between them.

One of the toughest jobs of parenting your teenager is knowing when she's "playing" and when she's "serious." If you think she's being serious when she's playing, it's another clear indication to her that you're clueless. For example, you overhear your daughter greet her best friend by saying "Hey bitch, what's up?" You may think she's being rude, but if you say so, she'll dismiss you as clueless: "That's just the way we talk to each other. It's not a big deal."

I struggle all the time trying to figure out when girls are being serious. Things you would think are serious often aren't and sometimes your daughter sounds casual precisely because she's covering up what she really feels. Depending on your daughter's intention and the power dynamics between her and her friend, there could be lot more going on than even she understands. How do you tell which one is which and how does your daughter? I assure you, there are times when your daughter isn't sure, but doesn't want to admit it to anyone, especially herself.

Playing or serious teasing depends on the power dynamic between her and the friend.

There are three different kinds of teasing:

- Good teasing (where everyone involved feels respected)
- Unintentional bad teasing (where the teaser doesn't intend to hurt the other person's feelings)
- Intentional bad teasing (where the teasing is used to put the person down and/or silence her)

Good Teasing

Good teasing is one of the cornerstones of great friendships. Someone who cares about you, knows you well enough, and is comfortable with you can tease and joke around with you, "with" (not "at") being the operative word. With good teasing, there's no intention to put the other person down. The person being teased feels confident that she'll be listened to if she asks that the teasing stop.

How does your daughter know?

- She feels liked by the teaser.
- She doesn't feel the teaser's motivation is to put her down.

ARE BAD WORDS A BIG DEAL?

Actually, they are. Most parents tell their daughters they don't want them using bad words because, first, it's rude, and second, it's an uneducated way to communicate. Both are good reasons, but there's another. Words have power, especially words that become part of everyday language. "Slut" and "bitch" are words your daughter hears every day. This means she constantly says or hears words that describe women either as sexual objects (sluts) or as aggressors who need to be put in their place (bitches). These words have the power to silence your daughter, to deny her a voice. And your daughter can use them to turn this power against others. How can your daughter learn about healthy sexuality and self-expression if she equates that with being a slut? How can she learn to stand up for herself and learn respectful assertion if she equates that with being a bitch? Educate her how to critically analyze why certain people are described with particular "bad" words. Explain why using those words puts girls and women down. Teaching your daughter that bad words are unacceptable is a battle worth waging, but it's only a valuable lesson if you explain the meaning behind the words.

There is a time when you should encourage your daughter to say bad words. For example, if someone called her a slut and it's upsetting her, it's important that she can say that word in front of you without worrying that you'll be shocked and she'll get in trouble. To solve a problem, you have to name it. Assure her you won't be shocked and she won't get in trouble. You always want her talking freely and openly.

- If she decides she doesn't like it, she feels she can say something and it will stop.

Unintentional Bad Teasing

It's easy to tease someone and not know you're hurting her feelings. We've all done it and we've all been on the receiving end of it. It's always hard to tell someone you like that you're not happy with something they did. In particular, it's extremely difficult for girls and women to be in situations like this because we're taught to not make waves. But when the intent isn't malicious (which isn't to say it couldn't be insensitive), once the teaser understands the impact of her behavior, she'll get over her defensiveness and make a sincere apology because she recognizes she's hurting someone she cares about.

How does your daughter know?

- Your daughter feels that the person doing the teasing truly doesn't know how she feels.
- She doesn't feel the teaser's motivation is to put her down.
- Although she may have to gather her courage to say something, her reluctance to speak up isn't a reflection of her fear of confronting the specific person who's teasing her but of the difficulty of confrontation in general.
- She doesn't apologize for the person's actions or blame herself in some way.

Bad Teasing

Teasing is most effective when it pushes buttons. Who knows how to do that better than the people we're closest to? I can move my head a particular way and my brother climbs the walls. Your daughter may be closer right now to her friends than to her siblings; therefore the clique has the most power to exploit her insecurities.

However, bad teasing happens both inside and out of the clique, and either way, it's ugly. The teasing is done precisely to put the recipient in her place (i.e., below the teaser on the social totem pole). First, she's relentlessly teased about something she feels insecure about; girls always seem to know exactly what to say to cause the most humiliation. Second, she's dismissed or put down when she defends herself ("Can't you take a joke?" "What are you making such a big deal of this for?"). Often the result is that she ends up apologizing for speaking up in the first place ("I'm sorry, I'm such an idiot") or swallowing it lest she lose her place in the clique.

A girl can't tease "up" the ladder. If she does, girls with more power can become enraged and the only way things get back to normal is if someone puts her back in her place. Sometimes it's the girl who puts herself down by making a self-deprecating comment or apologizing profusely, which restores the equilibrium in the group.

The Queen Bee isn't the only one who teases within the clique. Actually, the Sidekick and Wannabe do a lot of teasing because they need to build their position in the group. The Queen Bee gives her approval by a quiet comment that backs them up. The most likely girl they'll go after is the one least likely to fight back. Your daughter can't petition the Queen Bee to back off unless she's willing to risk being kicked out of the group. If she's willing and can really stand up to the Queen Bee, she'll know it and back off. But most often if your daughter is in this situation, she'll be too intimidated to be alone with the Queen Bee to make the request.

Teasing Outside the Clique

Especially in sixth and seventh grade, girls change cliques frequently. When this happens, it's common for girls who used to be friends to turn on each other, and the bad teasing can be brutal. Girls' friendships, while fickle, are intense. So when a girl leaves one group for another, the friends she's left behind feel as though they've been rejected by a lover. Their feelings of rejection often cover seeds of self-doubt. Why did she leave? Am I not cool enough? How does her leaving reflect on me? Dee demonstrates how challenging this can be for girls, even when she's trying to write a letter of apology.

> Dear "Friend,"
>
> I'm sorry that I talked about you behind your back. I thought you were cool and stuff before you got involved with Mary and Caitlin's group. I once even compared your hair to a greasy dish rag (only to one person though). I'm really sorry I said these things even though I still might believe them. Sorry.
>
> Dee, 12

Dee is still licking her wounds. Her disappointment and ambivalence over the breakup of her friendship with the other girl resulted in teasing so rough that it provoked a confrontation and, later, an apology that sought to make her point again.

The other bad teasing outside the clique occurs when one or more girls inside the clique go after a loner who doesn't have the safety of other girls as her backup. This is the "piling on" we know from *Carrie* and other teen movies, where the girls in the clique try out their own power by picking on someone who's relatively defenseless.

Perversely, there's a benefit to being teased by someone outside the clique. At least there's no confusion about what the teasing means, and the target can admit to herself that she doesn't like it. If it's happening to your daughter, she won't have the same conflict of interest as she does if she's being teased within her clique ("I'll take the teasing so I can stay in the group"), but she can be equally paralyzed.

Teasing can be very frightening. Girls tell me how they're scared to go to the bathroom or walk down a hallway where they're more likely to run into the teasers. They walk home later, earlier, or on different routes — anything to avoid facing these girls. They can't concentrate on schoolwork because their attention is focused on their dread of and strategies to avoid these girls. Why would your daughter be so reluctant to ask for help? Because she probably assumes that if she snitches things will get even worse; adults won't take teasing seriously; and she should be able to take care of her own problems.

No matter who's doing the bad teasing, if your daughter is on the receiving end, it'll fit one of the following:

- She feels smaller than the teaser.
- The teasing is relentless.
- If she complains, she believes the teaser will dismiss her feelings or tease her more.
- She feels it isn't worth saying anything because nothing will stop it.
- She feels she has to laugh along.
- If she complains, she ends up apologizing.

Sometimes I would make a pretty feeble attempt that probably came off as whining that no one took seriously. And these girls were sup-

posed to be my friends. . . . If the girl protests, even weakly, the
teasers will say "We're just joking with you. Don't be silly. Stop mak-
ing such a big deal of this."   Jordan, 17

If she really stands up for herself she destroys the comfortable feel-
ing with her friends.   Becky, 15

That "comfortable feeling" Becky refers to is the feeling she needs in
order to sit comfortably in the life raft. The more fuss she makes, the
closer she gets to the raft's edge.

These girls are my best friends. I can tell them anything. They'll back
me up. But if we're so close, then why do they tease me all the time?
If they really are my friends, then why do they make me feel bad? Why
am I so frightened to say anything?   Rhoda, 14

Things would be a lot easier if your daughter could ask herself these
questions. But she often doesn't want to admit these questions to herself,
let alone you. She'd rather make excuses for her friends or convince herself that she really doesn't care so she won't have to take action. It's also
hard for her to get all of those feelings organized into thoughts.

Her biggest problem is that it looks like a no-win situation. She's
trapped hanging out with friends who make her miserable. If she says
nothing, she'll be angry with herself because she can't hold her own
against bullies who masquerade as her friends. Keep this in mind later
when you ask yourself why your daughter dates someone you don't think
is respectful to her. *She is learning to be silent in the face of intimidation*
right here.

Remember, unless your daughter can see a different recourse, her goal
is most likely to remain in that life raft.

GOSSIPING

Gossip is like money. We exchange it, sell it, and lend it out. It's what
we have of value.   Jane, 16

I'm never mean to people without a reason.

Anonymous Queen Bee, 12

Let's face it. We all gossip: on the phone, at parties, meals, and family reunions. I think the best thing about family get-togethers is the gossiping we do when everyone has gone home. Girls are no different. In fact, why do you think adults are so good at it? Because we've been sharpening our skills since we were teens and it's almost impossible to stop. So do I tell my friend to stop when she calls me at work with some juicy information? Of course not. But there's a difference. While gossip still has the ability to ruin your day, its impact on your adult life is usually superficial and fleeting. Hopefully, you shut your mouth when you know you'll hurt someone. But it's very different when you're a teen. Along with teasing, gossip is one of the fundamental weapons that girls use to humiliate each other and reinforce their own social status.

Gossip is so humiliating because girls' natural self-focus means that they literally feel like the whole world notices everything they do, and what's said about them and their social status in school often serves as the basis for their self-identity.

Most likely you've seen your daughter's egocentricity in full bloom when she becomes embarrassed by something you've done or said in front of others. In *Reviving Ophelia,* Mary Pipher describes the "imaginary audience syndrome" where a girl was humiliated by the way her mother clapped at a play. In reality, no one but her daughter thought she

LANDMINE!

When your daughter reports being humiliated by gossip at school, don't say "It's not a big deal; no one noticed but you" or "Don't worry, everyone will have forgotten about it by tomorrow."
As far as she's concerned, there is no tomorrow. She needs you to understand that she's hurting right now, and it *is* a big deal. Try to convince her otherwise, and she'll think you're hopelessly out of touch.

was clapping strangely, and even if they did, who cares? However, this girl truly believed that everyone was totally focused on her and, by extension, her mother.

If you can embarrass your daughter by doing something no one notices, imagine how she feels when rumors are spread about her. She feels as if she's wearing a neon sign advertising her shame and humiliation.

Come back with me again to the Empower classroom. There are ten minutes left in class. We have spent the entire time discussing gossip. For the last exercise, I ask the girls to sign a pledge not to gossip for any amount of time they think is realistically possible. They giggle and argue. Is it possible? Can they do it? Why would they want to? Most are doubtful they can make it past thirty minutes. During this time, they are encouraged to think about how much of their conversation with friends revolves around gossip. Here are some of their pledges:

> *"We the class of 8B promise not to gossip or be exclusive when we walk to our classes today."*

> *"We the class of 6C promise not to backstab, lie, gossip, or spread rumors about each other for two hours today, April 2."*

Occasionally, the girls aspire to greatness.

> *"We the class of 9B promise not to gossip for three days."*

I don't assume the girls will uphold their pledge. The purpose is for them to realize how much of their daily conversation revolves around gossip. Through this exercise, they get it. Their most frequent comment at the next class is "It was weird to realize that gossiping is all we talk about!"

What do girls gossip about?

In Sixth Grade
Friendships
Conflicts with friends
Rivalries in cliques

Rivalries between cliques
Boys and crushes

In Ninth Grade

Who's trying to become friends with the seniors
Who's popular
Which parties you're invited to and which ones you aren't
Who's drinking, doing drugs, or having sex

In Eleventh Grade

Which freshmen girls are throwing themselves at the seniors
Who got together at the last party
Who had sex at the last party
Who got drunk and/or did drugs
Who's getting used

REPUTATIONS AND IMAGE

Gossip and reputations can't exist without each other. Reputations are a by-product of constant gossiping and, good or bad, they trap girls. Like cliques, your daughter will probably perceive reputations more rigidly in her early teens than in her later teens. When I first discuss reputations with girls, I ask them the following three questions: (1) If a girl gets a bad reputation, is it her fault? (2) Once you get a reputation, good or bad, will you always have it? (3) Should you back up a friend when she gets a bad reputation?

The majority of younger teens believe that you're to blame for the reputation you get, you will always be stuck with it, and they're torn about backing a friend. Older teens know that many people get reputations without "doing" anything to deserve it and sometimes you can leave your reputation behind; even if that means you have to switch schools. They're more likely to back their friends.

For our purposes, it doesn't matter which word you use; the impact of reputations and image last throughout your daughter's teen years, because somewhere along the way, girls start believing their press. Who they are (their character, sense of self, and personality) gets tangled up

LANDMINE!

When talking to your daughter, use the word *image* instead of *reputation*, which usually prompts the simultaneous eye roll and sigh. Girls have a harder time talking about reputations than they do the image a particular girl projects.

with their reputation and image. This is another reason why girls are often confused about their own motivation when they know they're doing something foolish and/or dangerous. Because they want to please their friends, boys, and/or you, they will do things against their better judgment to uphold their image. For example, a girl who's afraid to be seen as less than perfect will starve herself to feel in control. A girl will stop participating in band because her friends tell her it's uncool.

The following is a compilation of different reputations I've seen or heard girls talk about. There are various ways a girl gets a reputation. Other girls and boys gossip about her, then she's labeled with one of the reputations outlined below. The social hierarchy and a girl's clique can protect a girl from a bad reputation. For example, a girl in the popular clique can duck a reputation as a slut even if she's frequently having sex. In contrast, if a girl who isn't liked by other girls gets that reputation, it'll stick. There are variations on every story. Your daughter could doubtless add to the list.

In-Your-Face Angry Girl

She's not afraid to dress differently and be "bitchy." She is dramatic, interested in zines (magazines authored by teens and printed and/or posted on the Internet). She has no patience for popularity and the people in the popular cliques. Sometimes she says things just to freak other people out. She can be cause-oriented and talk about her issues constantly. She comes across as cynical and not easily impressed. Notwithstanding her hard exterior, she's easily hurt by others and feels like the world is against her. She listens to music that reflects these feelings of isolation and alien-ation, music that other people think is "dark" and "gloomy."

Other teens often accuse her of listening to satanic music. I've heard extremely serious discussions between girls about X artist's pact with the devil. Sometimes the In-Your-Face Angry Girl and the Quiet Morose Girl, described below, are into the occult, often precisely because it gives them a feeling of power over other students who make them miserable. A dramatic curse can go a long way to get the "in people" to leave you alone.

Quiet, Morose Girl/Loner

She's similar to In-Your-Face Angry Girl, except she's usually most com-fortable observing other people and expressing what she sees and feels through dramatic poetry or journals. She feels helpless to stop what goes on around her, so she comes across to her peers and adults as withdrawn, depressed, and sullen. She's prone to wearing all black (including lipstick and fingernail polish). She also can be very active in social issues.

Big Girl/Tomboy

In the sixth grade she played football with the boys, but by eighth grade the boys won't play with her—and neither will the girls. She's often phys-ically bigger than other students. She's reluctant to join groups, is quiet, and often feels out of place. She can speak out defiantly if she has to, but then goes back into her shell. It's common for her peers to spread rumors about her being gay. Parents and teachers (myself included) can have a really hard time getting her to open up.

Jock

Girls get this reputation if they excel at sports and have a masculine appearance and/or demeanor. The Jock's peers often see her as asexual. She can come across as tough and unemotional and can have a hard time admitting when her feelings are hurt. Big Girl and Jock aren't the same thing, but they sometimes blend into each other.

Social Climber

She's the chameleon. She changes herself constantly to fit in with girls she emulates. She looks to others for her opinions because she's afraid to express an original thought. She can be horrible to a target and is easily manipulated by more powerful girls. She can also be targeted for trying too hard.

Teacher's Pet

The reputation that won't go away. Girls don't trust her and, for the most part, teachers don't like her either. The Pet often makes things much worse for herself by becoming the rules enforcer when the teacher isn't there. Girls find her incredibly annoying and don't take her seriously.

Perfect Girl

Everyone looks at her and wants to be her. Meanwhile, she feels like a fraud and thinks that at any moment someone will pull back the curtain and expose her. She tries desperately to avoid making any mistakes and is impossibly hard on herself. She finds fault with herself easily and never thinks she's doing enough. She runs herself into the ground trying to keep up with her image.

> *I should be what other people want me to be. I should act how they want me to act or else I won't have any friends.*   Jane, 16

> *I don't think she sees who she is anymore. She is becoming a compilation of everything the girls say about her.*   Jane's mom

Boyfriend Stealer

Some girls think this girl is cool as long as boys aren't around. She acts ditzy around boys even if she's smart. Other girls know that boys are her priority, so they don't trust her.

If I was dating someone and my friend flirted with him, or at least other people thought so, people would label her as a tramp. No one would talk to her or trust her.   Kate, 15

Tease

A girl is called a tease for the most arbitrary of reasons. If she wears stylish clothes, even ones that aren't tight, if she won't make out with boys and she's pretty, she can end up with this reputation.

It's scary what girls will do to be liked. Girls like the idea of people thinking they're attractive but not the promise behind it, which is you have to put out.   Morgan, 16

Lesbian/Butch/Dike

This reputation is closely associated with the Big Girl/Loner, and it often doesn't have anything to do with whether a girl is gay or not. Generally, it's not so much if you really are a lesbian but how you present yourself. If you're more masculine in appearance, people will give you a harder time than if you look more feminine. Unfortunately, homophobia still runs rampant in schools, and when you don't look stereotypically girly enough, things can get uncomfortable and even physically dangerous. Girls have told me about being tripped, shoved, and even pushed down stairs while other students utter homophobic slurs. These girls feel that they have to look and act tough to survive, and the dike label comes with that territory.

Some girls have adopted a "butch" look because that's how they feel most comfortable. Some adopt the look to desexualize themselves. If you're being felt up while walking down the school hallway, dressing like you aren't a girl gives you some degree of space and safety. At one school where we teach, a group of girls march down the hallway together in a line and people are scared of them. Together, they're presenting a united front. Alone, they're vulnerable to attack.

In schools where the adult leadership implicitly condones homophobia by looking the other way, gay students are constantly harassed, humiliated, and often physically threatened. If the adult leadership strives to make a safe environment for everyone in the school, the harassment decreases (and other forms of harassment and bullying decrease as well) and these girls can thrive more easily.

Square

> She likes school, has had a boyfriend for three years, and is one of those preppy, peppy annoying people. She's on all the committees.
>
> Angie, 16

She could be a genuinely happy kid, but she also might be covering. Watch out on this one. Don't be so caught up in her accomplishments that you don't see the warning signs that she feels she's nothing without them.

Actual Happy Person

Not every girl is miserable. There are actually genuinely happy girls. People look up to them. The cliques cut them a lot of slack. I don't come across them very often, but they do exist.

The Über-Rep: The Slut

Ho. Freak. Whatever. There are few other words that carry so much weight, have so much baggage, and control a girl's behavior and decision-making more. One of the biggest inner conflicts I have with my work is encouraging girls to be proud of their sexuality while making sure they understand how vulnerable they are in a world that constantly exploits their sexuality. The most frequent way girls are trapped in this conundrum is when they accuse each other of being a slut. This über-rep also makes girls more vulnerable to sexual coercion and violence from boys.

When it comes to the "slut" reputation, girls accuse each other of two things: acting like a slut, and being a slut. The fear of being accused of acting like a slut controls girls' actions in a particular situation. For example, when your daughter chooses what to wear to a party, she's trying to balance looking sexy while not coming off as slutty (i.e., being attractive to boys yet not incurring the wrath of other girls).

> *I was playing basketball with three friends. One of my friends was a girl and the other two were boys. We had been playing for a while, when a girl in our school who was in seventh grade asked us if she could play. We said yes. After a while, she took off her sweatshirt and pants and she was only wearing a jog bra and shorts. I mean, she had breasts and everything! We kept playing, but the boys couldn't pay attention. I thought she was really showing off and flirting with the boys. The whole thing got really weird. I think she was acting like a total slut.*
> Brett, 11

When I asked that girl how she felt watching this scenario unfold, her reaction was far more complex. As much as she didn't approve of the seventh-grade girl's behavior, she was conflicted because she envied the boys' attention. Girls often feel they have to choose between being themselves and displaying a sexy costume. It's a huge conflict. If a girl opts for the costume and acts the part, she'll get the boys' attention, but she'll also incur the girls' wrath. She might also feel weird inside because she'll think she's selling out. She'll try to achieve the impossible by pleasing groups with two competing agendas. She might also feel that once she interacts with boys in a sexual way, she'll lose the ability to just hang out with them as people. These conflicting emotions and confusion over how to act spill out when girls accuse each other of acting like sluts.

For younger girls, the threat of being called a slut defines the limits of acceptable behavior and dress. They use it to describe a girl who is perceived as flirting "too much" and dressing too provocatively. They're easily and understandably confused about their own personal comfort level regarding how they come across to others because they're literally transforming from little girls into women in a world that often perceives them first and foremost as sexual objects. It can be confusing, exciting, and terrifying all at the same time. What usually prompts girls to accuse one of their own of being a slut is recognition from the world (meaning boys) that she's not a friend but a "girl."

So, acting like a slut is a label a girl gets from her appearance and behavior in "public" places like the school hallway, the movie theaters and malls teens frequent, and parties. Being a slut is a reputation a girl gets when there's gossip about whether she's making out or having sex with someone, usually preceded by people seeing her drunk and/or "throwing" herself onto someone.

Even Eleven-Year-Olds Will Accuse Each Other of Acting Like Sluts

It's 8:00 A.M. on Wednesday, and I'm walking down the school hallway to teach a sixth-grade class. I'm surrounded by the normal chaos that is sixth-grade girls when three girls run up to me in obvious distress. "Ms. Wiseman, we really need to talk to you before class." We walk down the hall for privacy as they explain, interrupting each other constantly. "There's a rumor spreading around the whole grade that is totally untrue. People are saying we're sluts because we were hanging out with some seventh-grade boys. There's even a rumor that we kissed the boys in a basement. We want to talk about it in class. Can we?"

These girls are part of the most popular clique in the class. Teachers would call them social butterflies on their report cards. As confident as they usually appear, it's clear they're very upset. We prepare what they'll say and walk into the classroom.

The rest of the girls are sitting in a circle ready for class. The three stand up in front of the board, look at their classmates, look at each other, take a deep breath, stand silent for a few tortured seconds, and begin. They start strong, confident, and indignant as people do when they have been wrongfully accused. But as they express their anger, the power of the rumors becomes clear. They're embarrassed, humiliated, and desperately want the girls in their class to believe their innocence.

The other girls can see how upset they are. The atmosphere in the room changes. How can these popular girls be hurt? These invincible girls are vulnerable. Rumors are things whispered in the halls, publicly private. But even though everyone knows what's being said, it's hardly ever brought out into the open of a classroom. It's a powerful lesson that the über-rep of being a slut trumps anything else—it can even rattle the girls at the top of the social totem pole.

In this situation, the powerful girls were vulnerable because it was sixth grade and the other girls are simultaneously terrified, disgusted, and excited about the "sex" stuff that's starting. Gossip about boys and kissing buzzes like bees around a hive—everyone wants in. The popular girls' slut reputations will probably not last long because their social status gives them some degree of immunity.

The accusation of being a slut most often doesn't come until eighth grade, when more girls are likely to be exploring kissing, making out, or even having intercourse. Then the slut reputation is more about pointing fingers at a girl's sexual activity, whether she "gives it up" easily, fools around with a lot of boys, etc. It's an image that's almost impossible to shake because the accused is the repository of everyone's judgment, jealousy, curiosity, and fear. When I work with girls with bad reputations, they're initially wary of me. Why should they trust me? They've learned to build big walls around themselves to block out the judgment and rejection they so often feel from others. I'm the teacher who is supposed to talk about girls' friendships? Please. They're walking advertisements for how cruel girls can be to each other.

When I have girls like this in my class, I can usually pick them out by their defiant, sour expressions. The worst expressions come from girls who aren't only on the outside of the "Act Like a Woman" box but are really suffering at the hands of the other girls in the group. At first, talking about these issues can feel dangerous for them. We're talking about things that hurt them, and they have no reason to believe I'll do right by them.

Picture me teaching thirty-five tenth-grade girls. Kate walks into the classroom about ten minutes after the class starts. Her expression is both challenging—she's waiting for me to call her out for being late—and hostile—she's anticipating that the class will be boring. She starts off by sitting in the back of the room, but within five minutes she moves right in front of me. The "Act Like a Woman" box is on the board and the girls are discussing the different roles girls play in cliques. Kate, scowling, says something I can't quite hear. When I ask her to repeat herself, one of the popular girls says, "Oh, don't pay any attention to her. That's just Kate." Kate's face clouds over and her back stiffens as she repeats herself, "I said that I hate girls. You can't trust them. Girls are petty, stupid, and jealous. Like in this grade, the girls are just jealous because I get more attention from the boys. I know I'm known as a slut but I don't care." As she speaks, you can feel the ripple of anger and resentment in the classroom in response. There are few things popular girls hate more than being accused of jealousy.

Kate transferred to another school at the end of the year. But she hasn't left her troubles behind just because she's away from a hateful, accusing clique. It isn't just that she doesn't trust girls and that she's a target for cliques' envy. The bigger problem is that Kate's mistrust makes her vulnerable to a dangerous combination: low self-esteem and social isolation, which can lead to sexual coersion and/or violence at the hands of boys.

Here's how it happens: Kate, for many possible reasons, needs attention, especially from boys and men. She learns how to get this attention, as we all do, and acts and dresses accordingly. Now consider this quote from a senior girl remembering what it felt like to see girls like Kate.

> In seventh grade, I watched a girl who constantly flirted with boys. The problem was that she alienated herself from other girls. She pretty much accepted the slut role that people made her into. The boys she flirted with didn't take their relationships with her seriously. Even though I didn't want to be treated like she was, I wanted the attention she was getting. But whenever I was around her, I felt incredibly prudish and uptight. Skye, 17

Girls are at best uncomfortable with girls like Kate, and at worst treat her like dirt and refuse to have anything to do with her. In turn, Kate doesn't trust girls and she has good reason not to. They have rejected her. In her mind all girls are bad. But her mistrust of girls clouds her thinking about which boys to trust. Her experiences with girls are a constant reminder that she's a social liability. Naturally, she seeks out people who'll make her feel better. What is the easiest, fastest way for Kate to get the attention she wants? By hanging out with boys. But which boys will want to hang out with Kate the most? The ones who need to prove their masculinity by interacting with girls only as sexual objects. Naturally, they see Kate as an easy way to prove their masculinity. Kate, not wanting to turn away the attention she's getting, will do what the boys want. She won't reject someone who isn't rejecting her. By the time she learns that she's valued for what she can "give up," not for who she is as a person, she may feel it's too late to do better for herself and she'll take what she can get . . . hence,

> *Boys may call me a slut, but at least they call.*   Sasha, 14

Where Do Kates Come From?

Don't think these girls just come from poor families. In my experience with thousands of girls, rich and poor, I've found that these girls generally have parents who are disconnected from them, show them love inconsistently, or make them feel ashamed for who they are. The girls have come to the conclusion that they're on their own and can't depend on anyone but themselves. However, this doesn't mean they don't romanticize love and sex. They're still girls caught up with wishing someone will rescue them and see them for who they really are. Every time they have sex, there's a little part of them hoping this person is the one who will.

CHECK YOUR BAGGAGE

Teasing, gossip, and reputations understandably make parents really uncomfortable. I've talked to moms who took greater offense and forgave less easily than their daughters.

> *I want to kill them! I still remember the girl who was mean to my daughter . . . and I think it bothered me more than it bothered her.*
> Mary

- Is there anyone you would run away from if you saw them now?
- Did you ever feel trapped by a reputation you couldn't shake?
- Were you ever teased? What were you teased about? How did you handle it?
- Did you ever spread gossip and get caught? Were you ever gossiped about? How did you handle it?

Write down a list of your daughter's closest friends. Do you think they support her or discourage her?

If you were a mean girl, what would you tease your daughter about? How do you think your daughter would respond?

Do you gossip and tease other people today?

Does your daughter hear you gossip on the phone?

What You Can Do About It

The first step you can take to help your daughter is to acknowledge the role of teasing and gossip in your own life. As I said at the beginning of the chapter, if you gossip and tease meanly, you're modeling that behavior for your daughter. Turn off the gossip shows, stop reading the gossip magazines and columns, and if you have to indulge, don't do it around your daughter. If you do get caught, use it as an opportunity to talk with your daughter about how it's easy to get wound up in the excitement and intimacy of gossip and forget how painful it can be to be the object. Talk about how much truth there is in gossip—is it okay to pass along a rumor you have no way of substantiating?

Now you need to arm your daughter with a battle plan for when she's been the object of bad teasing or saddled with an unfair reputation. Let's use a true example that one of my students shared with me recently to show you how to proceed:

> When I was in junior high, there was this new girl that a bunch of guys liked. Two girls in the grade went around with a petition they made all the boys sign that said, "I will never go out with the megawhore, Lori Shore." After a while, one of her best friends told her about the petition. One of the girls flat out said, "Yeah, I did it and what are you going to do about it?" The other girl was a really good friend of Lori's and kept denying it and pretended to be her friend.   Hope, 17

As despicable as this story is, it suits our purposes because it involves all the issues we've been discussing. Let's assess which girls did what:

- The Queen Bee (the girl who admitted she did it) is the one who passes around the petition because Lori, the new girl, is getting too much attention from boys. The petition's purpose is to bring Lori down and to demonstrate the Queen Bee's power over the other kids.

- The Wannabe/Pleaser is the petition-passer who keeps denying she did it. She's intimidated by the Queen Bee and too ashamed to come clean with Lori.
- The Messenger is the girl who told Lori about the petition. From what we know, it seems that she genuinely believed that Lori had the right to know.

If this happened to your daughter, how would you handle it? First things first. You're allowed to hate the Queen Bee. You might fantasize about killing her. If you were Lori's parents, you would definitely want to scream and blame her parents. Your first instinct would be to pick up the phone and let them know what a horrible troll they've raised. That won't solve the problem. It'll make it worse. Your daughter won't learn to deal with problems herself, you'll make the parents defensive, and she'll have to deal with the same girl at school the next day, but now it'll be worse because everyone knows she can't fight her own battles.

If Your Daughter Is the Target, Don't Say "Just Ignore It"

Choosing when and how to confront teasing and gossiping is always difficult. As I mentioned earlier, many parents are tempted to tell their daughters to ignore the teasing and it will stop or the gossips will move on to someone else. Even though this sounds like a reasonable, mature strategy, it's exactly the kind of parental advice that makes girls feel that their parents don't understand the world they're living in. When girls have problems, they need help right away. Immediately. Imagine if you were Lori. You wouldn't care about anything else but how you were going to show your face at school the next day. Lori isn't thinking in the long term. Next week may as well be next year.

Clearly, Lori is faced with bad teasing. Using that definition, she knows that the girls who passed around the petition aren't going to leave her alone if she ignores them. In fact, they and everyone else is watching closely to see how she'll respond. She has to know what to say, how to hold her body, and what tone of voice to use. If she can't work it out on her own, she needs to be able to tell you or another adult if she can't concentrate in school, she's scared to run into her teasers, feels trapped and powerless, or doesn't want to go to school.

Finding Out She's Upset

If you're Lori's parents, unless Lori comes home crying (which is possible because this is such a horrendous situation), it may be hard to know that something's wrong, or what that something is. Review the strategies in Chapter 2 for how to tell if your daughter's upset. Remember, anytime your teen daughter wants to talk, you should be prepared to drop everything and pay attention. You're ready to talk when she's ready to talk.

If your daughter wants to talk to you but also couches it as "no big deal," don't believe her; it's a big deal. If you know she's upset and she doesn't approach you directly, approach her gently: "You seem upset. Anything I can help with?"

If she approaches you and you absolutely can't talk to her that minute, tell her when you can. However, always remember that by the time you're ready, the opportunity may be gone, because in the interim she'll have talked to her friends and/or reconsidered whether talking to you is a good idea in the first place. If you have to postpone, set up a time as soon as possible and don't forget to keep your promise! She has to know that you'll come through when she asks for help.

You have two goals: The first is to have a productive conversation with her. This means that through the process of your conversation, you want to affirm her and confirm that you're a good resource and a nonjudgmental listener. The second is to help her come up with realistic strategies to confront the problem effectively. You'll never accomplish the second goal without the first.

Here's how the conversation might go:

YOUR DAUGHTER: *Um . . . well . . . can I talk to you for a minute?*

YOU: (paying bills, balancing checkbook, in the groove of getting things done) *Huh?* (Your brain slows and the gears start to shift) *Oh, yeah, sure, no problem.* (Stop what you're doing, physically turn your body away from the task at hand, and sit down so you're looking at her with your full attention.) *What's up?*

YOUR DAUGHTER: *Well, it's nothing really. I mean it's not that big a deal, but there're these girls at school who are bothering me.*

YOU: *I'm sorry about that. How are they bothering you?*

YOUR DAUGHTER: *I don't know. They say mean stuff.*

YOU: *Can you describe some of the things they do or say?*

YOUR DAUGHTER: *Okay. But you have to promise not to get mad.*

YOU: *Well, I can't promise that because I don't want anyone to be mean to you, but I can promise you that I'll help you think this through.*

YOUR DAUGHTER: *This girl at school made up a petition that she had all the boys sign that said "I promise not to go out with Lori Shore the megawhore" and all the boys signed it.*

YOU: (Take a deep breath! Don't freak out. She's watching you closely. Now empathize and affirm her pain.) *That's terrible! I'm so sorry! Okay, I have to admit I'm really angry. I can't believe anyone would say that about anyone, let alone you, but I'm so glad you told me. I can totally understand how upset you would be. If it was happening to me, I would be upset, too. Let's figure this out together. . . .*

On to the Second Goal

With your support behind her, what can your daughter do about it? There are five options, listed in order of priority; if the first option doesn't work, go to the next one. It's far preferable to teach your daughter to handle these problems effectively herself using the first or second options; this both bolsters her self-esteem and broadcasts to victimizers that she's not an easy target. For our purposes, I'm calling the Queen Bee who perpetrates the teasing and gossiping the RMG (Really Mean Girl). Here are the five options:

- Your daughter can confront the RMG
- She can ask a teacher or counselor for help
- You can call the RMG's parents.
- You can talk to the teacher
- You can talk to an administrator

Option 1: Confronting the RMG

Step One: Preparing Your Daughter

To get started, take your daughter to a quiet place and suggest she write down the specific details of the teasing, including dates, times, what was said to her, and what she said or did in response. She should include how she felt in the situation, her feelings now, and what she wants to happen so the behavior stops. Every step of the way, I always encourage girls to write this information down so when they're facing their victimizer they'll be more prepared and less likely to lose their words.

There's another reason to document the misdeed. You never want to think the worst, but you want to be prepared for it. Your daughter needs to show a history of what happened and the steps she took to address it. For example, if the first three options don't work, when you go to the teacher, you have a written log of your daughter trying to get help from this teacher. If you can show specific dates and times, the teaser's pattern of behavior, and the steps your daughter took to address this problem, the school will take you more seriously because it's more difficult to dismiss it as a she said/she said conflict.

Next, have your daughter write down what she wants to say and then practice in front of a mirror. Her tone of voice needs to be calm and level and her eyes steady but not challenging. Her body language needs to be confident: standing up straight, face-to-face. You can even suggest that she practice the conversation with you or another adult she trusts.

The conversation has to:

- Describe specifically what's bothering her
- Request what she does or doesn't want
- Affirm the person and/or their relationship

Step Two: Confronting the RMG

If your daughter feels she's not in physical danger, I strongly recommend she talk to the RMG first. (If there's more than one, she should have separate meetings, since a one-on-one confrontation will be more successful, as I'll explain below.) She needs to choose a place and time where she can speak to the RMG alone, some place where she feels safe and secure. For many girls, the library is a safe zone; the librarian patrols there and it has a reputation for being a calmer place, but your daughter should choose a site she thinks is best.

When your daughter's ready, she should confront the RMG when she's away from other people so she's not making the RMG lose face and other girls can't buzz around them. If your daughter confronts the RMG in front of her friends, even if the RMG feels bad about what she did, her need to appear in control in front of her peers will trump the motivation to do the right thing. If the RMG is in a group, your daughter should request a private meeting. ("Hi, there's something I need to talk to you about in private. Can you meet me during study hall in the library at 11:00?") There's one thing to watch out for: Sometimes girls will bring their friends to a meeting like this for physical support. If that happens, your daughter must request that the other girls leave because this is a "private meeting" between her and the RMG.

Here's how the private conversation might go:

YOUR DAUGHTER: *Can I talk to you for a minute?*

RMG: *What about?*

YOUR DAUGHTER: *Look, I know about the petition, and it really hurt me. I don't know why something like this would happen, but I want it stopped and I know you have the power to stop it.*

RMG: *Well, too bad, and obviously people agree with me because they signed it, too.*

YOUR DAUGHTER: *I want it stopped. I don't know why you don't like me so much, but there's nothing I can do about that. I would like us to be civil to each other and respect each other.*

RMG: *Whatever.*

YOUR DAUGHTER: *If you ever want to talk to me about why you did this, I would like to hear it. Again, I'm asking you to stop and I really think you have the power to stop it.*

In this scenario your daughter was specific about what happened, how it made her feel, and what she wanted stopped, and she finished by saying something positive. She lost nothing by admitting that the other girl "won." In fact, it can mollify the RMG because it acknowledged her power; your daughter's appeal to the RMG's Queen Bee status, and therefore her ability to call a halt to the victimization, increases the likelihood that it'll stop.

Notice that the RMG concluded the conversation by saying "whatever." That's probably as good as it'll get. Girls often feel they've failed if the RMG doesn't immediately apologize and then the two become friends. Girls crave reconciliation because it regains "that comfortable feeling." But they haven't failed if they don't reconcile—and reconciliation usually happens only if your daughter capitulates. The immediate goal is to stop the RMG's behavior. The only way she'll do that is if Lori communicates that she's not easy prey. Just like any predator, RMG goes after easy targets first, and Lori's proving to be too difficult. The unfortunate reality is that your daughter can't control the way an RMG will respond to her. She can only control her own actions. If the RMG acknowledges her evil ways, so much the better, but don't count on it. (Apologies are more likely if the RMG is a friend inside the clique rather than a teaser singling out a loner.)

> *Everyone wants to talk about everyone else and use you as a topic of discussion, but at the same time they don't want you to get mad at them. Everyone's a coward. Most of the time people vehemently deny they said anything. If I find out that someone is spreading rumors about me, I go up to them immediately and say, "What the hell is wrong with you?" They usually say, "I didn't say that. Who told you I said that?" If I really have caught them and there's no denying it, then they usually say, "I'm sorry." On rare occasions, people fight back when you confront them by saying that they spread a rumor because you did something first.*   Zoe, 17

If the RMG tries to sidestep the issue by asking "Who told you that?," don't let your daughter get distracted. Girls typically avoid taking responsibility for their actions by blaming the person who got them into trouble. If the RMG raises this red herring, your daughter can say, "It doesn't matter how I know. What matters is that it stops now."

If the RMG is a friend inside the clique, your daughter needs to affirm that friendship, but spell out what it will take for the friendship to continue. "Look, I want us to stay friends, but that'll only work if you understand how much that hurt me. Friends don't do that to each other. If you want to talk more about why you did it, I'm listening."

Option 2: Talking to the Teacher

If your daughter feels that her conversations with the RMG aren't working, the next step is to talk to a teacher or counselor, someone she trusts
but who doesn't necessarily know the teasers. However, if a student goes
to a teacher, she has to assume that the teacher will want to get the RMG
"in trouble." This can be a big problem. Your daughter will probably
want the adult to make the problem go away without anyone knowing
that she told. It's very important that you talk to your daughter about this
possibility so she can be clear about what action she does or doesn't want
the teacher to take. Your daughter should choose a teacher she feels listens to her, respects her, and follows through on her promises. Here's how
the conversation might go:

YOUR DAUGHTER: *Ms. Wiseman, can I talk to you for a minute after class
today?*
ME: *Sure, is this something we are going to need some time for or privacy?*
YOUR DAUGHTER: *Maybe.*
ME: *No problem. Why don't you come back after last period today?*

After last period.

ME: *Hey Lori, what's up?*
YOUR DAUGHTER: *Well, some girls did something that really bothers me.*
ME: *What?*
YOUR DAUGHTER: *Well, I'm not sure what I want you to do about it, but
RMG and her friends circulated a petition that all the boys signed that
said I was a whore and that they wouldn't date me.*
ME: *I'm so sorry! Coming to school today must have been really hard. It
must have taken a lot of courage. How do you want me to help you?*
YOUR DAUGHTER: *I just want it to go away, but I don't want to get into trou-
ble for going to a teacher!*
ME: *Well, I know that's hard, but I'm really glad you came to me. Let's figure out together a strategy for dealing with this. Tell me what you've
done so far.*
YOUR DAUGHTER: *I told her to stop, but she wouldn't listen.*

ME: *I can talk to her. Let's decide together what you would like me to say.*
YOUR DAUGHTER: *Okay, but I don't want her to know I told on her.*
ME: *No problem. I can say I found out about the petition on my own.*

Your daughter should give the teacher a copy of everything she's written about the incident. Your daughter's goal is to come up with a mutual agreement between her and the teacher about what will be done and when. After the meeting, she should write down what the teacher said she would do and when. Everybody works better with deadlines. If the deadline passes, your daughter should ask the teacher a few days later about what's going on, get another deadline, and write it down.

If that deadline passes, it's time for you to get involved.

Option 3: Talking to RMG's Parents

Unfortunately, when parents talk to other parents, the problem usually gets worse. Avoid letting your natural desire to protect your daughter get in the way of effectively resolving the problem. No matter how tempting it may be to call RMG's parents and scream at them about their evil child, it should never be your first resort. Even if the other parents did exactly what you want—get off the phone with you, then scream at their daughter and ground her for a month—guess what happens next? The next day your daughter goes to school with an RMG bent on revenge. At some point, the RMG's and your daughter's paths will cross without adult supervision around. The harassment will escalate.

So your involvement is critical, but you have to be smart. Assume that the RMG's parents don't know what their kid is doing. Go to them asking for their help in solving this problem, not accusing them of bad parenting or having bad kids. Ask them for advice about how they would handle this situation if they were in your shoes. A great goal would be to work together to come up with complementary strategies.

YOU: *Hi, I'm Lori's mother. Lori is in the seventh grade with your daughter. Do you have a minute to talk?*
RMG'S PARENT: *Yeah, sure* (suspiciously).
YOU: *Look, I have to admit I'm uncomfortable calling, but I need your help.*

*My daughter came home today and told me that your daughter wrote
and circulated a petition that said my daughter was a whore. Lori came
home really upset and of course I am, too, so I'm asking for your help.*

RMG'S PARENT: *Well* (defensive tone of voice), *I mean, I'm sorry that she
did that, but I don't think it's that big a deal and I think they should
work it out on their own. In any case, how do you know my daughter
did it?*

YOU: (take a deep breath and remember the goal) *Thanks for the apology*
(sincere not sarcastic). *I know because your daughter admitted it. I'm
sure you realize that it's a big deal to me since Lori's feeling like she's
too embarrassed to go to school. Lori's already asked your daughter to
stop and that hasn't helped. I would really appreciate any help. I think
parents should really stick together in situations like this.*

RMG'S PARENT: *What do you want me to do?*

YOU: *Lori would like the petition to stop, and I would really like to request
that your daughter apologize to her. I'm also worried that when the
adults aren't around, Lori will get teased again. Do you have any ideas
so that won't happen?*

If You're the One Called

It's 6:00 and you're blissfully alone. It's quiet and calm. You have a few
moments to yourself with nothing to do . . . or maybe not. More likely,
you're desperately trying to get dinner on the table and get to an evening
meeting on time . . . when the phone rings.

LORI'S MOM: *Is this RMG's mother?*

YOU: *Yes . . . what can I do for you?*

LORI'S MOM: *Do you know what your daughter did to my daughter Lori?*

YOU: *No, I don't.* (You glare at your daughter, who is beginning to clue in
that this conversation is about her and it's not about what a good
Samaritan she is.) *What happened?*

LORI'S MOM: *I don't know how you raise your daughter, but she wrote, circulated, and made all the boys sign a petition calling my daughter a
whore. What kind of child have you raised? If you can't raise your
daughter with some morals, I'm reporting her to the school.* (At this

moment, you're angry in many directions. Angry at your evil daughter—could she really have done something so awful?—angry that you're accused of being a lousy parent, and angry that you'll now be late to this meeting. No matter how angry you are, immediately acknowledge the other parent's feelings and admit it's upsetting.)

YOU: *I'm really sorry if my daughter did something so cruel to your daughter. Can you tell me what happened and when? Can you give me more details? (Write them down.) Let me talk to my daughter, and then I would like to call you tomorrow. When is a good time? Thank you for calling. It's really hard to hear, but I'm glad you did because I want RMG to be held accountable for anything she did that was cruel. I would really like to work together on this.*

Because Lori's parent usually wants to vent, these calls can take a long time. If you must go to that meeting, apologize, tell Lori's mom about your meeting, and let her choose another time to talk. Then call *exactly* when you agreed.

> I listen to them and then listen to my daughter. It's her responsibility. I think it's wrong to be accused without seeing the accuser. I also don't use pronouns. For example, I will say, "A call came in . . . it reported X. Do you know anything about it?" Then I think my daughter has to make a choice. She can continue her crappy behavior or she can change. Now this doesn't work all the time because I'm so pissed off.
>
> Peggy

If you meet the parent in person, use the same strategies as you would on the phone. Stay focused on the goal and enlist the parent's help.

When you confront your daughter about her nasty behavior, tell her the facts as you know them. No matter what her excuse or justification, she should be punished in a way that communicates how seriously you take this issue.

Option 4: Parent Talking to the Teacher

If the first three strategies haven't worked, you'll need to meet with your daughter's teacher yourself. Before your meeting, familiarize yourself with the school's policies concerning student conduct, bullying, and/or harassment. With recorded information in hand, you're an advocate for your daughter. Approach any school professional with an attitude of collaboration and respect. Most teachers and administrators interact with parents only when something is wrong. As a result, parents are often perceived as defensive and unwilling to take responsibility for their child's actions. Teachers will be much more likely to help if you approach them as partners and not assume from the beginning that they're part of the problem.

Explain your understanding of the situation and your goals for the meeting. Be clear that although you're sure the teacher's busy, it's very important that your daughter feel safe in the school, and that your daughter has already approached the teacher for help and it's critical that he or she follow through. Confirm school policy and always try to work with the teacher to develop a strategy. Get a firm deadline from the teacher for action. If the deadline isn't kept, write a short note telling the teacher you are contacting the principal and then do it.

Option 5: Parent Talking to the Principal

If you're unsatisfied with the teacher, your last option is to speak to the principal. You're there to establish the following: Your daughter has asked for help from a member of the faculty, you've also asked for help, and help hasn't been forthcoming. There's a consistent pattern of behavior where your daughter is going to the school for help and the school isn't providing assistance. As a result, your daughter's schoolwork is suffering. The U.S. Supreme Court has stated that students have the right to go to school and be able to concentrate on their schoolwork in a safe environment. Request the principal's intervention.

What If Your Daughter's the Bystander?

Often your daughter won't be the victim or the victimizer, but an eyewitness to the mayhem. She'll be conflicted: Should she stand up to the RMG and risk censure by the group, or keep quiet? It's important to communicate to your daughter that you can relate to her dilemma. This is an excellent opportunity for her ally to talk to her (if your attempts to talk to her are failing).

YOU: *So I heard about the petition. You want to talk about it?*

YOUR DAUGHTER: *No, not really.*

YOU: *Well, I want to talk about it. Was there really a petition that said Lori Shore is a megawhore?*

YOUR DAUGHTER: *Yeah, I really didn't want to do it. I wish RMG would back off a little, but she never does.*

YOU: *Why does she do that? What does she have to gain by doing it? What do you have to gain?*

YOUR DAUGHTER: *I don't know.*

YOU: *Well, tell me if I'm wrong, but I'm sure it's hard to stop RMG when she sets her mind on something.*

YOUR DAUGHTER: *Well, maybe.*

YOU: *Well, I'd understand that it'd be really hard if I were in your shoes. But even though I know how hard it must have been, it's really important to me that you stand up and do what's right in these situations. I know you want to and I know you can. What do you think stopped you? What would have happened if you refused to go along? Let's figure out a plan of action.* (Then suggest to your daughter that she use the grid from Chapter 5 to plan her course of action.)

What If Your Daughter's the Nasty Gossiper

When my mom wants to talk to me, this is what I imagine . . . I have a shield, I'm wearing armor, and I have a stick that I am poking at her while I say "Back! Back! Stay back! Stay away!" Zoe, 17

It's hard to admit that your daughter has behaved like a jerk, but it isn't a reflection of poor parenting if you admit her misbehavior. Quite the opposite. Guess which parents teachers and people like me complain about? The parents who think their daughters aren't little angels or the parents who blame everyone else for corrupting their little darlings?

You overhear her gossiping to her friends. What should you do? First, wait until you're alone with her. Never humiliate her in front of her friends.

YOU: *When I was driving you to soccer practice, I overheard you calling Amy a slut. Why?*

YOUR DAUGHTER: *I didn't! I mean, well, Mom, I was just kidding! Do you have to make such a big deal out of this?*

YOU: *Well, yeah, I do. It's important to me. Why did you say that?*

YOUR DAUGHTER: *Mom, I didn't!*

YOU: *You aren't answering my question.*

YOUR DAUGHTER: *You should have seen her! It was disgusting! She was throwing herself at these guys!*

YOU: *Look, this is important to me. Calling Amy a slut puts down all girls—including you. I want you to stop calling girls sluts, whores, or whatever else you call them. I don't doubt that there are girls throwing themselves all over guys, and if you want, let's talk about it. I'll listen to what you have to say anytime. But that doesn't take away from the fact that it's very important to me that you don't tear other girls down. I love you and expect great things from you. Strong women don't call other women sluts and whores.*

Then have her apologize to the girl and afterward ask her how the apology went. Don't blow off this last step because chances are high that your daughter will agree to apologize and then not do it. Apologizing is an important skill to teach your daughter. Don't let her off the hook.

THE ART OF THE APOLOGY

Dear Samantha,

I think I really need to apologize to you. In the fourth grade, when I first met you, I had the impression that you were just a snotty, boy-crazy jerk. I hated how you always walked around in your clique. I guess I wanted to be included and instead of trying to be friends with you because I thought you thought I was a geek, I acted like a total jerk toward you. I know I have called you some pretty bad things to your face and behind your back and I feel pretty bad. I just hope that

you don't hate me so much that you can't forgive me. I really think we
should be friends.   Ilana, 12

Apologies are powerful because they're a public demonstration of remorse, an acknowledgment of the consequences of hurtful behavior, and an affirmation of the dignity of the person who has been wronged.

A true apology has to be:

- Given with a genuine understanding of the crime involved. Especially when your daughter is younger, make sure she understands what she's apologizing for. Otherwise, she may very well hurt the other person again. Don't let her put the best possible spin on her actions ("I didn't mean to say X to her, I think she just took it the wrong way").
- About the apologizer's actions alone—her apology can't include what she thinks the other person did or said.
- Devoid of any "last licks" in which the speaker buries another insult within the apology ("I'm sorry you were so clueless about the party that I had to tell you that you weren't invited").
- Given without qualification. It's not an apology if it includes "But I only did it because . . ." or "I wouldn't have said that unless you . . ."
- Genuinely contrite—there's nothing worse than an apology clearly rendered only because the girl was told to apologize ("My mom says I have to apologize" or "I guess I'm supposed to say I'm sorry").
- Given without the expectation of a return apology. If the listener has the grace or goodwill to say "I'm sorry, too," that's a bonus.
- Rendered with the understanding that it may even invoke further recriminations ("Yeah, well, you really hurt me! I can't believe you did that!")

However, encourage your daughter to realize that the art of the apol-
ogy, once learned, shouldn't be overused. I've had too many friends
that are way too apologetic all the time!   Nidhi, 16

Beware that apologies can be manipulated! Girls in lower positions in the social hierarchy apologize when they inadvertently challenge a more powerful girl. Then they aren't apologizing for something they did that hurt someone, they're apologizing for challenging the other girl's right to make her miserable.

Apologizing means taking responsibility for your actions. It's one of the most essential life skills you can teach your daughter.

Resilience

Teasing, gossip, and reputations regulate girls' behavior and make them afraid to be and become who they really are. Your daughter could use every strategy I've described and a girl will still be mean to her. There's no easy strategy that guarantees other girls will leave your daughter alone, but that's not the most important goal. The most important goal is that through difficult experiences like these, your daughter creates, maintains, and communicates her personal boundaries to other girls. If she's able to do this, the sting of cruel words will lose their venom and she'll feel stronger and more resilient, and proud of herself.

Power Plays

Group Dynamics and Rites of Passage

It's the beginning of the school day and all the eighth-grade students are hanging out in the hallway a few minutes before the first period bell rings. Morgan walks to her locker where she always meets up with her friends Melissa, Felicia, and Dara. As usual, they're standing together talking, but when Morgan walks up to them they fall silent. Morgan can feel the temperature drop in the room even as she feels increasingly hot-faced and self-conscious. Dara looks nervous and Felicia and Melissa look bored.

MORGAN: *Hey, what's up?*

FELICIA: *Nothing, we're just talking about history class. We should get going . . . the bell's about to ring.*

MORGAN: *Well, I'll see you all at lunch, right?*

MELISSA: *Um . . . Yeah, right . . . sure. See you then . . .*

DARA: *Come on, Melissa and Felicia, let's go to class.*

Morgan watches them walk away, wondering what she did wrong, but scared to find out.

WHAT YOU SHOULD KNOW

- It's inevitable that your daughter will experience these power plays. You can't stop them from happening, but you can teach her how to think through them so she doesn't feel she has to go along with the group.

- Just as these experiences are rites of passage for your daughter, they are also rites of passage for you as a parent. Don't underestimate how painful they can be for your daughter—or for you.
- Most girls aren't stuck in one role, which means your daughter will have experiences as the one who excludes and the one who's excluded.
- Reconciliations are often fleeting. Two girls can be in a fight, say that they've worked it out, and one can attack the other again the next day at school. This is especially true when the girl in the weaker position believes everything's okay.
- In early adolescence, best friends are inseparable and like most relationships, these friendships usually end with one person's heart broken.

I spend so much time teaching girls about the more hurtful aspects of cliques that it's easy to forget the positive aspects of girls' friendships. It's wonderful to see them in the hallways giggling, laughing, and walking with their arms flung around each other. I'm sure you feel reassured when your daughter gets invited to parties and sleepovers regularly, pals around with her best friend, and dashes to the phone because once again it's for her. Of course, if that were all there was to cliques, you wouldn't be reading this book. Every one of these joyful experiences has a devastating flip side: exclusion from parties, the breakup with the best friend, excommunication from the clique without a moment's notice. These power plays are all important adolescent rites of passage. As such, these experiences teach girls about themselves, their world, and their place in it. The goal for any girl is to learn how to navigate these painful experiences successfully and go through a process of self-reflection that leads to wisdom and the development of a personal code of ethics. As horrible as these rites of passage are, they're inevitable and they provide opportunities for growth.

Watching your daughter go through these experiences can make you want to bounce off the walls. Her friends walk all over her, and yet she always forgives them. Can't she just believe you when you tell her that she needs to find new friends? She goes to a dance with a boy who dumped her two months ago. Does this guy have to teach her about being used? Does she really have to make huge mistakes while you sit back and watch?

Most parents know intuitively that their role is to offer gentle guidance and support, but sometimes they can't help getting involved in nonproductive ways. Often parents step in to fix problems instead of letting their daughters take the lead in figuring out how to handle these situations, all the while racking up the bumps and bruises of the body blows girls inflict on each other. In this chapter I'll dissect the group dynamics of several typical power plays and rites of passage and offer some advice on how to help your daughter stand up for herself and get more support from her friends.

Uninvited: The Sixth-Grade Birthday Party

Few things are more devastating than not being invited to a friend's party. I still flinch when I hear about some great dinner party I wasn't invited to. But when you're eleven or twelve, forget it, you just want to hide in the closet. If you're the parent, you want to kill that nasty little girl who maliciously hurt your daughter's feelings.

Somewhere in early adolescence the birthday party morphs from the free-for-all at the Discovery Zone or bowling alley into a major social signifier that reinforces the girls' social hierarchy. Many girls want to have a party more because of the attention they get leading up to it than the party or presents themselves. The birthday girl gets to be Queen Bee for the day as she decides (in consultation with her best friends) who'll be invited and who'll be left out. (And if you allow your daughter to invite boys, as I'll explore further in Chapter 7, the drama escalates to a fever pitch.)

MARY: *Did you hear . . . Amanda's having a birthday party! Are you invited? I got the invitation in my locker this morning!*
ANA: *I don't know, I don't think I got an invitation . . .*
MARY: *Oh, I'm sure you're invited. I'll go find out and let you know.*

That afternoon . . .

MARY: *I'm really sorry. Amanda says that her mom is only allowing her to have a few people. You know, like her really good friends.*

ANA: *That's okay.*

MARY: *Maybe I can talk to Amanda and get you invited.*

If your daughter is in this situation, how should she think her way through this? Below I have diagrammed each girl's feelings, motivations, likely outcomes, and a better outcome (called "makes her folks proud") for a few typical power plays. I suggest to girls that whenever they have a conflict with friends, they use this grid to sort out competing interests and the roles girls play. Show your daughter this format and help her through a few examples so she understands how they work. Understanding girls' motivations can help her figure out what she wants to do. In the example above, Amanda is a Queen Bee (i.e., person with power at least temporarily), Mary is a Messenger (in the middle), and Ana is a Target (person left behind). Here's how the birthday party snafu would look:

	Ana	Mary	Amanda
Feelings	Rejected	Torn but feeling important because she's in the middle	Enjoying being the center of attention
Motivations	Torn—wants to be invited but doesn't want to beg	Torn—wants to help friend and affirm her own social place	Wants to have her birthday her way
Likely result	Feels she's at the bottom of the totem pole	Feels important	Gets what she wants
What she learns	Has to change herself if she wants to be accepted	Her Messenger position is powerful	Has control over others
Makes her folks proud	Recognizes it isn't a reflection on her	Feels torn, but doesn't make this an opportunity to feel important	Realizes she's hurt others' feelings and opens party to others

If you're Amanda's parent: This is a really difficult conflict for parents. You want to do something special for your birthday girl, but you don't want to make other children feel bad in the process. If your daughter goes to a large school, you're also not obligated, nor is it financially realistic, that she invite everyone in the class.

This is an opportunity to work together with your daughter. Know what your budget is, and discuss the upper limit of the head count. Always start by empathizing with her. You can understand why she would want only the people she likes best at her party, but in situations like these, it's very important that she makes decisions that are inclusive and respectful to others. You shouldn't force her to invite certain girls, but encourage her to explore how she'd feel if she were left out. I would encourage her to do something less grandiose so she can invite more kids rather than doing something exclusive, especially if that means cutting someone from the bottom of the clique out of the picture. If that isn't possible, make up the guest list together and stick to it. If a delegate comes to her on someone's behalf and your daughter changes her mind and invites Ana, be aware that it usually backfires. For example, Ana might come to the party only to find that the other girls are mean to her. Or end up hanging out in the kitchen with you after she calls her dad to come pick her up early. That double-snubbing definitely backs up the girls' social hierarchy.

If your daughter is a Wannabe and she's the birthday girl, the Queen Bee and Sidekick may look like they're deferring to her when making up the guest list. Don't be fooled. This is a tactic. They'll almost certainly try to get your daughter to exclude people they don't like or pressure her to invite boys (I'll discuss boy-girl parties in Chapter 7).

When distributing invitations, encourage your daughter to mail them. Yes, it's cheaper to stick them in other kids' lockers, and certainly your daughter wants the thrill of being the center of attention when girls start opening up the invitations and asking each other if they're going. But mailings to home spare the feelings of the uninvited. For the same reason, strongly encourage your daughter to restrict discussion about the party until after school. Again, ask your daughter to think about how she'd feel if she were one of the excluded.

It's equally important that when she's hosting the party she's gracious to all her guests, meaning she's not allowed to invite people and then ignore them at the party, nor intimate that they're only there because "Mom said I had to invite you" or "Dad made me ask all the kids."

If you're Mary's parent: Of all the parents in this scenario, you have the most difficulty discovering her involvement. If you find out what's going on, the primary question you should help her figure out is her motivation: Is she getting in the middle because she feels bad that Ana isn't invited or because it makes her feel important as a Messenger? When she describes the situation to you and she's the star of the story, she's more likely to intervene to solidify her position. If she is, you both should ask yourselves why it's important for her to be in this role. If her description centers on her empathy for Ana, then you have a great opportunity to discuss your values (i.e., Do you want your daughter going to a party where people are excluded? How does she feel about this?), what she gains from being invited and going (she feels popular), and what she loses (she's making decisions based on popularity instead of other people's feelings).

If you're Ana's parent: You'll know what's going on because she'll tell you or she'll be upset. Tell her that you can completely understand how awful she must feel. This is a good time to share a personal story if this ever happened to you. When the party day arrives, do something with her that she wants to do so she's reminded that there's life outside the party. Under no circumstances should you call the parents of the party girl to angle for an invitation. If you do this, you are teaching your daughter a clear lesson that social status is more important than her personal dignity and that parental love is based on her social value. As painful as it is to see your daughter excluded and as bad as she feels about it, it's more important to affirm her ability to cope.

THE THIRD WHEEL:
DIVIDED LOYALTIES AND THE TAG-ALONG

Jennifer and Jolene are in sixth grade and very good friends. Sometimes they play with Sara, a girl who really wants to be in their group. Jolene and Sara used to be really good friends, but these days Jolene thinks Sara is a little boring; she still acts like a little girl. Jennifer invites Jolene to her house for a sleepover on Saturday night. Sara overhears them talking about it and asks if she can come.

Jennifer tells Sara that she's a tag-along and she should make her own friends. Jolene doesn't like what Jennifer said to Sara, but she doesn't say anything.

On Sunday morning after the sleepover, Jennifer and Jolene are playing when Jennifer's mother marches into the room, obviously angry, and asks to speak to Jennifer alone. Right outside the room, Jennifer's mother tells her that Sara's mother called her and told her what happened at school. Jennifer's mother is really angry with Jennifer and she's now forbidden to have a sleepover for two weeks.

The first thing Jennifer does is self-righteously complain to Jolene.

JENNIFER: *Jolene, can you believe what Sara did? She cries to her mom and now I get into trouble. This sucks! I can't have sleepovers for two weeks!*

JOLENE: *Yeah, I can't believe it. That's totally lame.*

On Monday, Jennifer and Jolene are walking down the hall at school when they see Sara.

JENNIFER: *Sara, what did you think you were doing? You ran to your mommy so I would get into trouble! My mom thinks I wouldn't let you come over because that's what your mom said. Now I can't have anyone over for two weeks!"*

SARA: *What are you talking about?*

JENNIFER: *Don't pretend like you don't know that your mom called my mom.*

SARA: *I'm sorry. I didn't know. I mean, I'm so sorry. I was upset but I told my mom not to tell anyone. What can I do to make it up to you?*

JENNIFER: *You already did your damage. Come on, Jolene, let's go.*

Using the grid again, let's break down each girl's role.

	Sara	Jolene	Jennifer
Feelings	Excluded, rejected, upset, maybe angry	Depends on what kind of bystander she is: torn would feel guilty, powerful would feel justified and angry	Angry and defensive; wants to put Sara "in her place"
Motivations	Wants to be liked and is hurt by the other girls' rejection	Torn between friendships and doing the "right" thing	Got in trouble; doesn't want to be forced to be Sara's friend
Likely result	She'll apologize to the group, change her personality to fit with the group, or find other friends	Weakens friendship with Sara	Bullies Sara to stop hanging out with them and bullies Jolene to follow her lead
What she learns	She'll get in trouble if she admits that her feelings are hurt or confronts powerful girls; won't talk to her mom again	Jennifer is a strong Queen Bee; don't cross her	Bullying people works
Makes her folks proud	Stands up for herself by telling both girls how their actions make her feel; walks away proud of herself; knows that she should make new friends because the old ones come at too high a price	Tells Jennifer she doesn't like how she treated Sara and gives suggestions for handling the situation better	Takes responsibility for her behavior and apologizes to both Sara and Jolene

If you're Sara's parent: In this situation, Sara has learned that people in positions of power can bully weaker people and that if the victim of the bully "tells," it'll come back on her. Adults seem to forget something kids know very well: If you get the bully in trouble, at some point she'll find you and no one will be around to help. You must teach your daughter to fight her own battles. Your involvement should be limited to strategizing with her about what she wants to do and then affirming that she has the strength to carry it out. I admit it's a fine line. Your daughter needs to know that you're watching her back, but she also needs to know that you have the confidence in her to take care of herself. That means not calling the other girl's parents to complain about your daughter's exclusion and honoring her request to keep her complaints to yourself when she confides in you. If you keep trying to fix life for her, she'll learn that she can't do it herself, and that she can't trust you with her feelings.

Your first step, as always, is to empathize with your daughter. It hurts to be excluded, especially if you're put down as a tag-along and baby. It's hard to admit that other girls see your daughter as a nuisance. But if she is, you need to talk to her about it because otherwise, sixth through eighth grade will be very painful for her. Review your daughter's Bill of Rights with Friends (see below) with her. Ask her if she knew that Jolene and Jennifer felt this way about her. If she did, why does she still want to hang out with them?

The hardest question that both you and your daughter need to think about is: Why is this happening? Whatever the answer to that is, the next question is equally difficult. For example, if your daughter is annoying her friends because she's not as into boys as they are, is this something she wants to change about herself? I would say no. She should be interested in boys at her own pace and in her own time. On the other hand, if your daughter is annoying because she interrupts people and is constantly getting in people's business, then that may be something she needs to look at and change.

It's critical to get your daughter to understand the difference between her actions and her personality. She might want to change how she acts, but she shouldn't try to change who she is. Talk out why she thinks she and Jolene grew apart. Are they into different things? If so, is Sara feeling any pressure to "catch up" to Jolene's interests? Remind her that every girl has her own schedule, and Sara shouldn't give in to pressure to fake being into boys, clothes, or whatever else Jolene thinks is a more "mature" interest. At the same time, Sara needs to recognize that it's fair for Jolene to have her own interests and to want to hang out with girls who share them.

She shouldn't ask Jennifer to invite her, but she can tell Jennifer how she feels when she's left out. For example:

SARA: *Jolene, can I talk to you for a minute?*
JOLENE: *Sure . . . what's up?* (she probably knows something's up)
SARA: *This is hard to say, but I'm pretty sure that you don't want to hang out with me as much as you used to and I want to know if we can talk about it?*
JOLENE: *That's so not true! I don't know what you're talking about!*
SARA: *I'm not saying this to make you feel bad, I just want to talk about it because you're a good friend. Can you tell me why you don't want to hang out? I promise I'll do my best to listen to what you're saying.*

Sara may not get the response from Jolene that she needs. Encourage her to tell Jolene politely and directly how she feels and that real friendships are built on people honestly and respectfully communicating—even when what's being said is hard to hear. That said, she also needs to prepare herself for hearing something that may make her feel bad. But she's learning and implementing social skills that enable her to take care of herself.

It's painful to realize that a friendship may be ending, but remind your daughter that a lot of friendships have natural ups and downs, and that she and Jolene might be more in sync later. On the other hand, if Jolene is more interested in being part of a clique than being a good friend, Sara needs to assess whether this is a friendship worth trying to keep.

If you're Jolene's parent: What would you want Jolene to do in this situation? Girls do have the right to choose their friends. They just don't have the right to make the girl they don't like feel like dirt in the process. On the other hand, a girl can be too "nice." Of course, you want your daughter to be kind to others, but you don't want her to feel that she must always put other people's needs before her own. Being too much of a "people pleaser" can lead people to take advantage of her.

Even if you don't agree with what she did, remember to empathize with her first. I know that's hard and you should still hold her accountable, but you first have to get her initial defenses down. If Jolene were my daughter, I'm sure I'd be angry that she hadn't done the "right" thing by standing up to Jennifer the bully. But see it from her perspective. During adolescence, girls' loyalties are frequently divided. If Jolene sides with Sara, she'll earn Sara's undying loyalty, but she'll "betray" Jennifer. Betraying Jennifer makes her extremely vulnerable, because Jennifer will seek revenge by getting other girls to gang up on Jolene and exclude her. If she betrays Sara, there's no social liability, and most likely Sara will forgive her later. If you were twelve, in Jolene's situation, dealing with Jennifer and her friends all day, every day, what would you do? Going with Jennifer is often the only answer that makes sense. Jennifer is intimidating. Acknowledge how hard it is to stand up to someone who seems to hold all the cards.

Your next step is to get Jolene to take responsibility for her actions. Girls are masters at convincing themselves that their bad behavior is a result of someone else's actions. Jennifer believes she never would have been in that situation if Sara hadn't complained to her mother. Almost anyone in Jolene's position will back down and do anything to stay in the good graces of the powerful girl in the group. The girls' social hierarchy supports Jennifer's denial of responsibility because the other girls won't challenge it and the parents aren't there to know what really happened.

Girls always get angry with the person in Sara's position, but it's just a diversionary tactic; don't let your daughter get away with it. This is a great time to teach your daughter about the need to treat others with respect regardless of the social cost. She needs to admit that she should have stood up for Sara. Then ask her about Jennifer. Does she want to be a person other people push around? Does she want to be a person who says nothing when another person is bullied? Ask her how she would like to handle the situation in the future. Encourage her to talk through with you what she would like to say to Jennifer and Sara.

If she's really brave, the best thing she can do is apologize to Sara in front of Jennifer (see Chapter 4 for more on apologies). She should say to Jennifer that she didn't feel right about what happened to Sara (don't say "what Jennifer did to Sara" because, first, Jennifer will get defensive and, second, Jolene needs to take responsibility for her actions that backed up Jennifer).

If you're Jennifer's parent: You may be angry and embarrassed, but focus your energy on what lessons Jennifer can learn from this experience. Because another parent is blaming your child for bad behavior, it's easy to feel that your parenting skills are being questioned. Take Jennifer's behavior seriously, but also look at this as part of the unfortunate yet realistic parenting process. Thank Sara's mom for telling you and apologize for Jennifer's behavior. Then get Jennifer's side of the story (which will initially focus on how she was pushed to be mean because Sara wasn't listening to her). Empathize: "There's nothing wrong with wanting to spend time with Jolene alone, but that doesn't excuse or justify treating Sara the way you did." Just as if you were Jolene's parent, emphasize that it doesn't matter how she feels about Sara; it was wrong to be cruel. Tell her how you want her to act instead: "You don't have to be friends with everyone, but that doesn't justify being mean to people. The next time you are in this situation, I want you to first ask yourself why hanging out with this person is such a problem. What is making you not want to be with her? What is making you want to show her that you don't like her?" Ask her to call Sara to apologize for her rudeness (see the "Art of the Apology" in Chapter 4), and follow up to make sure she did. Have her call Jolene, too, and apologize for putting her in the middle.

BFF: Best Friends Forever or a Day?

I'm convinced that the best-friend relationships girls have in early adolescence can be the most intense relationships girls will ever have. In my estimation there are two different kinds. The first is largely tactical. Sometimes girls look for a best friend who offers protection from the social hierarchy. Girls can be in several cliques, but even if everyone else excludes them, they know they still have each other. These best friends are more vulnerable to the changing social winds than the best friends described below.

The other type of best friends are two girls who are truly inseparable. Other girls and boys perceive them as living in their own world. They have their own language and codes. They wear each other's clothes. They may have crushes at the same time on the same person (that may seem strange, but what better way to start exploring the scary boy-girl world than with your best friend). It's almost certain that they'll break up around seventh grade (if not before) when at least one will want to expand her social horizons.

And then they'll make up, then break up, then make up. . . . Sometimes your daughter will be the dumper, sometimes the dumpee. Both roles can be very painful. When your daughter is on the outs with her friend, first and always empathize with her. Discourage her from demonizing her friend or the friendship by focusing only on the negatives, and don't you do it either (where will you be when they're back together next week?). Again, remind your daughter that friendships have a natural ebb and flow, and she doesn't need to burn her bridges behind her. Help her appreciate that people can grow apart and still be genuinely nice. Don't minimize her broken heart over a lost friendship. There's little you can do to "fix" the situation; here's your chance to hone your listening skills and help your daughter realize she can survive the hurt.

Exile from the Promised Land

It all started in October. I began to feel left out of my group. One of the girls in the group, Brittany, was moving, and I wanted to be closer to her before she left. Every time I went near her, she ran away. I was very upset. So I expressed my feelings to her. She told me that I was following her. I agreed, I was. After we talked, I was happy because I thought I wouldn't be left out again. I was wrong. Then a soccer teammate of Brittany's told me she saw Brittany and my friend Brianna imitate me before their soccer game.

I decided I would hang out with Kim. The next day, I went to lunch with my head high, but when I walked into the cafeteria, Brittany and the other girls in my group were taking up all the seats. I was very hurt by what the girls did. I cried uncontrollably. I just couldn't stop crying.

When I talked to the guidance counselor, she suggested that we talk to one of Brittany's best friends, Krista. Krista was one of my close friends, too. Krista offered to have a party inviting Brittany and the others that were in my group. At the party, Brittany and I apologized to each other and were now friends again. The party turned out so well that I looked forward to Monday.

The next day at school, nothing had changed. Brittany, Krista, and the others in the group were still sitting at the opposite side of the table. So I said to Kim, "Fine! Let them sit there, I don't need them." And to this day, I have not talked to any girl in the group. Kim has stuck by me during the hardest time of my life. I'll always have eternal gratitude for Kim. She's a true friend.   Amy, 14

You're in. No, you're out. One day your daughter will go to school and her group of friends will have decided that she's no longer one of them. Or it may happen to one of her best friends in the clique. Sometimes there's a nominal reason for expulsion—she palled around with the "wrong" person, she took the "wrong side" against a Queen Bee or Sidekick, and/or she committed some other act of high treason. Sometimes there's no easily identifiable reason except that the leaders of the group decide she no longer belongs. Whenever and whyever it happens, it's devastating. Girls come away from these experiences learning that girls—even the ones you think are your true-blue friends—can turn on you on a whim. Ironically, as is the case here, this is also a time when girls can learn the meaning of true friendship.

Amy's mom told me her daughter's seventh-grade year was completely horrible. She watched her daughter go from relatively happy to miserable. Here's how I would help Amy and her mom break down what happened so Amy (with her mom's guidance) could figure out her next best steps.

If you're Amy's parent: I talked to Amy's mom, and she's really on the ball. She's honest in her assessment of her daughter ("She can be bossy and sometimes self-righteous"), but compassionate as well. She talked to

Feeling	Amy	Krista	Brittany	Kim
Feelings	Confused and rejected	Torn and grateful she isn't being excluded	Feeling special but anxious because she's moving	Loyal to Amy
Motivations	Wants to feel included, wants to express her feelings	She's the Banker	Queen Bee	Wants to be friends with Amy and willing to hang with a shunned girl

(cont.)	Amy	Krista	Brittany	Kim
Likely outcome	Loses friendships with rest of the girls	Becomes Queen Bee when Brittany leaves	Moves away and fits into another Girl World	Has good friends; may be seen as a social liability, but a "nice girl"
What she learns	Even when you think there's reconciliation, you're never sure. But she does have one good friend in Kim.	Being the social glue equals power	Control equals power	Girls are fickle
Makes her folks proud	Expresses her feelings to the girls calmly so she feels she did right for herself and learns about true friendship	Stands up to Brittany when she rejects Amy again	Apologizes and lets go of her Queen Bee position	She did!

her daughter, empathized with her, and supported her. She even called Brittany's mom because she thought Amy might have contributed to the problem. Unfortunately, Brittany's mom chose to act more like Brittany (she wasn't interested in working with Amy's mom to figure out how they could support each other). For more information on how to talk to other parents, see Chapter 4, but suffice it to say these are difficult yet critical conversations to have. You'll be more effective if you approach the other parent as an ally and resource.

If you're Krista's parent: Frankly, the counselor's idea to resolve the conflict by bringing Amy and Krista (instead of Brittany) together was a big mistake because it sends the message that Brittany is either operating under adult radar and/or is above the law. As a result, Krista's party became an opportunity for Brittany to steamroll over the other girls and call all the shots. If your daughter is in Krista's position and asks you if she can have this party, she may feel so excited about being the social nexus that she'll tell you what's up. If it's clear that she's doing this mainly to cement her social status, nix the party. If Krista explains that she was only trying to patch things up between Amy and Brittany, ask her why she joined Brittany in snubbing Amy at school. You need to get her to admit to herself what she is getting out of this situation. (Girls are never nicer to each other than when they're fighting with someone else.)

If you're Brittany's parent: Brittany may be feeling anxious because she's moving. Maybe she snubbed Amy because she wanted to confirm that her status as Queen Bee is secure; she's doing it just to prove that she can. In your discussions with her, talk about what's making her anxious and out of control. Your job is to make her see the connection between what she's anxious about and the things she's doing to feel more in control. Empathize with her about what's motivating her to act out in this way. Then insist she apologize to Amy. Follow up to make sure she not only made the apology but also continues to act consistently afterward. (Freezing Amy out at school clearly violates the spirit of the apology.) Watch out for this: Many girls agree to a truce or reconciliation and then start a war all over again as soon as they get the opportunity.

THE BETTER OFFER: BLOWING EACH OTHER OFF

Amber and Michelle are in ninth grade. They used to hang out all the time, but recently they haven't been spending as much time together because their interests are changing and they're hanging out with different groups—Amber is hanging out with the more popular group, while Michelle still hangs out with their old group. Amber likes Michelle, but when she's with her, she feels as if she's missing out on the fun things her new group likes to do.

Amber and Michelle make plans to hang out the next Saturday night. Michelle is supposed to come over at 7:00. At 5:00, one of Amber's new friends, Nicole, calls her and asks her to go to the movies. She also tells Amber that Will, a really hot guy in the group, is interested in her; he's going to the movies, too.

At this point, Amber has three options.

1. She can tell Nicole she wishes she could go, but she already has plans with Michelle. She tells Nicole to have a good time without her.

2. She can blow off Michelle with a lie and go with Nicole.

3. She can try to have her cake and eat it by getting Nicole to invite Michelle to the movies, too.

I've role-played this scenario hundreds of times with girls in my Empower classes. In all that time I've had *only one girl* stick to her plans with Michelle. About 20 percent invite Michelle along, and the rest lie. There usually isn't a moment of hesitation before they decide to lie, and the lie usually blames the mother: "My mom is so mean! She won't let me go out because I have to do chores for her/baby-sit/finish my homework." ("My grandmother died" is another popular option, which never ceases to amaze me—don't these girls think the truth will out?)

Whichever choice they make, girls learn critical lessons from this situation.

- If Amber sticks with her original plan to hang out with Michelle, Nicole may not respect that Amber is doing the right thing. If Amber stays with Michelle and is at all conflicted about it, she may resent Michelle for "keeping her down" and worry that Nicole will think she's not cool enough to hang out with again. Amber learns that "doing the right thing" isn't all it's cracked up to be, no matter what her parents may say.

- If Amber lies, Michelle will usually find out about it. (In our role-playing, we make the girls run into each other at the movies so that they learn that if you lie, you usually get caught.) Michelle will think that Amber is two-faced, but she'll also be confused about what she should do about it; wouldn't she have done the same thing in that situation? Or even if Michelle doesn't have the same social aspirations, it's a clear indication that Amber has been anointed by the powers that be (Nicole) that she's cool or on the way to being cool. It'll be harder for

Michelle to confront Amber now that her value on the social index has increased.

- Nicole brings a person like Amber into her group for a reason. Amber is most likely a Pleaser/Wannabe or Torn Bystander. Michelle is hurt and rightfully angry at being blown off, but the social pecking order is reinforced. Michelle learns that she should try to change herself to be more like Amber and Nicole so she won't get left behind. If she tells Amber how she feels about being blown off, Amber will probably accuse her of jealousy, so she learns to keep her mouth shut.

- Nicole, despite her high social status, often feels that the only way to maintain friendships is to make people prove themselves to her. She's just as trapped as everyone else, maybe more so. Girls in Nicole's position can get so caught up in maintaining their high status they can't even develop a sense of self to lose in the first place.

Let's diagram the situation:

	Michelle	Amber	Nicole
Feelings	Betrayed, rejected, and angry	Confused, defensive, and flattered by Nicole's attention	Say what? Amber should feel grateful she's being accepted into the group
Motivations	Wants things to go back to the way they used to be with Amber	Wants the status of hanging out with Nicole and the attention of the guy	Wants to demonstrate her power
Likely result	Gets into a fight with Amber where she has to justify her feelings and then gives up on Amber	Couches any apology by accusing Michelle of being jealous and holding her back	Dismisses Amber's friendship with Michelle and flatters Amber with more attention

(cont.)	Michelle	Amber	Nicole
What she learns	Popularity is more important to Amber than their friendship	She can't have friendships with Michelle and Nicole; she has to choose one	She's in control of Amber
Makes her folks proud	She talks to Amber and responds effectively to the accusation of jealousy. She feels good about how she handled herself.	She apologizes to Michelle and decides which friendship she wants and why. Is able to stand up to Nicole.	Realizes that she's making people choose her over others. Apologizes and stops.

If you're Michelle's parent: Empathize with her, but don't make her feel better by talking about how badly Amber or Nicole behaved. You need to help your daughter feel better about herself because she is who she is, not by putting someone else down. (Besides, chances are you'll come home in a week and see Amber hanging out with Michelle and then she'll worry that you don't like Amber.) Acknowledge how difficult this is right now, but point out that in the long run, her situation is probably less difficult than Amber's. Michelle doesn't have to change herself to be accepted by her real friends; Amber does.

Encourage Michelle to tell Amber how she feels and brainstorm how to respond if Amber tells her she's just being jealous. ("I know you think I'm jealous, but that's not the issue here. The issue is that we agreed we were going to hang out. Good friends don't blow each other off the second a better offer comes along.")

If you're Amber's parent: The biggest problem you have is a daughter who's willing to do things against her better judgment to increase her social status. Acknowledge that Nicole may be more fun to hang out with, but she needs to keep any commitment she makes, regardless of whether a better offer comes along. Ask her what she's giving up in the process. If she says "nothing," review her Bill of Rights with Friends (page 173). What does she want and expect from her friendship with Nicole? Can she be herself with Nicole or does she edit herself to please Nicole? If she assures you that Nicole is a really good friend, don't press the issue, because you don't want her to feel she has to defend Nicole to you. Let her think about it on her own.

Most likely, if Amber were your daughter, there's a chance you'd know about her plans with Michelle. If she changes her plans to go with Nicole, she has to figure out how to get past you (because you'd make her keep her plans with Michelle). You become the biggest obstacle in her way, and she might lie to get around you. Once she lies, you won't know where she is and/or who she's with. It's at this point, when Amber may feel more secure in the life raft than ever, that she's actually swimming in shark-infested waters.

In any case, Amber owes Michelle an apology, and if at all possible, she should tell Nicole how she feels. If she went with Nicole and blew off Michelle, then she needs to tell Nicole: "Look, I need to tell you that I made a big mistake. When you invited me out, I actually had already made plans with Michelle and I blew her off. I feel bad about it and I don't want to do that again. So next time, I'd like to invite Michelle."

If she invited Michelle along and Nicole was mean to her, then she needs to tell Nicole that she won't hang out with her if she's going to treat other people like that. Rest assured, there's a selfish reason to do this because if Amber stands up to Nicole now, Nicole will be a lot less likely to turn on her later. You need to impress upon her that there's real danger in trying to please everyone around you all the time, because it usually results in pleasing no one and losing yourself in the process.

If you're Nicole's parent: Your daughter will appear in control. Do some soul-searching before talking to her. What motivates her to build and sustain friendships like this? She didn't technically do anything wrong but try to persuade a friend to hang out with her. But when I do this role-play in class, the Nicoles can be very convincing because they make Amber feel like she's losing out on the opportunity of a lifetime. It's often presented as a choice that's not a choice: Either you can come with me and you'll have the keys to the kingdom, or you can stay home and spend forty years in the social desert. You need to hold her accountable for her behavior (and perhaps hold yourself accountable for encouraging it, too. Are you perhaps a little too invested in your daughter's popularity?). If you're convinced that your daughter is inviting Michelle along to be inclusive, that's something to be proud of.

CHECKING YOUR BAGGAGE

- When you were your daughter's age, did you blow friends off if a better option came along?
- What and how have you communicated your values about friendships and commitment to your daughter?
- How important is social status to you?
- What do you think your daughter would say if I asked her the same question about you?
- Do you have close friendships where you can tell people when you're upset with them and they'll respect what you're saying?

WHAT YOU CAN DO

You may feel that it's not worth making a federal case of not getting invited to a birthday party or letting your daughter blow off one friend for another. But these aren't trivial issues; they lay the groundwork for girls faking their feelings, pretending to be someone they're not, pleasing others at their own expense, or otherwise sacrificing self-esteem and authenticity. The skirmishes that in earlier years are limited to hurt feelings can transition into parents' worst fears: vulnerability to drinking, drugs, and sex. You can use these early power plays to help your daughter figure out why it's worthwhile to be true to herself and to think through what real friendship is all about.

Your daughter will almost certainly pass through the rites of passage I've just described, or variations thereof. In addition to the advice above, here's a general strategy for communicating with her about girls' power plays:

- First, empathize with her situation. Even if you think she's behaving abominably, appreciate the awful pressure of the clique and her fear of losing her social status.
- Ask her questions to articulate her motivations and those of her

friends. (Drawing a diagram similar to the ones in this chapter can help.)

- Have her review the Bill of Rights for Friends (page 173) to clarify whether she thinks her behavior or that of her friends has stepped outside bounds.
- Articulate your values and ethics and how you would like to see them reflected in her behavior.
- Brainstorm and role-play with her how she can respond so that she stands up for herself, communicates her feelings respectfully, and asks for what she wants clearly.
- Hold her accountable when she makes mistakes.

Give your own personal experiences to explain why you have these values and ethics.   Nidhi, 16

You should also appreciate that sometimes the values you teach your daughter will be in conflict with the way she feels she needs to act to feel comfortable in her clique. Let's suppose that you've always taught her that championing the underdog is the right thing to do; she should stick up for people who are being bullied or picked on. So then your daughter stands up for some unpopular girl, and the result is that her friends in the clique are angry at her. She's bound to feel burned; you taught her to do the right thing, she did it, and she ended up feeling punished. She needs to know that you understand how she feels. Acknowledge that sometimes doing the right thing will bring her grief in the short term, but that in the long term, it's more important to be true to her character and values. Tell her you're proud that she took the rougher road and that, sooner or later, she'll feel just as proud of her actions.

Talk to your daughter about what she should expect to give and get from her friendships with others. Every friendship will have its ups and downs, so there are benefits to encouraging your daughter to take a longer view so she doesn't burn all her bridges. That said, you should help her identify patterns of inconsiderate behavior that suggest rethinking the relationship. Help her clarify her expectations with the Bill of Rights for Friends:

Bill of Rights for Friends

- What does she want and need in a friendship? (Trust, reliability, loyalty, telling you when they're angry with you in a respectful way)
- What are her rights in a friendship? (To be treated respectfully, with kindness and honesty)
- What are her responsibilities in a friendship? (To treat her friends ethically)
- What would a friend have to do or be like for her to end the friendship? (Not listen to her, not honor her values and ethics)
- Under what circumstances would she go to an adult for help with a problem with a friend? (When the problem feels too big to handle alone)
- What are her friends' rights and responsibilities in the friendship? (To listen even when it's not easy to hear)

Then ask the hardest question: How do her experiences with her friends compare to her Bill of Rights? If they aren't similar, why does she have those friendships?

If and when your daughter makes the decision that her friend(s) aren't right for her, it'll be a very lonely time for her. She may know that she has made the right decision in ending a friendship, but that'll be only a small comfort. It takes incredible strength of character to decide to break up with a friend who doesn't respect her Bill of Rights and even more strength to remain resolute. Praise her courage.

DO ASK, DON'T TELL

It's very hard as a parent to hold your tongue when you can see your daughter being used or mistreated. You'll be sorely tempted to tell her what to do and summarily banish the evil trolls who steamrolled her heart. But remember, these situations give her a chance to test her own strength, hew to her own standards, and affirm her self-sufficiency. Let your daughter come to her own realizations. Beyond the Bill of Rights for Friends, sometimes a simple question—"Is this the way a real friend would treat someone?"—is all you need to ask. And when your daughter is the steamroller, you'll be tempted to control her behavior by grounding her or taking away her privileges. That may be appropriate, but it's not enough. Your most important goal is not to punish her for her actions but to get her to take responsibility for them.

CRITICAL THINKING

People often blame girls' low self-esteem as the root cause for the problems girls face. I respectfully disagree, and I'm asking you to look at it another way. What I have diagrammed in this chapter is a methodology for your daughter to develop the critical thinking skills she needs to think her way through these difficult rites of passage. If she is able to accomplish that goal she will develop social competency—the necessary coping skills to navigate the social hierarchy. From social competency comes high self-esteem. I see high self-esteem as a by-product, the end goal of all the work you and I are doing to raise healthy girls with a strong ethical foundation who can make sound decisions. This is hard stuff, and you have to manage your own reactions as you watch your daughter muddle her way through. Just don't forget that it's in the process that your daughter will figure out who she wants to be.

Boy World

The Judges and the Judged

Pete, Andre, and Jack meet up to go to the movies. Andre brings his girlfriend Maddy with him. While they're waiting in line, Maddy runs into a guy she used to know from her old neighborhood. She hugs him hello and is clearly happy to see him. As she steps out of line to catch up with him, Pete and Jack tease Andre about this new contender. When Andre tries to blow them off, they tease him harder, saying that he's whipped and they wouldn't let a girl disrespect them like that. When Maddy returns, Andre is angry. When she asks what's up, he accuses her of disrespecting him in front of his friends and throwing herself on the other guy. Maddy gets right back in Andre's face and tells him she can do whatever she likes and he can't tell her what to do. Andre, pretending he doesn't care about her, calls her a bitch and a slut.

Think this situation is ridiculous and out of hand? Happens all the time. Boys love to point out each other's insecurities and failures when it comes to "being a man." Many boys believe that a girlfriend is disrespecting you if she shows affection for another guy. While Andre might have been jealous watching his girlfriend talk to another guy, it was his friends' questioning of his masculinity that made him feel that he had to prove himself. Like most boys, Andre has no idea how to express his feelings without coming off as if he is trying to control her.

BOY WORLD: WHAT YOU NEED TO KNOW

- Boy cliques control boys just as girl cliques control girls.
- Boys' behavior, choices, and personal boundaries are largely dictated by their definition of masculinity.
- Most boys won't reveal their feelings and problems to their male friends. If they reveal their problems to anyone, it's usually to a female friend.
- Most boys aren't violent. A few are and the rest have no idea how to stop them.
- The more a boy believes in gender stereotypes, the more vulnerable he is to perpetrate violence.*
- The boy honor code values loyalty and silence over everything else.
- Just like girls, boys are often intimidated by and in awe of the leader of their group.

Teen movies and the media love to focus on bitchy, inner circle/outer circle Girl World, but Boy World is just as controlling and powerful. While boys' friendships and memberships in groups can be validating and supportive, important research and books such as William Pollack's *Real Boys* and Daniel Kindlon and Michael Thompson's *Raising Cain* have called our attention to the cultural expectations of boys and how they affect boys' relationships with peers and their behavior toward girls. For your daughter's happiness and safety, both of you must become experts on Boy World.

Whether your daughter is boy-crazy and dates constantly, or is never sexually interested in them, their presence in her life will be equally important. No matter where she falls along the spectrum of interest, it's your goal to teach her to form strong, healthy relationships with boys, either as friends and/or as young men with whom she is or will be intimate.

As a parent, you should appreciate two issues that have an especially powerful effect on boy/girl dynamics. First, boys are perceived to be the

---

*Empower Program and Liz Claiborne, Inc. Survey on Teen Social Hierarchies, December 2000.

judges who award the girl who comes closest to their ideal with the ultimate prize: their attention. Second, if your daughter has sacrificed herself
to please her clique, she'll likely do the same with boys, especially boys to
whom she's sexually attracted or thinks she should be. What you'll see in
the following chapters is that sacrificing herself to please others is the
most dangerous aspect of Girl World and fits all too well with the lessons
Boy World teaches boys.

So far in this book I've concentrated on the social pecking order of girls
and its impact on your daughter's sense of self. In the upcoming chapters
we'll focus on how these issues impact her interactions with boys, from
her first crush, rejection, and matchmaking, to how she can turn herself
inside out trying to be the girl she thinks boys want. Lastly, we'll look at
how this process can threaten her sense of self and make her vulnerable
to date rape and abusive relationships. To begin, it's important to clarify
how our society's definition of masculinity influences boys in much the
same way that our definition of femininity influences girls.

As I mentioned in the introduction, Empower works with boys and
girls in equal numbers. When I started teaching over ten years ago, I
thought that boys' and girls' perceptions and experiences were vastly different. The more I teach, the more I am struck by their similarities. Many
boys perceive their relationships with each other as structured on a strict
social hierarchy, the same as girls. They feel that they have to put up a
front based on gender stereotypes and sacrifice what they want or feel in
the process, the same as girls. Many boys, like girls, obsess about their
body image, chasing an ideal masculine physique. Boys still feel that they
have to laugh when their feelings are hurt, be always ready with a quick
retort, act smooth and confident with girls, be blatantly and obviously
heterosexual, and never appear to be sensitive and therefore "whipped."
They can't be weak and can never be a mama's boy.

William Pollack, in *Real Boys' Voices*, refers to the "big impossible"
where boys constantly try to prove their masculinity and society's expectations of males by

> *engaging in reckless or hurtful acts of bravado, or showing that they
> can handle physical and emotional trauma without uttering a word
> or conveying a single emotion. . . . For a young boy trying to forge his*

*own path, this pressure to fulfill traditional rules about masculinity can often feel overwhelming. It can lead him to tease, bully, or abuse others. It can cause him to make mistakes in how he treats girls and young women and become compulsive about seeking out sex. It can push him to drink alcohol and take drugs. It can prod him toward depression . . . it may even lead him to frightful, sometimes lethal acts of aggression and violence. In almost all cases it makes him want to limit the range of his personal expression or silence his genuine inner voice entirely.**

If you have a son, you need to know this so you can help him. If you have a daughter, you need to know this because these are the forces that guide boys' behavior toward her. The pressure to stay faithful to the image of their gender is just as hard on boys as girls. In Empower's classes for boys, we conduct the same "in the box" exercise as we do for girls. We ask them to place inside the box those characteristics that boys need for high social status and place outside the box the characteristics that give boys low social status and get them teased. These are their answers, the "Act Like a Man"[†] box:

Weak	Strong	Funny	Gay
Unathletic	In control	Aggressive	Acts like a girl
Sensitive	Money	Tough	Geeky/Nerd
Mama's boy	Car	Athletic	Cries
Trying too hard	Girls	Confident	

If you look closely, you'll see that "acting like a girl" is the basis for every characteristic outside the box. Anytime a boy's behavior was perceived as weak or sensitive, the boys' automatic perception was that the behavior was inherently female or gay. When I first started teaching boys, I was shocked at how often they called each other a fag for expressing feel-

*William Pollack, *Real Boys' Voices* (New York: Random House, 2000), p. 36.
†Paul Kivel, *Men's Work: How to Stop the Violence That Tears Our Lives Apart* (Canada: New Society Publishers, 1998).

ings or even admitting they had feelings in the first place. Obviously, I couldn't allow the boys to call each other names in class, but I knew that the problem was larger than this; somehow their homophobia was connected to their negative attitudes toward women and girls.

At first glance, it's not surprising that boys would construct this definition of masculinity, but its consequences are a serious problem for both boys and girls. It means that everything boys do is in part or whole a performance to prove their masculinity—on the playground, at a school dance, walking down the school hallway, having a girlfriend, and having sex (including the amount of sex and the number of partners). This performance also dictates how boys express their emotions, from frustration and anger to love.

Think of how boys express anger and frustration. In Boy World, it's more acceptable to vent your anger outwardly; not so in Girl World. Angry boys pick on someone smaller, they hit a wall, or they bottle it up and, in the extreme, sit on their rage until they walk into a school with a small arsenal of weapons and kill students and teachers. You may have read the American Association of University Women studies that show that boys get more attention (positive and negative) than girls in the classroom; this is one of the reasons why. It's easier to notice an aggressive boy disrupting class than a girl sitting in the back quietly writing poetry about hurting herself and/or counting all the calories she's eaten that day. But both may be equally desperate for help.

Many boys don't feel they can talk to even their closest friends when they're upset. When I talk to girls about boys, I show them the "Act Like a Man" box and draw comparisons between it and the "Act Like a Woman" box. Then I ask the girls to imagine struggling with these issues without talking to your best friend about it. Or to imagine that your closest friends are the people you're most reluctant to ask for help. That's what most boys are up against—unable to speak about anything that troubles them unless it's to joke about it or tease each other.

As a result, many boys would much rather talk to a female friend about their problems—because they fear their male friends will laugh at them or blow them off. The cost for boys is prohibitive. Asking for help is often the same as admitting you're weak and sensitive, which translates for boys into being feminine and gay.

BOY PROFILES

By junior high, the "Act Like a Man" box has shaped several basic boy personality profiles. It's a rare boy who has the capacity to choose a different role for himself. When I teach, I ask boys and girls to describe common boy profiles. Here are their responses:

Misunderstood Guy

This boy is intoxicating to girls because he combines the dangerous bad boy elements with sweetness. He acts hard and dangerous in public and then sweet in private with a girl. Because of this public/private persona, he makes her feel special. If she hangs by his side, she thinks, she can change him. This boy is especially attractive to an intellectual/academic good girl because she can play the role of helper and rescuer. He hangs out with Aloof Boy and Thug/Bad Boy.

> *My friend is dating a guy who's a mess. She likes him because she can be his mother. She can keep him on track. She thinks with her influence, he'll turn around.*   Ellen, 15

Thug/Bad Boy

This is a really dangerous guy who often says disrespectful things to and about girls. He could, however, be easily mistaken for Misunderstood Guy. A girl often dates this boy in defiance of her parents even when she knows he's not good for her. The difference between Misunderstood Guy and Thug/Bad Boy is that she believes if her parents and friends got to know Misunderstood Guy better, they would see what she sees in him. In contrast, she dates Thug/Bad Boy *because* she knows he's bad. She gets to tick off her parents, flirt with danger, maybe even shake that annoying "good girl" image—a trifecta!

Nice Guy

Often overlooked until at least the end of high school, this boy doesn't understand why the girls always say they want someone who will treat them nicely, but then pass him over for the bad boys. Once he realizes that girls like him, he usually reacts in two ways: He is either bewildered by the attention (eventually he'll recover and be a great boyfriend) or turns into Player Guy (see below) and tries to make up for lost time.

Aloof/Distant Guy

This is the boy who has figured out how crappy school is and just wants to get through. He has little tolerance or patience with alpha males and the "Act Like a Man" box or anything to do with the school's "spirit squad." He can be interested in girls but not in playing the game to get status from the "Act Like a Man" box. He's often cynical and has a dry sense of humor, and he often likes to smoke pot (but then again so does almost everyone). He can be friends with Misunderstood Guy. He occasionally hangs out with Thug/Bad Boy because it's cool to openly fight "the system," but at the same time he's wary because he doesn't want to get into the kind of trouble Thug/Bad Boy does.

Geek

He doesn't have the social skills or looks for girls to be attracted to him. Girls sometimes pity him or treat him like a favorite pet, especially if they can get help for homework and he has a car. If he's funny and easygoing, people will like him.

Desperate Annoying Guy

This is the person moms make you be friendly with. You dread every moment leading up to it and you're miserable every moment you're with him. He doesn't listen to social cues. He tends to talk too much, with way too much detail, and shows off his knowledge about odd topics. Now that I'm an adult, I feel bad for this boy, but he was so annoying in high school!

> *He's hopeless—do his parents love him? Is any girl ever going to like him? He chases girls out of his league. He's socially inept and in denial about his own personality. He doesn't know when he isn't wanted.*
> Ellen, 17

Player Guy

This boy is good-looking, girls want him, and he knows it. He'll hook up with any girl who shows interest in him, but he's not interested in commitment. He's very good at complimenting a girl at a party, getting her to drink, and hooking up with her. He hangs out with the alpha group of popular girls and similar guys.

> *If a girl gets together with this guy, she doesn't feel used, even though she is—until the next day at school.*   Ellen, 16

Mr. Unattainable

Sometimes he can be confused with Player Guy, but he's different. He doesn't hook up randomly with girls. He can be popular (the nice kind) and an achiever. He seems to girls as if he's above it all.

> *Everyone loves the chase. If you can get this guy, then everyone will think that's amazing. He has all the characteristics you want, so you think, "Why would he be interested in me?"*   Lily, 16

The Good-Boy Jock

This boy tries to be tough because he thinks that's what everyone wants him to be. Coaches want him to be strong and aggressive. His dad is proud when he gets in a fight on the field, and his friends admire his strength and talent. He works hard in school, but excuses his effort to his friends by saying he's only doing it so he won't get in trouble for poor grades.

> *He acts macho around girls but is the most genuine and sweet guy around. He just tries to live up to everyone's expectations.*
> Jane, 16

You could parse boys' groups almost indefinitely: the boys who play hacky sack; class clowns; goth boys who wear black and are usually incredibly skinny; stoners; all-around freaks; and so on. These usually also fit into the Geek, Misunderstood, Aloof, or Desperate Guy profiles. Despite their often daunting reputations, I have never known any of these guys to be a truly bad kid.

The driving force for almost all boys is the same—getting girls and getting respect from other boys. Unfortunately, if you review the profiles again, the ones who look most likely to snag the girl and the high-fives from other boys are the Thug/Bad Boy, Mr. Unattainable, and Player Guy. Not great choices for your daughter.

DO BOYS HAVE CLIQUES?

Of course they do. Boys just think it's too feminine to use the word *clique*, so use the word *group* and you're talking about pretty similar social structures. I asked the boys and girls in my Empower classes to name the members of the group.

The Leader

This is usually the one in the clique everybody wants to be. He's one of or a combination of the following: athletic, tough, able to get the girls, or rich (or able to fake it).

> *Those shoes that come out next week . . . he already has them.*
>
> Nigel, 21

He's an opportunist. He's well-respected among boys. He knows when to be aggressive and when to relax. He has enough power over the group that he can direct them into conflicts or stop one in its tracks. The leader usually defines the "Act Like a Man" box. Contrary to what you may think, he isn't always loud and doesn't have to obviously display his power.

> *In my opinion there can be more than one leader. The leaders can form a clique of their own and have everyone else scrambling, doing anything and everything the leader(s) want them to do.*
>
> Kevin, 16

The Flunkie

He is often challenged to remember he has his own brain and therefore can make independent decisions. He is most obvious and tries the hardest to fit in. He is easily convinced by the other boys in the group to do something that irritates other people.

> *He'll do something like touch a girl's butt if the leader or someone in the clique dares him to. He's the "Yes, boss" type. The only social skill he has is diggin' in someone else's pockets. Surprisingly, you'll find out he's the softest person in the clique.*   Nigel, 21

The Thug

Every clique has a Thug or a wannabe Thug. He sometimes appears dumber than he is. He communicates through his body by pushing people around, taking up a lot of space as he walks down the school hallway and street, and/or making physical threats. He can appear popular because people know you shouldn't mess with him.

The Get Wit's (G.W's)

Much like the Flunkies, "Groupies" just want to tag along. They may receive respect from their parents and teachers for being good boys, but they aren't getting what they really want—the respect of the boys in their group and attention from girls.

> *Many G.W's end up in jail for long periods of time wondering how the hell they got there. G.W's are the most dangerous people in the clique because they're trying to build a name for themselves; consequently, they'll do anything.*   John, 17

> *I think this social ladder is complicated because only the leader is a leader. The others go in between being a thug, a G.W., and a Flunkie. The thing that makes this social ladder interesting is that only the leader knows everybody's role, the rest of the clique is so proud to be*

a part of "the clique" that they don't even realize they're literally "ass kissers."

Neil, 17

Pot, the Group Equalizer

You may not want to hear this, but the great equalizer that breaks down all boy cliques is marijuana. Most boys and girls I talk to don't view marijuana as a dangerous drug, any more than they view alcohol as a dangerous drug. At a party, boys will cross party lines to smoke it.

Boys' social hierarchy breaks down around drugs. Almost everyone smokes pot, and whoever has it is your friend for the moment. But when you go back to school, everybody goes back to their groups.

Jack, 16

What Do Boys Think About Girls?

In our Empower classes, girls and boys talk candidly about what they find so exciting, confusing, and frustrating about the opposite sex. Here's what boys tell us when girls are out of earshot.

In fifth grade, girls were psycho. Things got so out of hand that the school brought in a psychiatrist to talk to them. It was a couple of girls that were in a war with each other and the other girls followed them. It was vicious and a big mess.

Josh, 15

Girls are messed up, especially over looks and weight. It always surprised me that the most popular girls would have the most self-image problems and a lot of them looked like they were twenty. I've had good friends caught in a downward spiral. It hurts me how girls never see themselves as beautiful and it makes me feel horrible. They feel so ugly and I can't do or say anything to make it better. I think it's much harder to be a girl than a guy.

Jake, 16

Girls are a big question to me. Sometimes they'll speak to you and sometimes they're in some mood and won't talk to me in the hallway.

Greg, 14

I know everyone is unique, but some girls will think they're more special than other girls because a certain guy likes them, but he likes a million other girls, too. Ely, 15

WHAT DO BOYS AND GIRLS MOST WANT TO KNOW ABOUT EACH OTHER?

At strategically placed times in our program (meaning when our students are capable of having a meaningful conversation without putting each other down or yelling over each other), we bring the boys and girls together and they write down anonymous questions to ask each other. Of course, some of our students can't resist asking questions that are meant to shock, and we weed those out first or ask the question in a more appropriate way. Then we let the boys have the opportunity to answer the girls' questions (without the girls' commenting) and vice versa.

So what do boys want to know about girls? These are their common questions and the girls' most common answers.

1. *Why do girls like assholes?* Girls' reason: Because he's hot and they can be really cool when they're alone. My reason: The asshole fits in the "Act Like a Man" box. He's the Misunderstood Guy who looks like he has things under control. Girls find it especially attractive if the asshole shows them his sensitive side and only they can understand him.

2. *What are girls looking for in a boyfriend?* Or "*Why do girls say they're looking for someone who listens and respects them and then date the guys that don't?*" Girls' reason: Because we're confused. My reason: The "Act Like a Man" box gives them bad boyfriend criteria.

3. *Why do girls always go to the bathroom together?* The girls and I agree: It's a big-time bonding opportunity. Girls check in with each other and gossip. If they're on a date, they discuss if they're into the date (or if not, strategize how to get out of it).

4. *Do girls think about sex like boys do?* The girls and I agree: Yes, and they talk about it with each other in detail. When girls say this, the boys giggle nervously.

5. *Why don't girls tell you what they're really thinking?* Girls' reason: We do, but you don't listen. My reason: For one of three reasons: (1) girls

think they are, but they're communicating in a way that makes their opinions unclear; (2) they're afraid to tell you something you may not want to hear; and (3) they're putting up a front.

6. *How do you tell a girl you like her?* The girls and I agree: Directly.

7. *Why do girls ask so many questions when you're dating them?* Girls' response: We don't, but every time we want to ask anything, you all freak. My reason: Because talking and sharing personal information makes girls feel they're getting to know you.

8. *Why do girls wear tight clothing if they don't want the attention?* Girls' response: Don't even go there! We have the right to wear what we want, when we want. My response: Girls do want attention, but not the kind that makes them feel like a piece of dirt and/or a slab of meat. When girls wear revealing clothes, don't make the assumption that they want to have sex. Wanting to feel sexy is not the same as wanting to have sex.

What do girls ask boys? Here are their common questions and boys' responses:

1. *Why are boys such jerks in front of their friends and totally nice with you when you're alone?* Boys' reason: I don't know what you're talking about. Girls want too much when my friends are together and it gets on my nerves. My reason: To get their friends' respect, boys put up a front that they're tough, in control, and funny. They may feel more comfortable showing their vulnerable side to a girl because a girl won't tease them.

2. *Why are boys so homophobic?* Boys' reasons: Because it's disgusting. [I'm sorry to report.] People can do what they want but not in front of me. My reason: Because they always have to prove their masculinity by being homophobic.

3. *How should I tell a boy I like him?* The boys and I agree: Directly.

4. *Why do boys get mad when you don't want to date them?* Boys' reasons: Because girls give mixed signals, play games, and never know what they want. My reason: Some boys believe that girls don't have the right to say no. Much more likely is that the boys' feelings are hurt, but they don't want to show it because it makes them look weak. Instead, a more masculine response is to adopt an angry "Who does the bitch think she is" attitude.

5. *Why do boys think about sex all the time?* Boys' reason: Because we're obsessed and we have no control. My reason: Like girls, boys have hormones and sexuality is new and exciting. Unlike girls, society more readily condones sexually aggressive behavior in boys, so they have more freedom to express it. For example, boys talk about masturbating more easily than girls.

6. *When a boy talks to you, why does he look at your chest?* Boys' reason: Because we can't help it, especially when girls wear things that make it impossible to look anywhere else. My reason: (1) He could be objectifying you because that's how he generally sees women. (2) He could be distracted by your breasts because he's attracted to you but really does like you.

7. *Why don't boys talk about their feelings?* Boys' reason: Because we don't make a huge deal out of things like girls. We have nothing to talk about. My reason: It's a sign of weakness. They feel that girls have power over them if they give personal information.

8. *Why can't boys ever be serious?* Boys' reason: Girls take things too seriously. My reason: "Serious" to boys often means emotional, which equals weak and vulnerable to public humiliation.

"TAKING IT LIKE A MAN"

Boys need the same sociopolitical movement that feminism has provided for girls. The many waves of feminism have been powerful catalysts for challenging our culture's roles for women and girls. We're just beginning to recognize the cost of masculinity for boys. The "Act Like a Man" box becomes increasingly confusing as boys grow. For younger teens, being in the box primarily means getting respect from their male peers, but it gets a lot more complicated in high school. A teen boy has to be both outside the box to attract women (i.e., sensitive, but not too much) and inside the box to maintain the respect of guys (so he doesn't get the reputation for being whipped). He has to know the styles that are current for his group, yet not look like he's trying too hard.

It comes down to men identifying themselves apart from women because the characteristics they label as gay are female stereotypes: weak, emotional, not in control, and such. This intense desire to be "not a woman" defines much of what boys do and don't do. For boys who have a limited definition of masculinity, being perceived as an emasculated man is their greatest fear.

Of course, as much as they don't want to be girls, boys need to "get" girls to prove their masculinity—not to girls but to other boys.

> *A guy has to be funny and act cool. He can look like a nerd, but he has to play basketball and have social skills.*   Theo, 15

> *If you're a pretty boy, that's bad because you can't put too much attention to your appearance. There's no way to win. Too much attention . . . you're like a girl. Too little and you won't get girls.*
>   Will, 16

HOMOPHOBIA, MASCULINITY, AND VIOLENCE

Homophobia is the invisible hand in Boy World that guides boys to assigned roles of perpetrator, bystander, or target. Some boys threaten and/or perpetrata violence to prove their power and control—their masculinity—daring other boys to stop them: What are *you* going to do about it? Boys who witness these acts have a choice. They can be a passive bystander by looking the other way; an active bystander who backs up the bully by words and deeds; they can run away; or they can stand up to the bully. Standing up to the bully by physically fighting him isn't too tough—that's completely condoned behavior in Boy World. Standing up to a bully by saying his actions are wrong challenges the foundation on which Boy World is built.

Homophobia, manifested in boys' fear of being called gay, controls how boys make those choices and how their choices trap them into being complicit in a culture of violence. One of the best but most disturbing ways I can explain this dynamic is gang rape. The perpetrator not only is the first to rape the girl, but is instrumental in convincing the others boys to participate as well. If they don't, then their masculinity and loyalty are questioned. Most boys who would never commit an act of violence like this alone will do it if the alternative is going against the group. Whether it's going after a boy who's weak, failing to speak up when another boy

threatens violence or is violent, not respecting women and girls, or per-
petrating horrible acts of violence, the decision-making behind boys'
behavior stems from the same causes—the effort to prove one's masculinity and the failure to challenge the ethical foundation, the "right-
ness," of that definition.

One of my colleagues, Jackson Katz, a leading antiviolence advocate
and educator, clearly articulates the power of homophobia to police boys'
behavior:

> *Boys and men who speak out against sexism or publicly support girls
> and women run the risk of being ridiculed by their peers as "fags," or
> as "sissies," "pussies," or in some circles, "sensitive new age guys." The
> often unexamined implication is that real men (i.e., sexist heterosexu-
> als) wouldn't willingly support sexual equality and justice. (Women
> and girls who challenge male power or assertively confront sexism are
> often labeled "dykes" or "male-hating lesbians," which effectively
> silences many girls and women.) This name-calling can have a pow-
> erful effect on boys' and men's willingness to break their complicit
> silence. They might have a well-grounded fear that if they speak up,
> they too will be targeted for abuse. . . . Many gay adolescents don't
> want to risk exposure by calling attention to themselves.*
>
> *One humorous approach I use is to ask . . . "Why do some people
> presume that men who care about women, who are upset by violence
> done toward them, must want to have sex with other men?" This
> invariably provokes a surprised silence, which is often followed by
> cathartic laughter.**

The irony of the prevailing cultural definition of masculinity is that it
represses courage—not the kind where a boy will fight someone if challenged, but the moral courage to raise his voice and stand up for what's
right. If he physically stands up for a girl, then he's a hero. If he stands up
(especially if he refuses to fight) for a weaker, more effeminate boy, he's

---

*Jackson Katz, *More Than a Few Good Men: Strategies for Inspiring Boys and Young Men
to Be Allies in Anti-Sexist Education.* Center for Research on Women, Wellesley College,
No. 291, 1998.

called a fag. One mother spoke to me about her quandary: Her fifth-grade boy didn't know what to do about his friend, who was conspicuously weaker and more "girly" than the other boys. When the other boys bullied his friend on the playground, what should he do? If he defended his friend, he'd be outside the box and labeled a fag like his friend. If he did nothing, it would look like he agreed with the bullies. What should he do: Lose his friend or lose his social status and possibly become a target as well? Boys face challenges like this every day.

Seen in this light, homophobia becomes much more than whether you "tolerate" or "accept" homosexuality. Homophobia is one of the cornerstones of the culture of masculinity. If you want your daughter to be treated well by boys and men, you have to actively take a stand against homophobia.

THE HONOR CODE VS. THE BOY CODE

We all know what an honor code is. It's a set of behavioral standards including discipline, character, fairness, and loyalty for people to uphold and live up to. According to Michael Gurian's A *Fine Young Man,*

> *Honor codes are essential to boys and men. Boys develop personal codes of honor, and they are sponge-like in their absorption of codes of honor suggested to them by their nurturing systems. They watch their parents like hawks. If parents, mentors, and educators don't provide them with honor training, they will learn honor codes from peers, who sometimes promote codes that are dangerous. . . . Honor is what we provide boys as a structure in the self by which a boy can act wisely and well when his compassion is not enough to help him do so.*[*]

Gurian writes that parents, mentors, and educators generally have to provide boys with a "good" honor code lest boys provide each other with a "bad" honor code. It's not that simple. Boys don't learn the bad honor

---

*Michael Gurian, A *Fine Young Man: What Parents, Mentors, and Educators Can Do to Shape Adolescent Boys into Exceptional Men* (New York: Most Tarcher/Putnam, 1999), p. 240.

code only from their peers. The boys-will-be-boys code continues to exist precisely because many parents, mentors, and educators believe it, too.

What's really going on is that boys learn two codes that exist in conflict with each other. The feel-good Top Gun honor code about discipline, fairness, character, loyalty, and "doing what's right," the code that guides our heroes, is the kind that gets printed in the official code of ethics that schools post on their walls. It's supposed to be a self-policing mechanism that supports the institution's ethics and principles. It's what Gurian assumes adult men will teach boys. But many adult men have the same definitions of masculinity that boys do.

The second and opposing Boy Code—the peer honor code—is a much more powerful self-policing mechanism. It silences boys and makes them turn their backs on "doing the right thing." Discipline and character are manipulated to suppress emotions. Fairness gets lost in the glory of competition. Loyalty to doing what's right is subverted to keeping your mouth shut when you see violent, controlling, oppressive behavior. This is the honor code that guides so much of boys' behavior. Combined with homophobia, the peer honor code creates and sustains Boy World.

A CONSPIRACY OF SILENCE

It's common for Empower students to share their personal experiences with violence. Although more people are speaking out about violence, victims are still often shamed into silence and the perpetrators rarely held accountable. The following story demonstrates how pervasive the culture of masculinity is. It silences parents and students, and convinces well-meaning school administrators to believe they're holding perpetrators accountable when in reality their actions teach the perpetrators that they can get away with anything. It occurred at a prestigious private school, where these things aren't supposed to happen. But it did, and it happens in schools like it all the time.

Empower was teaching a group of ninth graders. At the faculty orientation, two teachers told me there was a junior student who was sexually harassing girls, which included placing his penis on a cafeteria table during lunch. His punishment? Social probation (meaning he wasn't allowed to go to any school social events—a punishment students in any private school, including this one, believe is a joke) and he was sent to a counselor. The teachers stated that although "he was talked to, and his behavior had improved, they were afraid he was slipping back to his old ways." They asked what advice they could give the female students so that the student would take their concerns seriously. I gave them suggestions, but I walked away from the meeting concerned that the burden was on the girls to control this student's behavior.

Classes were going well, except that the Empower teacher was having problems with a group of boys who were bullying other boys in the class. It was so bad that we met with the bullies privately and told them that they would either have to apologize or leave the class. Only if the other boys accepted the apology would they be allowed to rejoin the class. At the next class, the boys apologized, their apology was accepted, and they rejoined the class. As the Empower teacher guided the group discussion, he asked if the boys had experienced bullying from other boys in the school. One of the readmitted boys raised his hand and described being a victim (with the three other bullies) of a horribly violent hazing ritual that had recently taken place on an athletic trip.

Immediately after class, I was notified and we talked with the students privately; they confirmed the story. The boys assured us that this was a school tradition. In fact, as frightened and violated as they felt, they also felt honored to be selected by their abusers because it meant that they were to take their perpetrators' place as team leaders when they became seniors. They told me that one of their perpetrators as a freshman was hog-tied, his face duct taped, and thrown into a pool. The boys admitted that they looked forward to continuing this ritual as seniors. Not surprisingly, Sam, one of the two ringleaders on the athletic trip, was the same boy the teachers had asked me about and who had exposed himself on the cafeteria table.

My repeated discussions with the head of school and dean of the school revealed their belief that the best course of action was the following: speak to the ninth graders to confirm the story, talk to the perpetrators again, and then have me do a short presentation on hazing with the coaches. The perpetrators weren't suspended or expelled. No outside authorities were notified. The victims didn't receive counseling beyond talking to the dean (who isn't trained to work with assault victims but is trained to cover the school's rear end), yet they had to see their abusers every day in school. Everything was taken care of in-house.

Of course, this incident wasn't included on the perpetrators' college transcripts and I would bet my professional reputation that Sam continues to perpetrate the same behavior at college—and it'll also never be recorded on a transcript. Unfortunately, the reality is that your daughter could go to a party and meet someone like Sam and have no idea what she's getting into, because no one held him accountable and he is entirely polite and charming.

This school had a written honor code that specified that any incidents of violence or abuse had to be reported. Nevertheless, the school didn't take appropriate disciplinary action against the perpetrators. It thereby sent a clear message to the student body that the written honor code is a sham. By its very tactics, the school further punished and humiliated the victims (giving them even more reason to recant any accusations if the situation ever became public) and taught the students to ignore the school's official honor code and rely instead on the well-entrenched Boy Code that demands loyalty by silence.

Here is a poem written by one of the ninth-grade victims.

No matter how cool you think you are
Tight with seniors you will never be
If you think you can avoid it
Wake up and smell the coffee
If you think I am lying to you
You are ignoring the reality
Hazing is a part of life
No one could ever be haze free
Because those who do it now
Were once puny like me
So they want revenge for what happened to them
And the lucky freshmen are we
Who take it . . . and think about what we'll do
When seniors we will be

WHY METAL DETECTORS WILL NEVER WORK

Unfortunately, there have been far too many reports from Columbine, Paducah, and other schools in which boys pushed to the edge opened fire on classmates and teachers. Consider these questions from the Safe School Initiative: An Interim Report on the Prevention of Targeted Violence in Schools written by the U.S. Secret Service National Threat Assessment Center in collaboration with the U.S. Department of Education.

> *Why expel students immediately for the most minor infractions, when expulsion was just the spark that pushed some students to come right back to school with a gun?*
> *Why rely on metal detectors and police officers in school, when shooters often make no effort to conceal their weapons?*

Can the culture of masculinity provide answers about the recent school violence? Absolutely . . . but only if we all take responsibility. The media has named the school violence of the last decade as "Teen Violence" or "Youth Violence." As usual, these titles completely obscure the fact that almost all the perpetrators are boys who believed themselves to be victims of bullies. The reality is that very few boys have brought a gun to school to get back at their tormentors. But since the ones who did have done so much real and psychological damage to their fellow students, teachers, and parents, we need to understand what's going on so we have a chance to stop it.

So far we're collectively missing the boat. Politicians and many school experts advocate a "zero tolerance" policy to combat this wave of violence. In concrete terms, this includes installing metal detectors in schools or suspending students who write violent essays. The media has conditioned us to respond to youth violence as if there are "super-villain monsters in our schools masquerading as children."* These solutions address the problem superficially and are really instituted to make us feel better and less frightened. If a student truly wants to blow up the cafete-

*Gurian, *A Fine Young Man*, p. 198.

ria, he'll do it. How could metal detectors stop someone when so many students in every school know a door or window that's broken or habitually left open?

What zero tolerance is really about is maintaining the status quo. I'm not condoning the behavior of boys who fight back violently. I'm not excusing their behavior. What I'm saying is that we have to understand that these boys feel invisible, powerless, and humiliated and have good reason to have no faith in the adults who are supposed to protect them. Consider the response of a parent who knew Andy Williams (the boy who killed two and injured thirteen at a San Diego school in March 2001) when he heard Andy was planning some act of revenge at his school. "I told him that if he was even considering anything that I was going to take him straight to the sheriff."* When boys are crying out for help, adults threaten and punish.

If we want to stop boys' violence, schools must create cultures that directly confront the social pecking order and hold bullies accountable. We must address the intersection of racism and boy culture and how that contributes to the problem. The alternative is to keep our heads in the sand, continuing to think that these are isolated situations and that they won't happen in our communities — until they do.

I want to reiterate that I don't make the assumption that most boys are violent, or would be if they knew they could get away with it. One of the unfortunate consequences of how our society has marginalized feminism is that many people who work for women's equality are assumed to be male bashing and that boys and men are assumed to be inherently violent. These insidious assumptions are barriers to open and honest communication within and between the sexes. I consider myself a feminist, but one who believes we must have the participation of male leadership to solve these problems. Where we all fall short (feminists included) is that we rarely perceive boys as what most are: bystanders or victims of other boys' violence. Likewise, when violence-prevention educators talk to boys about violence against women, they rarely, if ever, ask how *these boys* feel when women and girls they care about are hurt at the hands of other boys and men.[†]

*National Public Radio, "All Things Considered," March 4, 2001.
[†]Katz, *More Than a Few Good Men.*

Do the Right Thing

Most boys really want to do the right thing, they just have no idea how. They want to be loving, emotional, strong men. But how can they be when their role models are men who are idolized for being tough and always in control and when they themselves are vilified and emasculated when they demonstrate characteristics associated with women and girls? Where are the role models who look like the strong men they want to be but who are also emotionally open, articulate, engaged, and morally courageous? Russell Crowe and Tom Cruise may protect the beautiful woman from gunfire, but what are boys learning about empathy and "real men" when their heroes limit communication to a clenched jaw?

If we believe that most boys are out of control, uncaring, and thoughtless members of our communities, and if we believe that the best response to this problem is to control and punish them, we'll create a self-fulfilling prophecy. When we set the bar low, boys will meet our expectations. Instead, if we demand the best from boys, hold ourselves accountable for what we do that contributes to Boy World, and reach out to them with respect, we will raise strong men who believe that "being a man" is about standing up for what's right.

The Liz Claiborne/Empower Survey

In December 2000, a survey sponsored by Liz Claiborne and the Empower Program questioned 477 fourteen- to seventeen-year-olds and 456 parents of students to increase the understanding of the social environment in which teenagers in the United States live and to gauge the extent of teen dating abuse and violence.

The teen survey uncovered a clear perception among teenagers of inequity in the social environment at their schools.

- Of the teens surveyed, 77 percent believe that some students or groups of students are "above the rules" and don't receive punishment for the same actions for which other students are penalized.
- The vast majority (86 percent) also feels that some students have more influence than others with their classmates.

- Of those students who say that both of these phenomena exist at their schools, 83 percent report that the students who are "above the rules" are the same ones who have more influence with other students. While the dynamic of popularity or influence in teenage social environments is not new or surprising, the survey exposes the interesting and disturbing finding that many of the students leverage their status in the school to intimidate or embarrass others.

- A significant proportion of fourteen- to seventeen-year-olds (36 percent) report that the students with the most influence engage in the intimidation or embarrassment of students who are not part of their groups "all the time" or "frequently."

- Another 32 percent report occasional intimidation or embarrassment of this nature.

- Younger students are significantly more likely than older teens to identify intimidation at their schools. More than half (52 percent) of fourteen- and fifteen-year-olds surveyed note intimidation occurring "all the time" or "frequently," compared to only 36 percent of sixteen- and seventeen-year-olds.

- Interestingly, 56 percent of students at rural schools say that influential students intimidate other students "all the time" or "frequently," compared to 37 percent of suburban students and 39 percent of urban students.

- Only one third of respondents indicate that students who intimidate or embarrass other students usually get in trouble with teachers or school administrators.

- Only 16 percent of respondents report that other students usually intercede to stop an incident.

- More than four in ten teens (41 percent) say nothing usually happens to the intimidators.

What happens, if anything, when students are embarrassed or humiliated by other students?

- More than half of girls (55 percent) and more than one third of boys (36 percent) agree that the recipients of intimidation usually respond by isolating themselves.

- Nearly four in ten respondents (39 percent) say that the victims usually laugh along with the intimidators, despite feelings of anger.
- And according to a significant portion of respondents (29 percent), the victims usually plan ways to get back at the intimidators in the future.

What happens when these "influential" students try to intimidate or embarrass students who are not part of their groups?

- Half the respondents communicate that the victims of intimidation usually verbally confront the intimidator.
- One quarter indicate that physical confrontation usually follows the intimidation. Boys are more likely than girls to describe verbal or physical confrontation as the typical response to intimidation, perhaps suggesting that boys are more likely than girls to confront their peers.
- Less than one third of respondents (31 percent) indicate that the victims usually report the behavior to someone at the school, while only 13 percent say they report it to a parent.

What You Can Do

Talk about this chapter with your daughter. Show her the "Act Like a Man" box and ask her how it corresponds to her experience. Does she know boys who fall into the categories in this chapter? Ask her to imagine what it would be like to be a boy in today's society. Let her read through the questions boys and girls ask about each other. Did any of the answers surprise her? Talk to her about homophobia, and how it affects not only attitudes toward the gay community but how boys and men behave. Talk to her about how issues of race and religion intersect with boy culture.

Most of all, help her appreciate that boys are in their own life raft. Just like girls, they're looking to break out beyond the stereotypes and be appreciated for who they are. If your daughter can empathize with how difficult it is in Boy World, she can work toward seeing boys as equal partners on the path toward healthy adulthood.

Girl Meets Boy

Crushes, Matchmaking, and the Birth of Fruit Cup Girl

The Drama Begins

Emily and Kristi are seventh graders and both are in love with Brett. Each spends considerable quality time with Brett, including sending him notes, writing his name on their notebooks, calling him after school for tortuously long, awkward conversations, hanging out after school to see if she can bump into him, and "accidentally" walking by when his team practice is over. When the competition for his affections becomes unbearable, they make a pact that both will stop liking him. Neither girl has any intention of keeping her word, but each also believes that the other will. Each is also convinced that she has the right to be angry with the other if she goes back on her word. Which is, of course, what happens. Both girls quietly do everything they can behind each other's back to win Brett's affection.

Things become much more complicated when they discover that no fewer than four other girls in their grade like Brett as well. Making matters worse, one of the four girls, Liza, threatens to usurp Emily and Kristi's position as the front contender for Brett's affections. Emily and Kristi's response is to go after Liza, assured that they're in the right because (a) Liza knows they like him; (b) Liza is throwing herself at Brett; and (c) They staked their claim first. Within a day, the grade is abuzz watching the drama unfold. Messengers are dispatched. Queen Bees are consulted. Delegations confer in small break-out sessions.

In the situation described above, the parents of Emily, Kristi, and Liza are largely clueless that anything's going on. Brett's parents figure something's up because their phone is tied up all night with these girls calling their son, or else they pick up the receiver, hear giggles on the other end, then a quick "click" as the line goes dead.

I've talked to many parents like Brett's. They see their son as a deer in the headlights with these girls barreling toward him like a Mack truck. Is this true? Are the Bretts of the world clueless and terrified as girls vie for their attention? If one of these girls were your daughter, would you know about this drama? Should you? Why do girls turn against each other over a boy they may barely know? How does girls' competition for boys influence your daughter's future intimate relationships?

Let's put Girl World and Boy World together and see how they impact girls' first interactions with boys. Here is where you'll see girls begin to turn themselves inside out to figure out how to be attractive to boys. Your daughter will be impatient that her friend isn't keeping up because she isn't as interested in boys, or she'll feel insecure when all the other girls don't want to talk about anything else, and she's more interested in soccer. You'll see your daughter question her self-worth if she doesn't think she fits the model (pun intended) she thinks the boys want. She'll fall madly in love and not know why. She'll feel totally alone when a friend ditches her for a guy. She'll be terrified that she won't know how to act around boys she likes.

WHAT YOU MUST KNOW

- Around twelve years of age, girls' bonding often extends beyond navigating their friendships with other girls to include bonding over drama with boys.
- If one girl is getting attention from boys or is more "boy crazy" than her friend, it will strain the relationship and put pressure on the other girl to play catch-up.
- At some point, a girl will pretend to be not as smart, strong, or capable around a boy she likes. She may be embarrassed by her behavior but not know how to stop.
- Her girlfriends will see this, be embarrassed, and talk behind her back, but also wonder if this is the right way to get boys' attention.

- As in their friendships with girls, girls often communicate unclearly or don't say what they mean because they want to please the boy they like. To a girl, pleasing means doing what the other person wants, almost always at the cost of what she wants—or doesn't want.
- She'll have a crush on someone who doesn't treat her or other people well. She'll know this, but won't stop liking the person.
- Not all girls like boys. Some girls are sexually attracted to girls or question their sexuality early in their teen years.
- No matter what her sexual orientation, your daughter will likely have strong friendships with boys through her teen years. Some of those friendships can (but not always) become sexual, but that doesn't take away from the depth of the friendship.

BOY FRIENDS AND BOYFRIENDS

I'm sure you remember this concept from your teens. There were boys or girls who were friends and then there were *boyfriends* and *girlfriends*. Girls still makes those distinctions. Most girls have strong friendships with boys that they value highly, and ironically, girls don't seem to be so constrained by gendered behavior within these friendships. They can be themselves, feel comfortable saying what they feel and think. As Mike, age sixteen, put it, "My girl friends will tell me when I'm acting like a dumb ass." This is a good thing. It means his girl friends are telling him what they think. As I'll discuss in this and upcoming chapters, girls often hide their true selves as soon as the boy goes from being a boy who's a friend to a potential or real boyfriend.

We become so nervous that we don't know how to act. Nia, 17

Your daughter may not be interested in dating in early adolescence. She's perfectly comfortable hanging out with her friends, enjoying her usual sports and hobbies. She's aware of the boy/girl fray, but not stressed out that she's not yet a part of it. This is just fine.

I never dated that young! None of my friends did—and there were twelve of us—we hung out all the time. No boys invited. The kids I did know that dated (the popular boys and girls) just seemed to pass from partner to partner. Boys in our class really weren't that interesting. I've been in the Gifted and Talented Program since third grade. We bonded because we got a lot of crap from the other classes about being nerds. Most of the kids in the other classes had elaborate social lives involving parties, dating, and smoking pot. Very few of the GT kids had that. I think because we had to defend ourselves to the rest of the school, we ended up doing weird things. I also think we just weren't at that level of maturity. So we formed this really tight-knit gang of girls and stopped paying attention to boys.

— Anna, 17

CRUSHES

Sooner or later your daughter will be ready for her first crush — or it'll hit her between the eyes, ready or not. What would adolescence be without crushes? Crushes are ubiquitous. They're exciting and they make girls gloriously miserable. Girls love to have them. Girls fall in love with someone "who's so hot, you don't understand, I'm totally in love" and then overnight change their affections to someone else. These are typical descriptions of crushes from the girls in Empower classes.

I feel like I'm going to throw up. And I'm sure right in front of him.
I get butterflies in my stomach.
I get excited, can't breathe, and then I start to giggle uncontrollably. It's humiliating and also fun at the same time.
I'm so nervous. I'm sure I'll do or say something stupid.

The problem with crushes goes back to the "Act Like a Man" box in Chapter 6. Girls usually have crushes on boys who fit in the box. It's not hard to see why. Do you remember what boys were like in sixth and seventh grade? Maybe two are growing proportionately. The rest are awkward and gangly. If you were a girl, who would you fall for? Exactly. Even though the awkward ones now will be the hottest at the high school reunion, girls don't know that, and even if they did, why should they care? Girls want someone who's cute and cool *now*. Unfortunately, boys are also taught not only to aspire to the physical characteristics of the "Act

Like a Man" box but the behavioral characteristics as well. Girls are attracted to physically mature boys who often act like buttheads as well.

> *Those guys develop an ego. One of my best friends did this. The girls were all over him and he treated them like trash. They accepted it and came flocking back.*
>
> Jake, 16

OBSESSIONS

Crushes can come and go in a day or a week. One step up from crushes are obsessions.

> *I was obsessed with this guy named Scott. I have no idea why. I look back and laugh at this now, but at the time I was totally serious. I would write [in my journal] the different things he had done that brought me closer to the conclusion that he liked me. I would show off, try to be near him. Every day during recess, my friend and I would play tag near where he played soccer with his friends and count the number of times he smiled at me. It was pathetic.*
>
> Julia, 12

> *Obsession in middle school is worse because you have nothing to compare it to. Someone who humiliates you, you like even more. I was obsessed with a guy in seventh grade. I dated him and then he broke up with me. Then he fell in love with someone else and I hated it. But then she did a little Mexican hat dance on his heart by hooking up with five guys and I felt a lot better.*
>
> Angie, 17

> *In fifth grade I was obsessed with this guy. I naturally told my friends I was crazy about him and they spread it around that I liked him. He stayed as far away from me as possible and wouldn't say a word to me after that.*
>
> Nina, 13

POWER BROKERS IN PUBERTY: MATCHMAKING

Early adolescence is an exciting time to be a girl. Some girls eagerly anticipate when they'll be old enough to have boyfriends and all the accompanying drama. But they're also cowards (which is totally under-

standable). They want to check out the whole boy thing and be involved
in the drama, but without putting themselves on the front line. So in
many different ways, girls push each other to be the first one to jump off
the cliff. For example, *Julie, 11, is on her way to math class when one of
her best friends rushes up to her . . .*

ANI: *I was just talking to Jeremy and he says that Matt likes you! That's
so cool! You guys would make such a cute couple! I knew he liked
you!*
JULIE: *Are you sure? I don't believe it. What did Jeremy say exactly?*
ANI: *He said Matt thought you were really pretty and nice.*

*Julie is totally psyched. She has had a huge crush on Matt since the begin-
ning of the year but hasn't known how to tell him. After the class, she discusses with her two closest friends what her next step should be. Later that
afternoon, one of them slips the following note into Matt's locker.*

Do you like Julie? Please circle your answer: Yes No

*After school, Julie opens her locker to get her books to take home and sitting
there is a crumpled note . . . it's the response.*

If the response includes a circle around the "Yes" and maybe a request
to meet after school, this means high drama. Julie gets to figure out every
nuance of the note in full consultation with her friends, who get to offer
their opinion and analysis. She will be the center of attention the entire
afternoon, and it will seem to her that all is right in the world.

Or perhaps the drama will play out at one of the boy-girl school dances
that are the hallmarks of middle school. The girls are at one end of the
gym, talking and swaying to the music; the boys are at the other end, similarly engaged in herd behavior. Egged on by their cliques or emissaries,
Julie and Matt's friends practically push them onto the dance floor, where
they move awkwardly together and try to talk over the deafening music.
Everyone's looking at them! Julie's a star!

More often than not, Julie—and every girl in her situation—is quickly disappointed, because the meeting with Matt isn't nearly as responsive and dramatic as Julie and her friends anticipated. Where is the romantic boy from the magazines? Why is this boy answering in monosyllables? Julie and her friends have a set idea of how Matt should act garnered from movies, TV, and magazines; Julie's expectations for Matt are also based on her closest friendships. Remember, girls' friendships in early adolescence are often characterized by "best friends forever," endless conversation, and devastating breakups and reconciliations. Girls' reactions to the ups and downs of these friendships are as intense, if not more so, as they will later be in romantic relationships. It's hard for the awkward first crush to measure up to the ease and intimacy of girl-girl friendships, or even the camaraderie of friendships with boys.

A lot of girls' first crushes never even get to the stage where girl meets boy. Some follow dramatic trajectories from first inklings of attraction through flaming breakup without the boy even necessarily knowing he was the object of affection ("It is *so over* with Jason"). Some girls run through a series of "boyfriends" without any of the relationships advancing, as one girl put it, "all the way up to holding hands." What's often true of a lot of these early forays is that the reality is a little disappointing compared with the anticipation.

A WORD TO THE WISE

Call waiting and conference call capacity are dangerous weapons in the hands of young adolescent girls. Not only is it extremely frustrating for you to be cut off from the phone, it's too tempting for girls to have conference calls where one girl listens to the conversation without the knowledge of another. If it's financially feasible, get a separate line and don't get call waiting or conference call capacity.

What's the first thing a girl does after getting off the phone with her new boyfriend? She immediately calls a girlfriend to analyze every word of the conversation and discuss every nuance. In these early romances, she may spend more time talking to her girlfriend about the boyfriend than to the boyfriend himself.

Even though Julie may be disappointed, it doesn't mean love's labor is lost. These experiences, even if they're short-lived and awkward, are important and make a lasting impact. Your daughter's expectations and standards for intimacy are built on them. Relationships at this age often have more to do with social status than with the actual boy a girl is dating (but don't expect your daughter to agree with this while she's in the throes of her latest love).

But let's go back to why Julie and Matt are getting together in the first place. It may have been a mutual crush at first sight, but more commonly, Julie and her friends have collectively decided that Matt is a worthy object on which to experiment. Or perhaps Matt is a friend, and the group decides that Julie should be the canary in the mineshaft: Is he boyfriend material? Usually beginning around sixth grade, matchmaking becomes the prime directive. Girls love to be in each other's business as they dissect the boy mystery. What better way to deal with boy anxiety than setting up a friend? No matter who made the initial push, the whole group can analyze every stage of the relationship, from the first mutual flirtations through the intense phone calls to the inevitable conflicts that send the whole thing down in flames. As girls go through this phase in their lives, their friendships are solidified around these dramatic moments. And not surprisingly, the social hierarchy is operating at full force.

> In the social hierarchy, although I am not the super Queen Bee, I'm fairly close. I'm not hated by anyone (hopefully) and have many good friends. The people I've set up are not outcasts or dorks, but aren't the Queen Bees. The people close to the Queen Bees are the matchmakers.   Kim, 15

> The Queen Bee set me up and I didn't feel like there was anything I could do about it.   Molly, 18

Queen Bees are careful to regulate the popularity of other girls. When they set up another girl, one of the ulterior motives is to bind the girl more closely to the Queen Bee. The girl set up for her first boyfriend, and hence her moment in the sun as the focus of attention, is now beholden and bonded to the Queen Bee. The Queen Bee can also influence when the girl stops liking the boy. Real conflicts between girls occur when the girl who is set up begins to act independently.

In Julie's situation, she is likely a Wannabe, Pleaser, or Messenger, and Ani is a Banker or Queen Bee. Note that both girls' stock goes up when Julie gets her first "boyfriend." One way to solidify your place on the social totem pole is to be a Banker or Messenger whose information on who likes whom is vital to the unfolding drama.

But what if Julie really didn't want a boyfriend? It'll be hard for her to resist the encouragement of her girlfriends and the excitement of this new kind of intimacy. And if it's not working out with Matt, it'll be hard for her to admit it to the group or herself. This is a new level of peer pressure that can be very harmful if she doesn't learn to recognize it for what it is.

THE BIRTH OF FRUIT CUP GIRL

When I was twelve, my grade went on a field trip and there was this boy that I really liked, but I didn't know how to get his attention. I got my courage up and sat down at the same table as him for lunch. All my friends knew I liked him. It was so embarrassing. I didn't know what to say, so I pretended that I couldn't open my fruit cup and asked him to open it for me. Looking back on it now, it was sort of pathetic, but I still let guys beat me in races.   Leah, 14

The Fruit Cup Girl personifies girls' internal conflict between expressing personal authenticity and codified gendered behavior that gets them attention from boys. Girls fight the stereotype of Fruit Cup Girl because she's embarrassing and contrary to what they know they should be like. They know they're supposed to just be themselves, but the proven success of Fruit Cup Girl stops them from doing so. Here's the cost-benefit analysis:

Benefits of Being Fruit Cup Girl
• She gets the boy's attention.

- It's easy. Somehow she knows how to play the part (even as she may criticize herself at the same time for doing it).
- It works, even though everybody makes fun of it.

Costs of Being Fruit Cup Girl

- She feels ridiculous.
- Girls can and will make fun of her.
- She feels like a fraud.
- She fears the only way guys will like her is if she acts in stereotypically feminine ways, i.e., weak, laughing at their jokes, etc. She's afraid to show her real self.
- She's afraid people won't take her seriously.
- She conditions herself to be Fruit Cup Girl whenever she's around a boy she likes.

In early adolescence, acting like a Fruit Cup Girl gives a girl validation and affirmation from boys. But at the same time, most girls are smart enough to know they're selling out. Fruit Cup Girl gets the guy, but she feels like a fool. Your daughter may well catch herself acting like this and she'll be confused and disturbed; she'll feel the same way when she sees her girlfriends do it, too. Fruit Cup Girl makes girls feel ashamed to be girls. The birth of Fruit Cup Girl begins the schism between girls around guys.

> I constantly see girls act superficially around guys! It's amazing how girls instantly become charming and flirty when a guy steps into the room, as if they can't let down their guard for a split second and just be themselves. Although I hate to admit it, I'm sure I've done this before.
> Jenny, 17

> I guess girls act [superficial] around guys because they're nervous around them and I'm one of them. Girls feel they're not perfect enough and try to make up for that by acting. Same with me.
> Jessica, 13

When girls are younger, being a Fruit Cup Girl is the easy way to get a boy's attention. By eighth grade, girls know that acting like that is only going to get you so far without inviting the ridicule of other girls. As girls get older and become more interested in hooking up, they still think they need to use Fruit Cup Girl to get boys' attention, but now they need an excuse to openly fall back on her. And that's where drinking comes in. As long as a girl has a beer in her hand, she has an excuse to be the silly girl. The metamorphosis from Fruit Cup Girl to Beer Cup Girl (who now clutches a beer cup in her hand) sets the stage for girls to use alcohol and drugs as excuses for doing what they want to do but are too afraid to do sober because they'll get a bad reputation.

> *When I was twelve, I remember wondering why girls had to act so fake around guys. They would stand around in clusters and scream and giggle and shoot looks over at some guy. Maybe one of their friends would come over and give you a message. If they act like that now, I would think they were trying to hook up. It's obvious. No one acts like that much of a moron unless they want to hook up.*
>
> Patrick, 16

FIGHTING OVER BOYS

Sixth grade is a wild ride for both of you. Any sixth-grade class I teach in the fall is a totally different animal in the spring. Many of the little girls I see in the fall are seeing themselves as young women—or at the least budding teens—by spring. And one of the ways they show it is to fight over boys.

Six- and seventh-grade girls scare me. They'll sink as low as they need to to win the boy they want. I teach a semester course for sixth graders as part of their health class. Last year before the class started, a teacher gave me the low-down. The girls were off-the-charts cliquey and mean. They had already been talked to several times with no improvement. The teacher described one girl by saying, "I'm sure Morgan's the Queen Bee; I've been trying to catch her all year and haven't been able to." When I met this girl, she was tiny, pretty, and didn't say a word in class. Meanwhile, there was another girl in the class named Brianna, also tiny and pretty, who talked constantly in class and asked my advice after class. Of course, being a sucker for anyone who asks my advice, I thought Brianna was sweet and Morgan was evil. Well, I was wrong; they were both evil. They had been waging a protracted dirty war against each other all year and the pivotal battle peaked at a boy/girl school event in the spring. At this affair, where adults were everywhere but no one was officially chaperoning, Morgan and two of her friends met up with three popular boys who Brianna thought were "hers." When Brianna found out, she began a systematic campaign to get the boys to switch their allegiance back—and she was successful. Practically the entire grade was polarized between these two girls, with savage consequences threatened for any displays of disloyalty. Morgan vowed revenge, although she assured me her behavior was morally correct because it was "only equal to what she did to me." The only thing that stopped them was the end of the school year. Next year, many new students will join their grade, and they'll each have about a day to decide which girl they'll align with.

REJECTION: DUMPING AND GETTING DUMPED

Oh, the pain. There's nothing like it except being sucker-punched in the stomach. Breakups are painful no matter how old a girl is. When she's younger, it hurts because she's having these feelings and experiences for the first time and her inexperience can blind her to the warning signs of an impending rejection, so it's a cruel surprise. When she's older, her relationship may be more physically intimate and emotionally complex. Her life could be more intertwined with his because they have the same friends. She could feel that her image in her school community is tied to the relationship. Lastly, since a girl's sense of self is often tied to her perception of her sexuality, when she's rejected she could feel used, manipulated, and foolish.

When a girl is dumped, she usually tries to figure out what she did wrong and then change that part of her personality. Even if she knows that the person who dumped her is a jerk, most likely she'll still feel that he's cool. Or she'll take him back again and again, even if she knows he's treating her poorly.

In sixth grade he wrote a script to break up with me and read it to me in the lunchroom. He said, "Erin, it's over, I can't be with you anymore," and I said, "Okay," and he goes, "No you're not following the script! Your line is, 'I need you, don't leave me!'" What a lame-ass. In seventh grade I gave him another try. That time he tape-recorded him breaking up with me.

Erin, 18

Why do girls take back boys who dump them cruelly? Because everyone wants what they can't have, especially if you've had it once. Girls want easy, quick fixes that will reassure them that they fit in. The "Act Like a Woman" box is an obvious place for answers, and it tells them that a boyfriend is important to your status. So they turn themselves inside out trying to be the girl they think the boy wants them to be.

A breakup's silver lining is that it creates great girl bonding moments. The intimacy that comes out of these experiences can be intense. Especially if the dumped girl has been blowing off her girlfriends for her now ex-boyfriend, those friendships can experience a honeymoon period. The dumped girl can pour out her sorrows, anger, and confusion to her friends while they analyze the ex-boyfriend's baggage and problems that made him reject her.

Girlfriends can be similarly helpful when a girl wants to dump someone. They can help her sort through the pros and cons of the relationship and strategize what to do when the girl wants out. This is a hard task for girls. Since they're conditioned to please, they may date someone longer than they want, then find it impossible to communicate clearly when they want to end the relationship. They'll look for excuses so they won't have to say, "I don't want to go out with you anymore." Friends in the clique can help them find the backbone to confront the boy. Or the clique can allow a girl to abdicate responsibility for the unpleasant job by bringing the bad news themselves or supporting her while she simply ignores the boy, hoping he'll go away.

In the early stages of romance, girls may find themselves turning to their cliques for loyalty and support more than their boyfriends. Later, the balance may shift.

CHECKING YOUR BAGGAGE

• Close your eyes and remember your first crush: Where were you when you first saw this person? How did you feel?

- What makes you most nervous about boys and your daughter?
- What do you want to teach your daughter about boys?
- Were you ever dumped by a girlfriend or boyfriend? Where and how did it happen?
- Who, if anyone, did you go to for support?
- What are your attitudes about homosexuality? How would you feel if a good friend told you that her daughter is gay?
- How would you feel if your own daughter were gay?

HER OWN PACE, HER OWN TIME

Just as your daughter feels anxious if she's not developing physically at the same pace as her friends, she'll feel out of sync if she's boy-crazy and her friends aren't, or if they're off to the races and she couldn't care less. Validate her feelings, and remind her that there's no such thing as a "normal" schedule for becoming interested in boys, and that some girls never become interested in boys and that's okay, too.

Especially if her group of friends is caught up in hard-core boy frenzy, she needs to know that it's easy to get caught up in the swirl and feel pressured. Girls will tease each other about the boys they are friends with. If your daughter has close male friends (this seems to be especially true with boys she grows up with and/or who live in the neighborhood), tell her that she doesn't have to lose those friendships if they aren't romantic. I have talked to many confused girls who don't want to lose these close friendships but can feel them slipping away under all the scrutiny and pressure to pair up.

> *One of my best friends is a boy I have grown up with. My friends tease the two of us all the time and I don't know what to do about it. He's like my brother and all these people want us to be boyfriend/girlfriend.* — Rachel, 12

Here's how you can start the conversation:

PARENT: *Hey, I'm not sure if you want to talk about guys, but I'm guessing girls in your class are. I just want you to know that girls can feel differ-*

ent things about it. Some girls are boy-crazy, some girls are sometimes interested, some girls aren't sure, and some girls don't care and may never care. Wherever you, or any girl, fit on that spectrum is all good and fine.

Now you have an opportunity to lay the foundation for helping her handle peer pressure, the kind of foundation she'll need when she's older and handling weightier issues like sex, drugs, and alcohol.

PARENT: *However, no matter what, I want you to know what I believe is important to remember. It's up to you to decide when you are ready for dating. When you think you are, let's talk about what that means to you. What do you feel comfortable with? What do you feel uncomfortable with? You have no obligation to go out with anyone because your friends want you to. At the same time, friendships can really support you as you all figure this stuff out. It's important to trust and rely on your friends so you can share your feelings with them and know those feelings will be respected.*

LANDMINE!

Don't use the word *boy* when discussing the subject with your daughter; use the word *guy* instead. Don't say, "Who are you dating? Do you have a crush on anyone? Do you have a boyfriend?"

If you really want to ask, say, "Are you interested in anyone?"
Anika, 17

Just as you've brought your baggage from your own experiences with friendships, you'll do the same thing when your daughter begins to have crushes and wants to act on them. Somewhere in your daughter's adolescence you'll go from telling her what to do, with a good chance she'll do what she's told, to guiding her and recognizing that she needs the space to make her own decisions. Nowhere is this more true than with boys.

I asked younger teens what their parents have told them about boys; here are some responses:

> *My mom always says not to listen to what boys say because they're always wrong or lying (I love you, I want to be with you, etc.). But if you like a boy, you should treat him like a normal person, not an idol. I listen to what my mom says because I think it's true.*   Bianca, 13

> *My mom told me I shouldn't be obsessed with a guy who doesn't like me. He's obviously not worth my time if he knows I like him and won't talk to me. She told me that when I get older, in high school, if I was obsessed with a guy and he didn't like me, he might use me. If I'm crazy about him, that gives him the message that I would do anything for him. I learned that I should keep who I like a secret and only with my very good friends because if too many people know, they tend to mess with my relationship and chances of being friends with the guy.*
> Nina, 13

HER BILL OF RIGHTS WITH BOYFRIENDS

Don't assume that every friendship with a boy has romantic potential. Be careful about how you talk to your daughter about these friendships; they're important to her, so treat them with respect. Even if you see a male friend of your daughter's obviously smitten with her, don't push your opinion on her.

LANDMINE!

I know it's tempting, but don't tease your daughter about whether she has a boyfriend.

When you sense that your daughter is ready to start talking about an interest in boys—either because she comes to you or because you see the unmistakable signs, such as the new monthly phone bill—it's time for a discussion to clarify what she wants and has the right to expect out of any relationship. Your goal is to help her understand how her feelings when she likes someone may impact her Bill of Rights. Ask her how she feels when she has a crush. Then ask her what her Bill of Rights should be with someone she likes. If the discussion is too uncomfortable for her, suggest she write it down in her journal. It should look like this:

When I like someone I feel . . .	*My Bill of Rights with someone I like includes . . .*
Nervous	Respecting me and other people
Excited	Being kind to me and other people
Butterflies in my stomach	
Distracted	Listening to what I (and others) say
	Not treating me differently in front of other people than when we're alone

The question you need to get her to think about is this: If she has a crush on someone and he doesn't act according to her Bill of Rights, will she ignore it? She should have a Bill of Rights for her friendships with girls (see Chapter 4); ask her why she would hold a person she likes to a lesser standard than she would a friend. If the boy doesn't respect her, how can she respond? What kind of things might a boy say or do that could make her forget her Bill of Rights? How could she respond? Which friends will back her up when she feels too weak, scared, or pressured to stand up for herself? Reassure her that you're there to listen or to help.

A girl sometimes discounts her Bill of Rights with boys because she thinks if she lets him get away with more, he'll like her back. What she doesn't realize is that that will only make him respect her less.

Nidhi, 16

Remember, dismissing her Bill of Rights is the first step (or more accurately, misstep) your daughter can take toward believing that what boys want is more important than what she wants or feels is right.

DADS, PAY ATTENTION!

When your daughter starts to like boys, you have a crucial opportunity to reach out to her. If you establish rapport with her, she'll see you as a critical resource for the boy perspective. If your inclination is to sum up what your daughter should know about boys in the sentence "All boys want is sex," think again. Even if you believe this is the case, it's going to be very helpful to her if you can discuss her feelings about boys from your vantage point. For example: "I know this may be uncomfortable, but when you start dating (or now that you've started dating), if you want to talk to me to get the male perspective, I'm here anytime to talk." If she has a boyfriend, ask her, "So what do you like about him? What do your friends think?"

Here's a great time to talk about the first crush you had, what you liked about her, and so on. Your daughter needs to be reminded that you were her age once and you may have gone through similar experiences. Feel free to tell her what confused you about girls and how you figured things out. Invite her questions about what a boy might be thinking in certain situations.

> Most of the time there is so much focus on the special relationship that mothers and daughters share that dads kind of get pushed to the sidelines when it comes to their daughters. I know that I'm very fortunate to be as close to my dad as I am, because a lot of my female friends have rather strained relationships with their fathers. Dads play a really important role in their daughters' lives. Girls want their father's approval. There's something really powerful about being "daddy's little girl" and most girls don't want to tarnish that image. At the same time, it's also difficult to talk to fathers because it seems like they don't know what to say and they also seem kind of clueless sometimes. Dads seem to have a really hard time letting go of the image of their "sweet little baby girl" and fear what will happen when

guys start to find their "little girl" attractive, because dads know how guys think and "no one better be having those thoughts about my daughter." It's good to warn daughters that not all guys may have the best intentions, but it's also important to let her know that there are some good guys out there, because your dad can't be the only exception to the rule.

I've noticed that my friends who grew up with their mothers and have really bad relationships with their fathers end up having bad relationships with their boyfriends. It often seems like they date guys who share some character traits that their fathers have, and those are the very same things that cause the relationship to fail.   Ellie, 21

THE FIRST SEX TALK 101

There's no excuse for not talking about sex with your daughter several times throughout her youth. If you don't provide her with accurate information, she'll learn everything about sex from her peers and the media. For example, most of the girls I teach believe that boys can be physically injured from "blue balls" — if they don't have sex after getting an erection, they'll hurt themselves. Therefore, many girls believe they're obligated to have sex or masturbate the boy even if they don't want to.

Don't assume that her school will take care of "the talk." The teacher may not be good or the class curriculum may be restricted. There are parents who believe that talking to children about sex and reading books with sexual content will encourage them to have sex. In my years of teaching, I've never understood this perspective. I believe that denying girls information greatly increases their vulnerability to having irresponsible sex or making bad decisions that can lead to coerced sex. And how can you be sure your daughter understands your values if you don't communicate them directly?

Talking to your daughter about sex can be uncomfortable. But your discomfort doesn't outweigh her safety. You're also not off the hook by having one conversation with her that superficially covers the facts. You should first talk to her before she's a teen about the nuts and bolts. There are wonderful books to supplement the conversation; my personal favorite is *Where Do I Come From?*

Talk to her again in sixth or seventh grade. Review the nuts and bolts, and now incorporate what you think is important about how to make dating decisions. If your daughter has two people raising her, both people should talk to her. If it's really too hard for you to have this conversation with her, ask your ally to do it for you. Review with your ally the facts and values you want your daughter to learn. However, if at all possible, try to undertake this task yourself. You are the rule-makers and caregivers in your daughter's life, and she needs to discuss important things like this with you.

So how do you start the conversation about boys in such a way that you both won't freak? I would suggest starting with some of the following questions:

PARENT: *Boys can be really confusing, especially because they're usually as unsure as girls are and have to pretend in front of their friends. What's most important to me is that you ask yourself questions. Why do you like that person? Do you feel like anyone's pressuring you to like him? How do you want a boy that likes you to treat you? What will that look like? What happens if a boy you like doesn't treat you or others well? How should you treat someone you like? What would stop you from doing that? Think about it and whenever you want to talk, just let me know.*

Don't think you have to ask each question. Too many questions in a single session will overwhelm her. It's better to have a discussion about one topic than to push her to answer each one.

I've listed several good books on the subject in the resources section. If you haven't had any conversations, start now. It's up to you to clarify and communicate your beliefs about sexuality. When your daughter is a young teen, it's especially important to discuss puberty, hormones, changing and conflicting feelings, and the essential need to look for mutual respect in every relationship. As your daughter matures, you'll need to address the nuts and bolts of sexual responsibility. (I know, gulp. I'll talk about this more in the next chapter. You can start breathing again.)

Get over your queasiness. Your girl is growing up with or without you.

DISCUSSING SEXUAL ORIENTATIONS

Any basic discussion on sex should include homosexuality. Your daughter lives in a world where people can be many sexual orientations. Whether or not she's gay, chances are good she'll have family and friends who are. Some of the information presented here may be more appropriate when she's older. Use your judgment, but it's never too young to teach your daughter that all people are worthy of her respect.

Imagine being with a group of people you don't know and you're told to write the most private secret about yourself on a piece of paper. Then you are told that you must fold the paper and give it to someone in the room. That person is told that he or she can't read your paper, but you must turn your back so you can't see what he or she is doing. How does that feel?

That's an exercise we do with students to approximate what it feels like for girls and boys to hide that they're gay.

> I've known all my life but I acclimated and molded myself to be straight without knowing it. I dated a guy in seventh grade for a week but it was awkward and weird. By my sixteenth birthday, I knew. My parents have been good about accepting me, but I know people where there's been huge drama. One girl's mother was a psychologist who always said she would accept anything about her daughter and then when she came out, the mother freaked out.   Gabby, 18

There are gay people in your life. They are your family, friends, and acquaintances. They can also be your children. How should you respond if your daughter is gay or you suspect she is?

Research over decades suggests that sexual behavior, identity, and orientation exist on a spectrum where a minority of people are exclusively homosexual or exclusively heterosexual. Everyone else fits somewhere in the middle. As a result, it's possible that your daughter may struggle with questions about her sexuality. What's important to remember is that no matter if your daughter knows she's lesbian from as long as she can remember or she's questioning, coming out is a process—for both of you.

First, let's get clear on the definitions.

- Sexual orientation is the attraction one feels toward either or both sexes. This is usually defined as gay, lesbian, or bisexual.
- Gender identity is how our culture defines behavior ascribed to one's sex. For example, boys are expected to act masculine (their gender). Most recently "transgendered" has been added to describe people who identify as male when they are biologically female or who identify as female when they are biologically male.
- Sexual behavior describes the sexual activities in which an individual engages. For example, a man's sexual orientation can be gay because he's attracted to other men even though he's married to a woman and only has sex with her.
- Sexual identity is how one perceives oneself and is recognized by others. For example, a girl's sexual orientation is that she's attracted to other women and her sexual identity is that she identifies as a girl.
- Heterosexism is the assumption of heterosexuality unless otherwise advised and an assumption that the heterosexual perspective is universal.
- LGBTQ is the acronym for lesbian, gay, bisexual, transgendered, and questioning.
- A transvestite is a person who wears clothing and other markers for the other gender. A transsexual is a person who feels that he or she was born the wrong sex. A transsexual person is born a man but feels that he's truly a woman or vice versa. Transsexuals can undergo hormone therapy and surgery to become the sex they feel they truly are.

My Daughter's Not Gay, So Why Should I Care?

Seeing sexual identity and gender as fluid, changing, and existing in a spectrum of possibilities challenges the fundamental tenets of our society and culture. Seen in this light, it's clear why some can feel so threatened as homosexuality gains increasing acceptance. Please know, however, that whatever your opinion about homosexuality, there are children in schools across this country who learn to hate themselves and/or live in fear every day because they identify as gay. Homophobia is an essential ingredient for creating an unsafe atmosphere in our communities, because it makes girls prove their heterosexuality in dangerous, unhealthy ways.

Whether a girl is or isn't gay is less important than if and when homophobia is used as a weapon against a girl to put her down and isolate her. (remember shaving legs in the beauty chapter?). The consequence is that girls in this position are pressured to prove their heterosexuality, just as boys are pressured to prove theirs.

> *In eighth grade there was a girl in my clique no one liked. One of the girls spread a rumor that she was a lesbian with another girl in our class. I hate to admit it, but I was mean to her, too. She was forced out and then she started having sex with all these guys. Her parents didn't know what had happened but they knew something was wrong, so they took her out of school and home-schooled her.*
>
> Tonya, 15

Your daughter may have a friend who's gay. Casual comments and/or jokes about her looking too masculine can be devastating and send the message that your home isn't safe. Imagine how much more welcome the world would feel to her if you said something affirming like, "It must be difficult for parents to have gay children because they must worry about their safety. I don't know what it's like to have a gay kid, but I can imagine it must be hard. I wish people didn't feel that they had to keep things like that from friends." Teaching your child to value human dignity is one of the most important lessons you can teach.

I've taught in schools where it's expressly forbidden to discuss homosexuality, except if someone is expressing homophobia. I've also taught in schools where students feel relatively comfortable being "out." I've seen many people express homophobia in two ways: (1) Their religious teachings tell them to love the sinner, but hate the sin. The people who believe this are often convinced that gay people can "switch" their sexual orientation. (2) It's disgusting, but as long as people don't "flaunt" their homosexuality, it's tolerable.

Just as I have asked you to look at the world through your daughter's eyes, I'm asking you now to look at the world through nonheterosexist eyes. The best way I know how to do this is to ask the following questions, variations on those gay people are often asked.

Homophobia Questionnaire*

- What do you think caused your heterosexuality?
- When and how did you decide you were heterosexual?
- Is it possible that your heterosexuality is just a phase you may grow out of?
- Have you disclosed your heterosexual tendencies to anyone? Wouldn't it be more appropriate to keep these feelings to yourself?
- Why do so many heterosexuals seem compelled to seduce others into their heterosexual lifestyle?
- If you've never slept with someone of the same sex, how do you know you wouldn't prefer it? Is it possible that you just need a good gay experience?
- Why are heterosexuals so blatant, always making a spectacle of themselves? Why can't they just be who they are and not flaunt their sexuality by kissing in public and wearing wedding rings?
- Heterosexual marriages have total societal support, yet over half of marriages end in divorce. Why are there so few lasting heterosexual relationships?
- Given the problems heterosexuals face, would you want your child to be heterosexual?
- Why do heterosexuals place so much emphasis on sex?
- A lot of heterosexuals seem to be very unhappy. Would you consider some type of therapy to help you change?
- Most child molesters are heterosexual men. Do you consider it safe to expose your child to heterosexual males? Heterosexual male teachers in particular?

If You Suspect

Some parents have an idea that their daughter is a lesbian. If you do, give her space and subtle support. On your own learn about gay issues and

*Sexual Minority Youth Assistance League, www.smyal.org.

bring them up as a normal part of a conversation. For example, rent the movie *Ma Vie en Rose* to see how a family struggles with a boy who believes he is really a girl. *Get Real* is an excellent British movie about coming out, as is *The Incredible True Story of Two Girls Falling in Love*. To see how powerful homophobia can be, watch *Boys Don't Cry* (but bring tissues). You want to communicate to your daughter that people have the right to be free from violence and that people shouldn't feel shame.

If She Comes Out

Coming out is the term for when a gay person tells her friends and family that she's gay. Coming out is a process. First a girl comes out to herself and then gradually comes out to people she trusts and loves, and then the larger community. And she'll continue to come out throughout her life because she will constantly make decisions about who she'll share this information with. Parents go through their own coming out. Parents can feel shock, denial, and guilt. They can feel that they did something that caused their daughter to be gay. If you feel this way, remember that your daughter is a separate person from you. You might want to consider attending a support group, such as PFLAG. Even if a girl has the most supportive parents in the world, it can be a very frightening to come out.

> *Coming out counters what people assume about you. Being straight is accepted and the norm. Coming out to your parents is going against the grain.* Kirby, 18

Here's how you might consider a conversation if your daughter comes out to you.

YOUR DAUGHTER: *Mom . . . Can I talk to you for a second? I've wanted to tell you something for a long time. I know I've been distant, and part of the reason why I haven't talked to you recently is I've been trying to figure some things out.*

YOU: *OK. What's up?*

YOUR DAUGHTER: *OK, well, I need to tell you something . . . it's really hard. . . .*

YOU: *Whatever it is, if it's important to you, it's important to me.*
YOUR DAUGHTER: *I think I'm gay.*
YOU: *Okay, that's okay. I'm really glad you feel comfortable telling me. You know I love you and accept you for who you are, right? Do you want to talk about it?*

What Else You Can Say

"Is there anything you need from me?"
"I respect your privacy and I respect your decision to tell whomever, whenever you want."
"Whenever you want to talk, I'm here."

If You're Really Struggling

"This is difficult for me, but I love you and I want for us to find a way to share openly. We may not see eye to eye, but I value our relationship and I want to keep talking about it."

> *Don't ask questions you aren't prepared to hear the answers to. My mom asked me and I told her I was gay. She told me she was going to throw up.*   Lynn, 19

Your feelings about homosexuality aren't as important as loving your daughter and contributing to an environment where she's safe and nurtured. In the heated debate about homosexuality, we often forget about the feelings, dignity, and physical safety of the people involved.

As I said in Chapter 6, boys' violence and emotional suppression is intrinsically tied to homophobia. Boys' fear of being called gay stunts their emotional maturity and convinces them to look the other way and/or participate in the degradation of women and girls. Homophobia creates an environment where boys' violence as an expression of masculine control and power is condoned. Whatever you think about homosexuality, you can't condone the violence that accompanies it. According to the Surgeon General's report on sexual health,

- 80 percent of gay men and women report verbal or physical harassment

- 45 percent have been threatened with violence
- 17 percent have experienced a physical attack.* My work with boys and girls confirms this. Girls labeled dykes are tripped, pushed against walls, and thrown down school stairwells.
- 97 percent of students report regularly hearing homophobic remarks by peers
- 53 percent hear homophobic comments by teaching staff
- 26 percent of youth report having to leave home because of their sexual orientation
- 40 percent of gay youth report that their schoolwork is negatively affected
- 28 percent of gay youth drop out of school
- 42 percent of New York City street youth are gay
- Gay youth are twice as likely to be threatened or injured with a weapon at school and three times more likely to require medical treatment as a result[†]

Gay-Straight Student Alliances

Many high schools have student groups for LGBTQ students. They can be called Gay Student Alliances (GSA) or something else that clearly reveals the group's identity, but often students are so shy or afraid about being associated with these groups that they come up with another name entirely. Some adults have accused these groups of being dating services and are worried that these alliances will "promote" homosexuality. Hardly. Why would you want to join a group that is usually marginalized by everyone? These alliances give kids a safe space to feel accepted.

My advice to girls who are questioning their sexuality or know they're lesbian is to chill out and take your time. Don't fake anything with either boys or girls. Listen to your insides. This is your turf, so you get to set the parameters of what you do and don't want to say.

Kirby, 18

*The Surgeon General's Call to Action to Promote Sexual Health and Responsible Sexual Behavior, 2001.
†Gay Lesbian Straight Education Network (GLSEN), www.glsen.org.

When your daughter first comes out, she may be a pain in the butt for a while because it's all she talks about, reads about, and so on. You'll want to talk about a good movie you saw last night and she wants to talk about the latest battle she's waging against the school administration. If you don't talk about it, she'll accuse you of not accepting her. She's setting up hurdles for you to jump over (which look like ultimatums) that prove you accept her. But it's a good thing. She's coming into her own and she's figuring out incredibly important stuff. She's living in a homophobic world, and getting a grip on that is difficult. Give her the space to make coming out her own process.

She may also want to surround herself with gay people and that may freak you out. Appreciate that she's looking for role models so don't feel worried that she's cutting herself off from everyone else.

The first sex talks are understandably nervous-making, even if they don't include homosexuality. Frankly, you probably won't need everything presented in this section until she's a little older. But this is very important regardless of her sexual orientation. Never forget that your daughter wants your love and she wants to be true to herself.

THE GAMES BEGIN: THE BOY-GIRL PARTY

It's happened. Your daughter has just received her first invitation to a boy-girl party. Should you let her go? I would let her go if she wants to. If, however, there's a hint that she doesn't want to go but is feeling pressured to go, always give her that out so she can "blame" you for not letting her. If she does go and she's open about it the next day, try to have a conversation with her about it. But don't start by asking if she had fun. (That's like asking how her day was; it can be overwhelming.) Instead, ask her what she thought about it. Ask if people acted the way she thought they would, or if they acted differently. (If she answers that some of the girls acted like airheads, you have a great opportunity to ask her why she thinks girls act like that. Talk about Fruit Cup Girl; does this ring true for her?)

Now, suppose your daughter is in sixth grade and begs you to allow her to invite boys to her birthday party. She's relentless. Remember why this could be so important to her: Having a boy-girl party is a huge asset in ascending the social pecking order. In sixth and seventh grade these parties can have an amazing amount of drama. Girls will get upset over a boy, someone will make out in your basement, and your daughter will be at the center of it all. What could be better? I guarantee tears and fights culminating in a Messenger going back and forth between two cliques brokering a peace accord.

So why would you volunteer to be the sacrificial lamb/host here? To make sure the party meets standards you can enforce by your presence, and to model your expectations for responsible behavior. If you agree to have the party (or any party for that matter), her school is small enough, and it's financially viable, I strongly encourage you to invite all the kids in the class. Know that if you don't, you're contributing to your daughter's social hierarchy. If your daughter goes to a large public school and it isn't feasible to invite so many people, encourage her to limit the guest list in a defensible way that spares others' feelings because it's not personal ("I'm sorry, my folks said we could only have people from homeroom/drama club/Sunday school/Hebrew school"). Make sure your daughter understands your parameters for invitations and the importance of diplomacy in issuing them, especially if she can't invite everyone. This can be a tough call for girls. They know their stock goes up if they have a boy-girl party, and it's very tempting to broadcast that all over town, which increases the potential for others to feel left out.

LANDMINE!

Forget the swim parties where participants have to wear bathing suits. If you forge ahead, anticipate drama. Someone's bathing suit will come off, girls with big breasts will be teased. It isn't worth it. Go bowling instead.

Before the party, clarify with your daughter where you'll be during the proceedings. Will you stay upstairs with occasional policing forays? Or will you be constantly circulating? Circulating is one way you can mini-

mize drama. It could be tedious, but you could also use this as an opportunity to play anthropologist studying a tribe. See if you can spot the
Queen Bees, Wannabes, Players, and Misunderstood Guys.

Go over your house rules for appropriate behavior and what will happen if kids behave inappropriately. Adopt a zero-tolerance policy for cigarettes, drugs and alcohol, and nasty exclusive behavior. Most important,
make a plan with your daughter for how she can ask for your help if
things get out of hand and she doesn't want to lose face.

Your Role as Parent: The Eternal "Out"

One of the cardinal rules you want to establish with your daughter is that
she can always use you as the "out" and blame you for any rules she may
secretly want enforced but doesn't want to take the rap for in front of her
friends. "I'm sorry, but my folks would kill me if they found any beer
here." "No way, I'll be grounded for a month if you light that up here."
"My parents say absolutely no way is anybody going upstairs to any of the
bedrooms."

This rule isn't just for parties. Make sure your daughter knows she can
always pin it on you if her peers are pressuring her to do something she
doesn't want to do: "Sorry, but my mom doesn't let me go out on week-
days." "Sorry, but Dad would go ballistic if I went to the mall without his
permission." It's a fair deal: You're the fall guy, and she stays safe.

OFF TO THE MALL: RUNNING IN PACKS

It's normal for teens to run in packs. A lot of major boy-girl interactions
will take place at the mall, the movies, the bowling alley, or school func-
tions. It's also normal that once in packs, kids do things they never would
if alone. You can't stop her from running in packs, but you can guide her
about how to behave in the pack.

Check-in time is very important. Make an agreement (and you know I
think it should be written down and each one of you should have a copy)
about when she'll check in with you. Make sure she has access to a cell
phone, pay phone, or pager. If you say she needs to be home at 10:00,
then you have every right to expect her home by then. If not, apply appropriate consequences.

MAKE NEW FRIENDS BUT KEEP THE OLD

In the excitement of girl-meets-boy, it can be easy for your daughter to forget to maintain her friendships with girls and boys. Just as you've reinforced the lesson that it's not okay to blow off one girlfriend when an offer from another girlfriend comes along, make it clear to your daughter that it's not okay to blow off a girl when a boy comes into the picture. As you'll see in the next chapter, this is a crucial lesson. As intimate relationships become more important to girls, they're apt to marginalize the friendships with girls and boys who could support and protect them. Your daughter needs to realize that an intimate relationship isn't better or more important than one with her girlfriends. She needs a variety of relationships to nurture herself.

ONE ON ONE: WHEN IS THE RIGHT TIME?

It's pretty rare that a girl will go on a one-on-one date when she's in sixth or seventh grade. If she wants to be alone with her boyfriend, it will more likely be in the context of her larger group of friends; she'll break off with her boyfriend and the two will be like satellites orbiting the peer planet. If she does get a request for a date, talk to her about it. Does she feel ready? Do you feel she's ready? If not, be prepared to explain why you feel more comfortable with her running with her group of friends.

The Stomach Churner . . . Should You Allow Boys in the Bedroom?

Maybe the rest of the group took off, and it's just your daughter and her latest beau. Or maybe he came over to study. (You remember that one, don't you?) Are you uptight if you forbid your daughter from having boys in her bedroom? Who cares? It doesn't matter, because you're the parent. This is exactly the kind of rule you get to make.

My opinion is that you shouldn't allow your daughter to have boys in her room. It probably won't stop her if she's determined, but make the rule anyway. She may accuse you of not trusting her or thinking she's having sex with every boy she knows. Too bad. There are several reasons to have this rule. First, if you aren't home and she's with a boy she's attracted to, she may feel nervous about "going upstairs" with him. She can blame you—the "eternal out" again—and keep him downstairs. Second, when she says this, it also transfers critical information to him about you: this is a house with rules; your daughter respects your rules and so should he; you're reinforcing your values about personal space (yours and hers); it gives her the feeling that you're watching her, so he'll feel the same paranoia. Remember, respect and fear are good things.

WHEN IT'S OVER: HOW DO YOU MEND A BROKEN HEART?

As mentioned earlier, your daughter might run through several boyfriends, with varying degrees of seriousness, when she's in her early teens. Even if she is dating someone who turns your stomach, you have to support her when she breaks up with him. Encourage her to break up with him respectfully, clearly, and on her own (meaning no Messengers doing her dirty work for her). She can use the same strategies as the ones for friends that I've outlined earlier. She should state how she feels ("When you tease me in front of your friends and won't listen when I ask you to stop, I feel like a piece of dirt"). When there's no reason other than she just wants to move on, she can say, "I just don't feel in sync with you anymore." Then she should state clearly what she wants ("I don't want to date you anymore"). Recall that this is very tough for girls; she may be tempted to be unclear, "I'm not sure we should see each other anymore" or "Maybe it isn't a good idea for us to keep dating," and these fuzzy statements are invitations to dispute or misinterpret. Finally, she should affirm the boy. She doesn't have to say anything cheesy and patronizing (saying "I still want us to be friends" with a condescending tone isn't going to cut it), but she still needs to affirm him. She's communicating that her own needs matter and she can set her boundaries with respect.

When someone breaks your daughter's heart, what can you do to make her feel better? Not a whole lot. Tell her you're there for her and are available to talk anytime, then let her sulk and lick her wounds in her room. Let her cry, and when she does want to talk, just listen; don't rush in with your judgments. Empathize with her feelings even if you don't believe they could be that intense, even if she's only been dating him for two weeks and/or you're relieved the relationship is over. Give her some time. Offer to do something fun with her. If she says no, then wait for a while and ask again.

LANDMINE!

What not to say when your daughter is dumped:

- "You're too young for it to be too serious; you'll get over it."
- "He wasn't good enough for you."
- "I didn't like him anyway."
- "There are other fish in the sea."
- "It's better that you broke up."
- "You'll have a new boyfriend next week."
- "Remember So-and-So? You thought you were so in love with him, too."
- "You'll be over it in no time."
- "I told you so."

I'd be incredibly depressed and I would take it out on my family. They would probably think I was back in some phase or something. Which of course would be really annoying. Chances would be that my mom would know that I was dating him, but she'd probably be happy that I broke up with him. If I thought I was love with him, she would think I wasn't. So then I wouldn't want to go to her. Girls are going to talk to someone else or keep it inside. Nidhi, 16

Support your daughter without tearing the boy down. That way she learns that she doesn't have to put someone else down to take care of herself. Also, if she gets back together with him (which is quite possible), she'll still feel she can go to you without looking weak.

These early boy drama experiences set the stage for your daughter's expectations for and understanding of her personal rights in intimate relationships. As she gets older, these relationships become more mature, and her friendships will become even more important as a safe place to reflect and analyze these new and often confusing experiences. Unfortunately, battles over boys will continue. As her parent, your ability to guide her in these earlier times will be crucial as she takes her first steps into the complexity of intimacy.

Pleasing Boys, Betraying Girls

When Relationships Get More Serious

Rosa, sixteen, has been going out with Greg for two months. She really likes him and feels good about where the relationship is going. They go to a party with a group of their friends. At first, she's having a great time, but then she see Stephanie, Greg's old girlfriend. Not only is Stephanie tall and beautiful, she's with her popular group of friends and she's glaring at Rosa. Then Rosa sees Greg walk over to Stephanie and she's all over him. All of Rosa's friends are watching, waiting to see what Rosa will do. In one moment, Rosa has gone from feeling good about herself and confident about her relationship with Greg to feeling insecure and vulnerable. Sean, a friend of Greg and Rosa's, comes up behind Rosa and whispers, "Looks like you've got competition tonight!"

Now that Rosa's a quivering mess of anxiety and insecurity, what will she do? Will she drink—or frink more? Will she push herself to please Greg and solidify her position in the clique, or risk losing him? Will she get into a verbal or physical confrontation with Stephanie? Many girls in Rosa's position do all of the above.

No matter how many times you listened to "Free to Be You and Me" when you were a teen, understand that your daughter still lives in a culture where boyfriends are crucial validation for three interrelated reasons: they increase her sense of self-worth; her friends will hold her in higher esteem; and a boyfriend is proof that she fits into teen culture.

This chapter will discuss how the dynamics of relationships with boys change as girls get older. It will look at how the girls' social hierarchy increasingly traps girls in a cycle of craving boys' validation, pleasing boys to obtain that validation, and betraying the friends who truly support them. Girls' fights over boys are only one of the consequences of girls' social hierarchies. If your daughter was Rosa, how can you help her think through this situation? How can you guide and support her as she weathers the ups and downs of intimate relationships? How can you teach her to communicate more effectively so she can stand by the boundaries she's set for herself? How can you channel your own concerns and fears as she develops these relationships so she'll listen to you instead of tuning out? How will you know when she's in an abusive relationship, and how can you get her the help she needs? These are the questions that this chapter will answer.

WHAT YOU MUST KNOW

- Getting validation from boys boosts a girl's self-confidence and confirms that she's in the "Act Like a Woman" box.
- Girls understand that their social status and identity are tied to relationships with boys.
- Even when she knows better, she may sacrifice her personal boundaries to please a boy.
- In trying to please a boy, she may betray and sacrifice her friendships with girls.
- At some point, most girls will lie, connive, or backstab to get the boy they want.
- Your daughter may lie and sneak behind your back to be with her boyfriend, especially if you don't like him and/or forbid her to see him.
- Girls, just like everyone else, have trouble defining the difference between acceptable flirting and sexual harassment.
- Denial is a totally reasonable response to your daughter's developing sexuality. For her welfare, get over it.
- Your daughter can become trapped in an abusive relationship even if she's confident and self-assured.

We see sex everywhere and we wonder what it's like.   Kendra, 16

For most teenage girls, guys are everything. Boys validate their exis-
tence; they define who they are and where they stand in the world.
You can talk to boys differently than your girlfriends. Until they screw
you over, they can be really fun and comforting.   Ling, 17

DATING, HOOKING UP, AND GOING OUT

In the last chapter we looked at the manifestations of love among younger
girls. As girls get older, their relationships with boys become more serious.
Do boys and girls still date? Does it count as a date when people go out
in a big group of friends? First, let's define some terms. As you'll see from
the comment below, girls play fast and loose with them. (Ask your daughter for her own definitions, so you can be sure you're talking about the
same thing.) "Dating" means going out in the evening one on one.
"Hooking up" means getting together casually, with no strings attached,
on a given occasion. However, hooking up also refers to a spectrum of
behavior, from hanging out to making out to having sex. "Going out"
refers to a more long-term relationship. As I discussed in the last chapter,
when girls first become interested in boys, they're more likely to date and
group date; hooking up and going out become more popular options as
girls get older.

Group dating is the best. It makes dating a whole gray area. Group
dates are safer because you don't have to be alone with the person
and if you decide you don't like him, you can ignore him.
          Aliesha, 16

Girls travel in packs and boys know this. If you're out one on one, like
it's just him and just you, then he wants to mess with you. Maybe he's
a senior and you're a freshman and he asks just you to dinner with
just him, then he wants to mess with you. I have a friend who did that.
She was totally pressed for him and he asked her out to dinner and a
movie. At first it was nice, he didn't skimp out on her, like he got her
chicken, not a side salad. But once they got to the movie and on the

drive home, he tried to get with her the whole night and she was
totally freaking out. Another girl in my group was asked out by a guy
that we hang with all the time. He didn't even take her out. He wanted
to be alone with her to get some.   Ariel, 16

The quality of your daughter's experiences with boyfriends and her perception of her choices within those relationships are based on four things:
(1) what you and other adults she's close to have role-modeled, (2) what
she gleans from the media, (3) her past and current friendships with girls,
and (4) her role in the clique.

Being in a clique is an easy way to meet boys. Whichever clique she
belongs to, there's a boy group that goes with them. If she strays out-
side of the accepted group of guys, then that's a problem.
                                                            Portia, 18

There's often a boys' group that's linked to the girls' clique, and the girls
may date those boys. Relationships usually don't develop by going on
one-on-one dates, but rather when both cliques hang out together. By the
end of high school, it's common for boys and girls within a large group to
have hooked up with almost everyone in the group. This doesn't mean
they're having sex with each other, but sexual interaction is often a
vibrant part of the group dynamic. Although your daughter may not realize it, dating boys within the group is another way to reaffirm her place
within her own clique.

Dating outside of the teen pecking order can be very difficult. If a girl
dates someone who has higher social status, then she can move up the
social totem pole, but it won't be easy. Like so many teen movie plots,
ugly things happen.

If she's in a lower social status, and she dates someone higher than
she is, then other girls who are higher will be nicer to her (than when
she was low), but they'll make sure that she feels unwelcome in little
ways. They'll look down at her. They'll make side jokes that make her
feel out of the group or have inside jokes about her.   Nia, 16

The senior girls don't like freshmen hooking up with "their" [senior] guys. The girls of higher social status feel like this girl who isn't as cool or pretty as they are takes "their" guys. They feel threatened. If they're close to the guy, the girls make comments to the guy when the girl isn't around or they'll try to hook up with the guy not because they like him, but because they want to get the "lowly" girl away from him.   Ella, 18

Two years ago there was a seventh grader going out with a popular eighth-grade guy. Some of my classmates were good friends with this guy. One of the girls had a crush on him and was saying that it was so stupid that he would ask a seventh grader out. But even more, she was saying that the seventh grader was a slut for going out with an eighth grader and that she was ugly, fat, and looked like a duck. But then, a couple days later, I saw the same girl talking to the seventh grader about how cool it was that she was going out him. It was so hypocritical. She talked behind her back and degraded her, but when she was with the seventh grader, she was all nice and fake.   Remy, 15

The girls' social hierarchy can dictate how much flexibility a girl has in her choice of dates. To a certain extent, a powerful Queen Bee has dating immunity; she can date whomever she wants because the guy she anoints as her current love interest automatically becomes cool. But at the same time, she'll be careful to be interested in someone who has some of the "Act Like a Man" box qualities because she has her image to protect.

It's gossip central [if a Queen Bee dates outside the box]. People will joke and say, "Is he paying her?" Or they'll ask her "What are you doing?" They won't be supportive of it until she breaks up with him.   Dawn, 15

Girls learn that one of the fundamental criteria for group acceptance is dating someone who has the group's approval. There's powerful pressure for a girl to discount her feelings and her own personal standards for whom she wants to date, either giving up someone she cares for and who treats her well or staying together with someone who superficially looks the part even if he doesn't treat her well.

SECURITY BLANKETS

There are always a few couples who date exclusively throughout high school. Parents and teachers think they're cute, and other students refer to them as married. But often, one of the two eventually wants to hook up with other people but is unwilling to let go of the security blanket that the old relationship has become. If the boy wants to play the field ("I really think we should see other people, but I still want to see you, too") and the girl doesn't want to let go, she may feel that she has to go along with what he wants. She'll put up with his being nonexclusive in the hopes that he'll come back, because it's better to have something than nothing. She'll say she doesn't need or want monogamy when she really does. She doesn't communicate what she really wants and hopes for the best.

The result is that they're still a couple but they aren't technically going out. They can use this technicality to treat each other like dirt. They can still have casual sex with each other, but it will be casual to one and not to the other. The girl in this situation is in a terrible bind. She's upset about the status of the relationship, but knows that she has no "right" to complain. If she does, her "agreement" will be thrown back in her face ("You said it was okay if we saw other people"), her feelings will be dismissed, and she'll have no one to blame but herself. The only thing she can do is create dramatic situations where she either drinks too much, does a lot of drugs, or does something reckless so he can come to her rescue. And he will, because he does still care for her and her request fits in the "Act Like a Man" box. He feels special because he's the only one she wants to rescue or soothe her. The end result of these dramatic moments are long (I'm talking hours) tear-filled conversations, often at a party where the happy couple locks themselves in a room to discuss their relationship problems.

MATCHMAKING AND THE OLDER CLIQUE

By fifteen, most girls have one or two very close friendships—the kind people develop when they go through boot camp together. But most also continue to have the kind of friendships with other girls that are an extended, although more sophisticated, version of their friendships in junior high.

It's hard to convince older girls that their individual behavior is still affected by cliques. They believe that after eighth grade, the clique no longer has the same impact. It's still there; it's just more sophisticated and flies under their radar. Matchmaking in late middle school and high school is a place where girls still feel it. Older Queen Bees now focus their attention on boys as the final arbiter for measuring their power among girls.

> *A Queen Bee doesn't often act as the matchmaker because she believes that the more guys she knows, the higher status she has. If she sets up her friend, the Queen Bee is afraid that the boy will like her friend better than her, decreasing her popularity.*   Remy, 15

> *The summer before my sophomore year, my best friend set me up with her boyfriend's best friend. I felt obligated to go out with him but I didn't like him. He was extremely sexually aggressive, and he really scared me. Alyson said it was "cute" to have two guys who were best friends go out with two girls who were best friends. I would consider Alyson a Queen Bee and I would be the Pleaser. When I told her what the other guy was doing, she said that I was being a prude, so I just shut my mouth and kept going out with him. I was miserable. Finally, I talked to her boyfriend about it. He understood and apologized for setting us up. He helped me break up with my gross boyfriend. It's really hard to be the girl being set up. I said no numerous times, but she kept pushing!*   Ella, 18

Here you can see the direct connection between girls' friendships and girls' unhealthy experiences with boys. Ella, in spite of being miserable, dated and couldn't break up with a boy she was frightened of because she wouldn't risk going against her friend. She was more afraid of displeasing the Queen Bee than being with a scary boy. People often link girls' vulnerability to sexual violence to their difficulty standing up for themselves with the boy. Yet one of the reasons Ella found herself with this sexually aggressive boy is that she was unable to hold her own with a girlfriend. Think of the power of that fear.

WHEN BOYS ARE THE BETTER OFFER

In previous chapters I discussed how girls often jockey for position within their cliques by blowing off friends for a better offer—a better party, a chance to see the new hot movie, or something similar. As girls get older, more and more the "better offer" involves boys. A girl makes plans to hang with her friends at someone's house, then "he" calls, and all bets are off. Because the Girl World values boyfriends over almost everything else, a girl is allowed to blow off girlfriends for a guy. Girls don't like it. They'll complain and talk behind the back of the friend who blew them off, but girls will almost always take her back.

> We all do it to each other. It's understandable. It's part of the code. If she ditches us, then we talk behind her back and say she has no self-esteem and how lame she is, but we'll take her back. Sometimes it gets out of control [with the boy] and we never see her anymore.
>
> Melanie, 14

> We have to forgive each other if we hope to be taken back.
>
> Ellie, 21

Ironically, girls blow each other off for similar reasons that girls blow off their parents—it's safe. A girl knows her parents won't reject her if she decides to go out with her friends instead of staying home and playing Scrabble with them. Likewise, her friends won't reject her because she's choosing a boy over them (although they might grumble a bit). It's the rare girl who will stand up and tell a girlfriend how hurt she is that she was dumped for a boy. There's a point in most friendships where the girl being blown off won't take it anymore, and it can cause huge fights between close friends. This dynamic sends girls the message that their friendships don't count as much as romantic relationships. It teaches them to discount themselves and to value themselves as less than males.

Boyfriend Stealing

By high school, girls' friendships are often made or broken over boys, and the effect on the support girls can expect from one another can be chilling. Some girls become so mistrustful of other girls that they shrink down their circle of friends, confiding in only one close friend, or deciding that only their diary is trustworthy. Getting together with another girl's boyfriend is one of the most common conflicts between girls and is often the reason why girls' conflicts escalate to physical confrontations.

When a girl betrays another girl by hooking up with her boyfriend, she has violated a sacred bond between girls. No matter who in the new couple took the initiative, rarely do girls blame the boy as much as the girl, if they blame him at all.

> *Girls will excuse his behavior by saying that the girl was all over him, she was being a slut and what was he supposed to do.* Amanda, 17

Many girls are conditioned to believe that boys are less capable of fidelity, so they don't hold them to the same standard they would a friend. Since girls' friendships are still often more intimate than the sexual relationships they are having with a boy, the feeling of betrayal often runs correspondingly deeper. Girls excuse boys' behavior. They don't excuse girls' behavior. This double standard of not holding the boy accountable has repercussions in other aspects of intimate relationships, as we'll see shortly.

Two things happen when girls can't trust each other. First, they turn away from each other and look to boys for more gratifying relationships. Second, they become much more vulnerable to sexual violence. The more girls watch out for each other, the less likely they'll be date raped, assaulted, or trapped in an abusive relationship. Take away that support, and girls lose a vital layer of protection.

Many girls I teach believe that boys are dogs, but girls are the enemy. It's this belief that makes girls turn the other way when they see a girl so drunk she can barely stand get taken to a room to have sex with a guy she met a few hours ago. It makes them blame a girl for "being so stupid and weak" when she's abused by her boyfriend. It makes them look at each other with cold, hard eyes, sizing each other up as competition and blaming anyone who makes a mistake.

Of course, not all cliques or friendships turn toxic over boys. One of the lessons I try to teach girls in Empower is the importance of standing by each other.

> *I had a friend whose boyfriend treated her really badly. After they broke up, her group of friends united against him to show him they were mad. Since he wanted to remain favorable with them, he started being nicer to her.*
>
> Joanna, 17

> *I have about five close girl and guy friends who have stood by me during this long process of trying to break free from my ex- and now-again "boyfriend" (this word would entail responsibilities, none of which he possesses, so I have trouble referring to him as such). Rather than tell me I'm stupid and weak and shouldn't care so much, they have tried their best to understand that the relationship is hard to break free of because he was my first everything. No matter how much pain he causes me, my friends understand that he has played an important role in my life and understand why it's a long and winding road. This, to me, is major support and tolerance.*
>
> Brooke, 18

RELATIONSHIPS ON ANY TERMS: PLEASE PLEASE LIKE ME

> *I hooked up with someone who told me from the beginning that he was not interested in monogamy. I said it was fine because I thought I could be happy with what I could get, but I wasn't. When he hooked up with friends of mine, I'd get so jealous and so angry, but I couldn't tell him why. It ruined our friendships because I couldn't be honest.*
>
> Zoe, 17

Think about the many dynamics intersecting when girls begin to be more interested in boys. They want true love the way they see it in the movies. They want boyfriends to show off to their friends and to increase their social status. They want to explore the excitement and drama of romance. They want to feel grown up. In the course of achieving these goals, they learn that you can get away with blowing off your friends for a date with a boy, that you can't always trust a friend not to take your man, and that ultimately the more valuable relationship is with a guy. Their focus shifts from pleasing their friends to pleasing boys. Pleasing boys controls what girls say and their perception of their power within a relationship. The desire to please affects the way they date, how they communicate what they want or don't with a boyfriend, even the way they dump a guy. Girls are looking for an insurance policy against their own insecurity. When Girl World is set up to riddle your daughter with insecurity, she'll seek validation from a boy and can become desperate to please him.

DIRTY LOOKS AND BAD VIBES: COMMUNICATING WITH BOYS

Of course, it's harder to please a boy if you can't figure out how to talk to him. Communication moves to a whole new level when girls have to figure out whether boys are being nice because they genuinely like them, or flattering them because they're physically attracted to them. By the time they're ready to date, girls have had years to hone the fake compliment. Girl World compels girls to compliment each other, so girls realize how hollow words can be. Picture yourself in the fitting room at a clothing store; the saleswoman tells you with a fake smile how great you look in a skirt that obviously makes you resemble a large bran muffin. You know she's lying, but there's some small part of you that wants to believe her. When a boy compliments a girl, it's the same thing. She wants to believe him, even if her gut tells her that there's an ulterior motive. She'll feel grateful and then obligated to him.

> *Although she realizes he's only voicing his opinion to get some action, it's still probably his honest opinion. His opinion is more honest than a girl's would be, anyway.* —Nidhi, 16

> *Girls always have to compliment each other, so I never believe them. If a guy tells me I look good, I can believe it. But at the same time, when boys compliment me I always get suspicious because they must want something.* —Rosa, 17

Your insecurity kicks in. At some point the fact that the guy wants something sexual doesn't matter because getting the validation is more important. Zoe, 17

As Deborah Tannen so eloquently put it in *You Just Don't Understand,* males and females often seem as if they're speaking different languages. Many girls initially capitulate to boys and agree to things when they may not want to; later it makes them angry with themselves and resentful toward the person and situation. They start to smolder and simmer, waiting for the boys to understand and reach out to them. Of course, boys rarely do this, because they've been trained to dismiss what is stereotyped as overemotional behavior or because they're clueless about what girls want.

Girls tell me how confused they are in these communications. Many feel they have to cater to boys, so they let them speak first and set the agenda. They want to suss out what boys are thinking before they say what they want. They think the boys should be smart enough to recognize they're doing this and anticipate their needs. But then they get pissed off when the boys don't get it. When the pleasing thing gets old and the girls want to rebel, they may not know who to rebel against, or how.

Boys are most frustrated that girls don't tell them what they're thinking. Girls make guys guess and then get angry with them if they don't guess right. They wait for guys to figure out what's going on with them. Some girls will put up an upset front and won't directly say it to you. Guys will get anxious and worried and then yell and then that will give her reason to yell back. Girls say there's nothing wrong. Guys don't know what's going on. Sometimes I think it's all about dirty looks and bad vibes. Jake, 16

Many of us feel that our negative emotions aren't as worthy as guys'. This is certainly true for me and it's aggravating. When I finally tell my boyfriend how I feel, I immediately apologize. So we [girls] end up saying yes when we really mean no. I think a lot of girls also feel like they need to keep up this mystique—it's in everything we do. We cover ourselves in makeup, we wear clothing just short of being completely revealing. Most of us (including myself) never let down that

barrier when it comes to our emotions. We don't say "It hurts me when . . ." Or "I feel like . . ." We just aren't speaking up and very few boys listen when we do.
Anna, 16

You're either supposed to know everything about everything or be an innocent little angel. There's no in between. I'm confused a lot.
Katiah, 16

Communication is another place where the expectations girls bring from their intimate relationships with girls inform their relationships with boys. Girls define a great relationship as one in which the other person knows what you're thinking and you can finish each other's sentences; you're totally in sync with each other. This is essential to girls' closest friendships. They think they're going to get it with the boys they like, and when they don't, they feel betrayed. They want to be understood without having to explain everything.

Isn't it easier to hope someone will guess how you're feeling than gathering your thoughts in your mind and bringing it up? Even now I watch my mom do the same things with my dad.
Jordan, 18

LET ME MAKE MYSELF PERFECTLY UNCLEAR

I wanted to break up with this guy and I just couldn't. It was so hard! I sat down with him and gave him a million excuses why I couldn't go out with him anymore. "I'm having a lot of personal problems right now, I just can't handle it right now." The more he questioned me, the more excuses I made up.
Ella, 18

All this miscommunication is the stuff of romantic comedies and the subject of best-sellers. Part of the joy of a girl's first more serious relationship is figuring out how to get on the same page as the boy. And it does happen. But the process is hampered by a girl's ingrained need to please and be "nice." Even when girls are trying to break up with a boy, they would rather blame themselves than tell the boy what bothered them. Pleasing boys has a lot of code words and phrases, for example: "I didn't want to hurt his feelings," "I didn't want to be rude," "I didn't want to assume what he was thinking," and "I didn't want to tell him what I wanted because I didn't want him to not like me." The result is often a seriously mixed message, and it's more of a problem in relationships among older teens because the stakes are so much higher.

A sixteen-year-old girl recently asked my advice about how to tell a boy she wasn't interested in dating him. Part of her liked him and part of her didn't, but she was fairly sure she didn't want to be his girlfriend. On the phone, she had told him that she couldn't date him because her parents wouldn't approve, and because she had to get to know him better. But because she felt obliged to explain this to him in more depth, she made plans to have dinner with him alone—something her traditional parents wouldn't have approved of, so she lied to them about what she was doing that night. She told me she believed that she had clearly communicated to this boy that she wasn't interested in being his girlfriend. I really don't think so. First, instead of explaining her own feelings, she blamed the lack of relationship on her parents. When the boy heard this, he could reasonably assume, "If we get rid of this obstacle, then we're back on." When she said, "I can't date you until I get to know you better," what did the boy think when she made plans to go out to dinner with him? That she wanted to get to know him better. What she said and what he heard were totally different. Now imagine your daughter is having this conversation secretly with a boy in her bedroom.

FLIRTING VERSUS SEXUAL HARASSMENT

Flirting is a time-honored ritual. It's how teens test their fledgling romantic social skills, and it can be a lot of fun. It can also be another haven for miscommunication. Hardly anything about teens is subtle, and flirting is no exception. Walk down any school hallway and you'll probably be disconcerted by the way teens overtly display their bodies, talk to each other in sexually explicit ways, and constantly touch each other. It's a huge part of teen culture, but that doesn't mean that all teens like it.

This is the environment where sexual harassment occurs. And when does flirting cross that line? Flirting makes both people feel good, and sexual harassment makes the recipient feel small, uncomfortable, power-less, and/or intimidated. The law defines two types of sexual harassment:

1. The quid pro quo—"I'll give you an A if you have sex with me."
2. The creation of a hostile environment—an environment that nega-tively affects your ability to work, be a student, and so on. You have the right to be free of sexual harassment in school so you can concentrate on your work and activities. A hostile environment can refer to the drawings and graffiti in locker rooms or bathrooms that describe a particular girl as being expert on giving oral sex. This girl doesn't need to see the graffiti to be sex-ually harassed by it because boys will interact with her differently because of it. If someone says or does anything that makes it difficult for her to con-centrate on her school responsibilities, that can be sexual harassment.

When I give presentations on sexual harassment at high schools, I ask the students to give me examples of sexual harassment separated into cate-gories of verbal and written, visual, and physical examples. These are their responses:

Verbal/Written	Visual	Physical
Sexually explicit notes	Hand gestures	Pinching
Cat calls	Licking lips	Grabbing
Showing lewd pictures	Staring at body parts	Hugging/kissing
Calling someone bitch or ho	Flashing	Blocking a path
"Can I get some of that?"	Grabbing crotch	Rubbing
		Grinding (when boys grind their bodies against girls at dances)

Then I ask the students if everything on the list is always sexual harass-ment. The answer is always no, but it never fails to spark a heated argu-ment. The key to understanding why sexual harassment is so confusing is appreciating that it's defined differently by different people, and that only the target of the harassment has the right to define it as harassment. There are several criteria that determine whether the action in question is considered sexual harassment: what relation the person doing the action has to the target; how comfortable or uncomfortable the target feels; the boundaries and personal space of those involved; and the threshold for harassment. If the target is attracted to the other person, she might have a higher threshold for what she considers sexual harassment.

Girls and boys each have distinct and different reasons why it's often hard to tell a harasser to stop. The following are two stories that may shed some light on these difficulties.

Girls Are Silent Because . . .

Jim, Craig, and Jess are friends who have a history class together. One day during class Jim convinces Craig to write a note to Jess that details the various ways they want to have sex with her. Jim encourages Craig to give Jess the note after class. When Craig hands it to her, he realizes that she's upset by the look on her face as she reads it, but she doesn't say anything. Craig immediately realizes how stupid it was to give the note to her and just hopes she'll blow it off. However, when she leaves the classroom she tells her friends. She didn't realize that boys she considered friends would think about her like that. With the encouragement of her friends, she tells the principal, who then suspends both boys. The boys are infuriated. If Jess is as upset as she claims, why didn't she say anything to them when she first got the note? Why did she go to the principal first instead of telling them?

Why didn't Jess tell the two boys off? First, she was so flustered—guy friends of hers think *that* way about her?—that she couldn't think of anything to say, much less the perfect comeback. Second, these boys didn't pick her by chance. They picked someone they liked but weren't intimidated by. Jess is a quiet pleaser. It would be hard for her to stand up to them. Jess is programmed to be polite; she doesn't want to make a big deal out of it. What if people think she's uptight, frigid, or a bitch? She's confused about the boys' motivations—maybe they meant it as a joke, or even a weird kind of compliment?—and her own reactions—maybe it's good that someone thinks you're sexy, even if the note makes you feel dirty? Insecure to begin with, Jess says nothing to them to their face. Only when she has the support of her clique does she feel she can take any kind of action.

Time and time again, I teach young women who seem self-assured but when confronted with sexual harassment become paralyzed. When we talk about it, it's clear that in addition to feelings of confusion, they also feel physically threatened. Why? If a guy says something obnoxious, stares at your chest instead of your face, or calls out to you as you walk down the street, he isn't threatening you. Or is he? I would argue that he is, or at the least is asserting his right to do so, and down deep, girls know it.

No matter how much equality women have achieved in our society, most girls believe that in a physical confrontation with a man, a woman will lose, and they'll be safer if they can depend on men for their physical protection, especially men they're close to. If they take self-defense courses, the enemy they're trained to defend themselves against is inevitably male and too often a stranger. But the statistics have always reflected that the person who will hurt them is more likely a man they know. Seen in this light, sexual harassment, especially by "known" people, makes women doubt themselves, and it's a powerful reminder and enforcer that men (even men you're close to) can take away women's safety whenever they want. Every whistle as a girl walks down the street, every cartoon on a boys' bathroom stall reminds girls that men ultimately have power over them. Even though statistically boys are more likely to be the victim of an assault, girls are raised in a world that tells them they must always fear for their physical safety. Even if Jess isn't consciously thinking that Jim and Craig would ever hurt her physically, it's one of the factors that makes her feel intimidated.

As you'll soon see, boys and men can be and are sexually harassed, but more often the harassment is contained to a single event or situation. It doesn't usually bring up the dread of "where is this going to end?" that it so easily does for women.

Boys Are Silent Because . . .

I was teaching a coed class on sexual harassment with junior and seniors. The girls had just explained how violated they felt when they walked down the hallway and boys tried to put their hands up their shirts. When I asked if there were any boys who had been sexually harassed, a handsome guy raised his hand. He was on the track team and when he was practicing, girls would call out suggestive things to him as he ran by or slap his butt. He didn't like it.

The same girls who'd complained of harassment moments earlier now screamed with laughter. This is the double standard boys are up against. Some girls and boys don't believe that boys can be sexually harassed because they "always want to have sex with anyone at anytime." If a boy complains, he's called gay.

> I can't be sexually harassed because I like it.   Luis, 16

It comes down to this: Boys can never say they don't want sexual attention for fear of being called gay and girls worry that if they say they don't want sexual attention, they'll be called frigid or a bitch.

Let's go back to the school auditorium. Examples of sexual harassment are written on the flip charts, and I think the students are getting it when a boy stands up and challenges me. "What about people's first amendment rights? Don't people have the right to say what they want? If they want to talk about a girl in the boys' locker room, that's their right and how does that hurt the girl?" I pressed him, "Why would you want to have the right to say something that would make someone else feel bad? Why is it so important that you have that right? And do you think people will like you for exercising this right?" He answered with, "You're trying to control the things we say. You can't do that." I said, "You're right. I have no control over what you say, but don't you want people in your community, including yourself, to be able to walk down the school hall and not be preoccupied with what someone is going to say to you?" A teen girl gave a very eloquent summary of how that locker room chat does indeed violate a girl's rights:

> *The first amendment gives you your personal rights as long as, in practicing them, you don't take away someone else's. A guy should have the sense of responsibility enough to know that talking to a bunch of random guys about a girl will have repercussions on that*

girl, and those repercussions will violate her rights of expecting
safety and comfortable surroundings in a school environment. He will
indirectly take away her sense of safety and security in an environ-
ment where she should be concentrating on studying. However, it's
not that indirect because he knows that she will get a disrespectful or
some type of sexually harassing response from the guys in the locker
room based on what he tells them.   Nidhi, 16

Most sexual harassers don't realize the impact of their behavior. There
are also people who do realize and don't care, or are intentionally using
sexual harassment as a way to intimidate. How can your daughter tell the
difference?

- An unaware perpetrator doesn't realize the consequences of his or
  her actions, but will stop if told in an effective manner.
- An insensitive perpetrator harasses to impress his peer group and
  can dismiss girls' feelings by laughing or making stereotypical comments, for example, "You are so emotional. You are so uptight."
- An intimidating perpetrator most likely intimidates boys as well
  through verbal and/or physical bullying, can be very charming with
  excellent social skills, and is usually intelligent. He'll usually harass
  when he is alone with the target.

Some people think sexual harassment is totally blown out of proportion
by the media and a few overzealous school administrators and teachers.
We've all read about the five-year-old boy suspended for kissing a girl in
his class. Forget about the extreme cases. The goal, as I say to students, is
to have a school environment where people feel safe and comfortable. If
there are students who feel uncomfortable because other people are
doing something in a sexual manner that they don't like, shouldn't we
want to address the problem? We all have to be honest. Girls and boys
both act inappropriately with each other all the time—usually because
they're trying to figure out what is appropriate. Girls rub up against boys
as they're pushing them away and saying "Get off of me!" and they mean
both. Boys are often deaf, blind, and dumb when girls send clear but non-
verbal messages like tensing and pulling away when they're hugged or

running away when someone asks if they can be their boyfriend. While it would be better if all girls could tell a boy directly when they don't like his behavior, it doesn't help the problem when we blame the girl for not speaking up or accusing the boy of being insensitive.

Instead, our goal should be to create a way for girls and boys to live together in a civilized, respectful way. The challenge is to educate girls and boys about the obstacles they face that make listening to each other so difficult. They have to know how the "Act Like a Woman" and "Act Like a Man" boxes guide their behavior and take responsibility when they behave in confusing, threatening ways.

HAVING SEX

Okay. Let's just dive in and talk about sex and your daughter. Scared? Grossed out? Flipping out? Resigned? Whatever your feelings, you need a lot of information so you can handle what your daughter is up against. And like anything else, the less you know, the more frightened you'll be. Get educated; you'll be more likely to make sound decisions.

In some ways, it may not be as bad as you think. In some ways, it'll be worse.

- Most young teens haven't had intercourse: eight in ten girls and seven in ten boys are sexually inexperienced by age fifteen.
- Most boys and girls begin having sex in their mid- to late teens. More than 50 percent of seventeen-year-olds have had intercourse.
- Every year, three million teens—about one in four sexually experienced teens—acquire a sexually transmitted disease (STD).
- A sexually active teenager who doesn't use contraception has a 90 percent chance of becoming pregnant within one year.
- Teenage girls' contraceptive use at first intercourse rose from 48 to 65 percent during the 1980s. By 1995, use at first intercourse reached 78 percent, with two thirds of it condom use.
- The overall U.S. teen pregnancy rate (still higher than in other developed countries) decreased 17 percent from 1990 to 1996. While 20 percent of this decline is attributed to decreased sexual

activity, 80 percent is attributed to more effective contraception practices.*

- Of girls who become pregnant, many feel that pregnancy will solve their problems. Instead, over 70 percent of pregnant and parenting teens are beaten by their boyfriends.†

- One in four girls have been sexually abused, physically abused, and/or abused by a date or a boyfriend.‡

Losing Her Virginity

When I was a teen, losing your virginity meant vaginal intercourse. Not now. Girls define it in a lot of confusing ways. The one thing that has stayed the same is that no matter how girls define "losing it," it's a big deal and the ultimate rite of passage that leaves childhood behind.

To be honest, girls sometimes lose me in their definition of virginity:

> *To me, it's a very big deal. Actually, wait. I take that back. It depends on (to paraphrase Mr. Clinton) how one defines "losing one's virginity." Because if you say that and you mean actually penetration, then, yes, it is a big deal to me and to most girls I know. That kind of crosses the line between "messing around" and risking pregnancy, STDs, etcetera. But if losing one's virginity is just having "sexual relations," then I think it becomes a little less important. Maybe. It depends on the girl, the situation, any number of things. For some girls, giving a boy a blow job at a party deems her a whore, despite the lack of any penetration. But if she were to, say, give her boyfriend—someone she'd been seeing for a week or more—a blow job, it may not be such a big deal. She's still a virgin. So it really depends. Girls who go around blowing every guy in class would not under any circumstances be referred to as "virgins." But even that sort of promiscuity is miles away from actual "sex." Basically, no matter who you are or who the boy is, if you are penetrated, you are no longer a virgin. Because now you have made yourself vulnerable to*

---

*Alan Guttmacher Institute: Teen Sex and Pregnancy 1999, see www.AlanGuttmacher.org.
†U.S. Health and Human Services report on Violence Against Women 1997.
‡Commonwealth Fund Report on Girls Health 1997, see www.commonwealthfund.org.

other risks (despite the fact that you can get many STDs without pen-
etration).

So, a girl who's pregnant isn't a virgin; a girl who has done every-
thing with all her boyfriends short of penetration may or may not still
be a "virgin." But don't ask me to define what makes a boy a virgin.
Girls fall victim to public opinion—everyone but us gets to decide our
sexual identity. Boys, on the other hand, get to define for themselves
what being a virgin is. Arrrgh!   Anna, 16

Here comes pleasing and trying to keep up, again—trying to keep up with
your sexually active friends; trying to keep up with your boyfriend, who
wants to have sex; trying to keep up with a society that pushes girls to be
mature and sophisticated even as it wags a finger at them for being slutty.

It's weird when you have a friend who has had sex and you haven't.
Definitely very weird. They have entered a whole new realm of being.
They're like light years away from any sort of sexual experience I
might have had.   Ilana, 16

Girls I know have sex to feel popular, so a lot of times it's at a party
with the hottest guy there. Guys know exactly what to say to the girls
to get exactly what they want. It's almost like they are predators and
know every girl's weakness, and when no one is looking . . . they
attack. At school, they may even deny any kind of association with
the girls depending on who they are, their social status, looks,
etcetera, and of course, what the boys' friends' opinions/reactions
are when they hear the "rumors." If a girl wanted him because of his
status and looks [and had sex with him], she'll tell everyone and will
be in shock when he denies it. Sometimes [she has sex] with a
boyfriend because the girl fears that the guy will "move to greener
pastures" if he doesn't get what "he deserves" or what "he needs."
The girl doesn't realize that even if she has sex with him, this type of
guy will still leave her eventually. She will just be prolonging the
detrimental relationship and causing herself more suffering, shock,
and pain.   Jane, 16

Just as younger girls can push each other to take the plunge and call that boy on the phone, older girls can encourage one of their friends to be the test case for sex. Or a more "experienced" girl can push other girls so she won't be the only nonvirgin. Of course, all girls aren't explicitly pressuring each other to have sex. If there's a clique and one of the girls isn't having sex and the rest are, it's not like the girls are going to tell her she's a loser for not having sex. Older girls are too sophisticated for that, and they know having sex has a lot of risks. But the girl who isn't having sex may still feel the pressure. Where does that pressure come from?

> There's a lot of kinship between girls who have had sex. It's another thing to bond with each other because you can tell each what you like and don't like. If there's a girl in the group who isn't sexually experienced, then you wouldn't feel comfortable sharing that kind of stuff with her.   Monica, 17

> Most girls are more supportive of each other than [to pressure someone to have sex]. Having sex is a really personal thing. It's an internal battle for what she's ready for. You will always want to know what you're getting yourself into. If one person in the group has hAd sex then the rest of the group doesn't think it's so scary.   Mariel, 16

It always comes down to sitting in that life raft. Getting through adolescence is scary. A girl finds a group to sit with and wants to stay put. Friendships are built on going through these rites of passage with each other. Sex is a pivotal right of passage; it can feel lonely being left out.

ORAL SEX: ARE THE STUDIES TRUE?

> Girls are doing it so they don't have to have sex. It isn't seen as part of sex but a part of foreplay. A lot of ninth graders do it because the older boys will like them and think they're cool.   Kim, 16

> Guys say things like, "You're so pretty and this would really make me feel good."   Alisha, 15

*Personally, I'm totally against it. I think it's humiliating. It compro-
mises your dignity and you're being used.*   Britt, 17

Talk about an issue that flips parents out. When the media began reporting a few years back that a large percentage of young girls were casually
engaging in oral sex, a lot of people freaked out, but it didn't ring true to
me. From the reports, you'd think ten-year-old girls throughout the country were cavalierly engaging in oral sex. In reality, there have never been
enough data collected to confirm or deny the assertion.* But here's a rep-
resentative sample of opinions from the girls I work with:

- It's gross.
- It's demeaning.
- Oral sex isn't "sex."
- Girls are sometimes willing to give boys oral sex to please them.
- Oral sex is a bargain—girls don't think they risk getting an STD
  (they're wrong about that) and they know it won't get them preg-
  nant.
- When people talk about teens engaging in oral sex, they're really
  talking about girls performing oral sex on boys, not the other way
  around.

The furor today is a reflection of a clear generational difference between
adults and girls. A generation ago, women grew up thinking oral sex was
equal to or more intimate than vaginal intercourse, and they primarily
feared pregnancy. Girls today fear not only pregnancy but HIV and a host
of other horrible STDs their mothers didn't have to face.

Fears of HIV and pregnancy have flipped the value many girls place
on vaginal sex and oral sex. Many girls see oral sex as safe and emotionally distant, vaginal intercourse as something you "save" for someone special. Adults assume that because girls don't see oral sex as sex, they have

---

*Alan Guttmacher Institute, "Oral Sex Among Adolescents: Is It Sex or Is It Abstinence?"
32, no. 6 (November/December 2000). The last credible data was collected in 1982. In
1992, the U.S. Senate stopped appropriations for additional surveys. In an amendment
sponsored by Senator Jesse Helms, funding for an adolescent sexual behavior survey was
prohibited because it would "legitimize homosexuality and other sexually promiscuous
lifestyles." www.alanguttmacher.org.

a cavalier attitude toward sex in general. When I compare what girls say about oral sex and what adults have deduced from the studies, I think adults' discomfort with girls' sexuality deafens them to what girls actually say. While it's true that many girls don't think oral sex is the same as sexual intercourse, it doesn't mean all girls are doing it or that it means nothing to them.

What is clear to me is that many girls believe that the dynamics of oral sex reflect the power difference between boys and girls. Repeatedly I'm told how degrading it is to be so submissive to a boy. That the only way a girl can maintain a good reputation and give a boy oral sex is if she's in a committed relationship with him. Otherwise, it's usually seen as a desperate attempt to please a boy she likes but who may not like or respect her in return.

> At my school, most girls don't just go around blowing guys left and right. You can do that with your boyfriend and that's about it. Sometimes you hear about a girl doing it at a party, but she's either drunk or has a reputation for that kind of thing. Because once that happens and word gets out, everyone looks at her differently.
>
> Anna, 17

> There isn't a lot a girl won't do to make a boy like her.   Maria, 15

> One of my friends was battling over a guy with another girl—and my friend was losing. So she went out with this guy and some other people and they were all in a car. She was in the back seat with him. They stopped and everyone got out but them. She gave him head! And people could look into the car! I think she did it because she felt like she had to do what he wanted or else he would like the other girl more.
>
> Robin, 17

Why do girls comply when they don't want to? I think one of the hardest things to do is ask yourself questions you're afraid to ask. It can be more important to maintain the illusion they're with someone who respects and cares for them, so oral sex is okay, than to say they don't want to give oral sex but acquiesce anyway. Many girls are afraid to raise their voices because they're afraid of what they'll hear.

The Bad Boyfriend

Unfortunately, it's almost inevitable that your daughter will date some duds, maybe even some jerks. Your daughter doesn't have to date someone who physically abuses her to cause a serious blow to her self-esteem. Here's my criteria for a bad boyfriend:

- When they argue, he questions her perspective and feelings.
- He tells her she needs to lose weight or makes other denigrating remarks.
- He questions her intellect and makes her doubt herself.
- He calls her a slut or a bitch.
- He insults her.
- He humiliates her.

So many girls I teach have been in relationships with someone who fits the above criteria. All relationships have drama, but anytime your daughter is in a relationship where she is made to feel "less than" or smaller, where her perspective is questioned, she shouldn't be in that relationship. Later in the chapter I'll offer some advice on how to help her handle that situation.

Positive Relationships

I realize I've focused in this chapter on the more negative aspects of relationships; these are the issues girls most often ask about, and addressing them is the core curriculum of Empower. Of course, not all boyfriends are bad. Your daughter can have a wonderful boyfriend. (And although you might not want to admit it, she can even have a sexually healthy and responsible relationship with that boyfriend.) Remember, girls develop their personal standards for relationships from watching you, their friends, and the media. What many girls lack is a clear idea of what a respectful, responsible relationship looks like.

To me, a healthy relationship is one where the people respect each other and can be themselves without being criticized or corrected. I

*think I may have trouble being in a healthy relationship because I
have no idea what to look for in a guy.*   Caroline, 15

CHECKING YOUR BAGGAGE

- Close your eyes and remember your first serious love: Do you remember the first time you saw this person? How did you feel? What did it feel like to be alone with your first love?
- Did you ever date someone your parents didn't like? How did you react to their disapproval?
- Have you ever been sexually harassed? How did you handle it? How do you think your daughter would? How would you want her to?
- Did you ever go along with something a romantic partner wanted because you didn't know how to say no?
- Did you ever feel pressured to have sex before you felt ready—or pressured someone else?
- What has your daughter learned from you about relationships? What have you modeled, for better or worse?
- Have you ever been in an abusive relationship?
- What would you look for to know that your daughter was in a healthy relationship?

WHAT YOU CAN DO TO HELP

There are six "boyfriend" areas where you can focus your parental energies.

1. Teaching your daughter to not blow off girlfriends for a boy
2. Helping her create criteria for dating on her own terms and on her own timetable
3. Helping her communicate clearly in intimate relationships (interpreting what boys mean, saying what she means, including break-ups)
4. Helping her respond to sexual harassment when flirting goes too far (including talking to boys, to you, and to authorities)

5. Thinking about sex. Is she ready to be responsible? Can she say no if it's not what she wants?

6. Recognizing when she's in an abusive relationship and knowing how to help her get out

1. Teach Your Daughter to Respect Friendships with Girls and Boys Equally

As mentioned in the last chapter, you should clearly communicate to your daughter that it isn't right to blow off someone when a better offer comes along. It doesn't matter if it's the love of her life; keeping her commitment to what she's promised is more important. Ask her about the unwritten code that says it's okay to blow off a friend for a guy. Where does it come from? What would happen if she told a guy she liked that she already made a commitment to someone else? Why would she want to date someone who couldn't accept that?

2. Teach Your Daughter to Respect Her Own Timetable for Dating

Each girl has to go at her own pace. Your daughter needs to identify her own pace, be able to talk about it, and appreciate where her friends are at as well. Please don't think that girls are telling each other, "To be cool, you have to have a boyfriend" or "If you want to hang with us, you have to date X." The pressure isn't that obvious. And it gets more intense if her friends have paired off with people and she feels left out. If everyone's with someone and you're not, then you'll feel dismissed and childish. Ask your daughter if she feels that kind of pressure, and how she can talk back to it.

3. Help Your Daughter Become a Better Communicator

In my Empower classes the girls often role-play how to break up with a boyfriend in a way that's respectful and clear. So many girls end up marooned in relationships in which they're not happy because they don't want to hurt the boy's feelings or are afraid of his reaction after the breakup. If your daughter wants to break up with someone, encourage her to think through why and then how she wants to communicate it. Let's review and expand on the steps your daughter can take when she's talking to the boy she wants to break up with:

- Describe what she doesn't like (sound familiar?) (e.g., "I don't feel respected when you're around your friends and you want me to do everything you say.")
- Request what she wants or doesn't want (e.g., "I don't want to date you anymore.")
- Remember to be direct; don't blame a third party or plead temporary insanity ("My parents don't want me to see you anymore" or "I'm just really messed up right now. I have a lot on my plate"). This sends the boy the message that if only he can overcome this obstacle, your daughter will want to keep dating him
- Affirm the person *without reaffirming the relationship* (meaning he should feel respected as a person but still know that the relationship is over: "There are many things about you that I like, you're great when we're alone because I feel that you're just yourself, you listen to me . . .)

She can follow the same strategy when she has a disagreement with someone.

Unfortunately, breakups are rarely clean and dignified. Most boys aren't going to feel comfortable having an extended conversation about why your daughter doesn't want to date them any longer. Most will run away and lick their wounds privately. Sometimes when they do, they'll get angry and retaliate by spreading rumors about her. If your daughter has this experience, here's an example of what she can say:

YOUR DAUGHTER: *You've been saying that I'm a slut/frigid bitch who wouldn't give it up. I have the right to break up with you without you saying mean things about me to other people. I can't stop you from doing it, but I'm requesting that you stop immediately. If you feel I disrespected you or you didn't have the chance to talk last time, I'm open to it, but only if you treat me respectfully. If you keep this up, you will force me to go to (person in school who can help).*

4. Help Your Daughter Respond to Sexual Harassment

If someone who harasses your daughter doesn't realize that what he's doing is a problem, then she can say a version of the following. Remember, as long as she feels safe to be alone with him, it's always better to have a conversation like this one on one, at a quieter time of the day (not when they're switching classrooms).

YOUR DAUGHTER: *Todd, can I talk to you for a minute? This is a little difficult for me to say, but I really need to talk to you and for you to take me seriously. When you hug me in the hall, I often feel like I'm being felt up. It makes me uncomfortable and I want you to stop. As my friend and someone I really care about, it's really important to me that I'm truthful with you and let you know when you do something I don't like. That's what I think friendships are built on.*

If he gets defensive or accuses her of sending mixed messages:

YOUR DAUGHTER: *You're my friend, and as my friend it's important for me to tell you when something is bothering me, that it's respected, and that you feel I'm doing the same for you. I'm sorry if you think I've sent mixed messages, so what do you want me to say if it happens again?*

If he knows that what he's doing is a problem:

YOUR DAUGHTER: *Todd, can I talk to you for a minute? I want you to stop making comments to your friends when I walk by your locker. Maybe you believe girls like that kind of attention, but I want to be clear to you that I don't. Now that I have said this to you, I assume you'll respect my request.*

If he laughs at her:

YOUR DAUGHTER: *Let me be absolutely clear. I want you to stop. If you won't stop, you will force me to go to (best person in the school) for help.*

If he does it again, she should go to her adult advocate in the school for assistance.

You Don't Like Her Boyfriend

> *I'd make a huge effort to get to know him better by inviting him over to dinner. If I still didn't like him, I'd give her a factual list of why, like if he smokes or he's lazy about grades, not that he burps at dinner.*
>
> Nina, 17

> *I have a policy that my best friend and I devised which originated sophomore year when I dated this guy named Rick who I was really into, but he could never get it together to call or see me. I knew he liked me, but he was just dumb. But my parents would always be on my case about it, and thus I would end up defending him! We then created the "Defending Rick" philosophy, which has come to describe just about every relationship I've encountered since then. The worst has been with Dylan (the one I'm struggling to break free of) because I've had to defend him in order for people to understand why I've let him back in my life after he broke my heart nine months ago.*
>
> Carmen, 18

Parents tell me that standing by and watching their daughter date a jerk is one of the toughest trials of the job. Especially if you've done time with a "bad boyfriend," it's unbearable to watch your daughter date someone you believe is unworthy.

Or is he? Before you pass judgment, co-opt the enemy. Invite the boy over to dinner and be on your best behavior as you get to know him a little better. Maybe he has more piercings than you would like, his posture stinks, or his speech won't nab any trophies for oratory. Forget all that. Does he treat your daughter respectfully? Is he polite? Does he seem to value her opinions? Many kids with green hair and tongue studs turn out to be terrific guys. Frankly, I'd worry more about the smooth charmers.

Okay, you've tried your best and you still can't stand him. The thought of him makes your skin crawl. What can you do? You know that if you voice your disapproval, she'll stay with him forever. So, as much as you can, keep your mouth shut and wait for her to come to you. Girls want their parents and people they respect to approve of their boyfriends. When asked, you can be honest, but first check your baggage. If you don't like what he wears, forget about it. If you don't like the way he talks to your daughter, that's something else entirely.

If you don't like him for a superficial reason, you can say: "I may not like him, but I respect your right to make your own decisions and I have faith that you that want to be in a relationship with someone who treats you with respect. But please come and talk to me about it anytime and don't feel uncomfortable bringing him around."

If you don't like him for a really good reason, you can say: "I would like to talk to you about Seth. Yesterday, when you came home from school together, I was really worried about how he was talking to you. Maybe I'm wrong or making too much of something, but I felt like he was belittling you. You have the right to have a boyfriend, but you also have the right to have a boyfriend that doesn't tell you things that make you feel bad about yourself or doubt yourself. Life is too hard as it is for the people who are supposed to care about you to make you feel less worthy than you are. What do you think about what I just said?"

To which your daughter will say, "Thanks, Mom/Dad, for telling me what you were feeling. I didn't see it before, but now that you've said it, you're right and I'll break up with him right now." Yeah, right. And then the Lotto van will back up to your driveway with your jackpot winnings, you'll fit into your high school jeans, and your gray hairs will disappear.

Or perhaps your daughter will flip out and tell you that you don't understand her relationship. Then you need to respond with: "I'm not asking for answers or telling you that I don't like him or want you to stop seeing him. All I'm asking is for you to think about what I've said and talk to me later."

> *Relationships in high school don't last. Don't say anything and it will go away in two days.*   Zoe, 17

5. Have another talk about sex

I could pretend that there are rules you can give your daughter about sex that she'll follow, but of course I won't. She'll respect the values you've taught her only if she's internalized them so they've become her code of ethics—for herself and others. Again, you'll have to clarify your own values about sex so you can share them with your daughter. I'm assuming they'll be based on the assumption that when the time is right, your daughter should know how to act responsibly, respectfully, and consensually—and expect the same from her partner. Please see the books listed in the resources section for more in-depth discussion of these issues.

> *I don't think there're any rules you can give her. Once she decides she's mature enough to have sex (regardless of whether she is or not) she will, and there's nothing to do to stop it. I know this isn't the "right" thing to say, I think she should stay with her boyfriend in your house because then you can keep an eye on her.* Helen, 17

Oh, God, They're Having Sex

The worst, most ineffective things you can say to her are:

> *You can never see him again.*
> *He's such a bad influence.*
> *He's making you do . . .* (because girls don't like to be told they are controlled by anyone)
> *You're a slut/whore/tramp.*
> *If I catch you doing this again . . .*

> *The times when I get into trouble are when I'm sneaking around and can't talk to my parents.* Grace, 16

What should you do if you find condoms?

> *At least she's using protection. Parents can't stop her. I'd sit down and talk to her about safe sex, and offer birth control.* Megan, 17

If you find condoms, you have to admit to yourself that there's a strong probability that your daughter is having sex. But even as uncomfortable as that may make you, it should reassure you that she's at least practicing safer sex. And if she's not having sex now, finding condoms is a clear sign that she's definitely thinking about it.

Some parents confront their daughters when they find condoms. If you do, here are some common things you'll hear.

I was buying them for friends.
An HIV/AIDS/sex-ed teacher was giving them out as part of the presentation.
Someone gave them to me as a joke.

Please notice that none of these explanations is a denial that your daughter is having sex. They could all be true. She could be buying them for friends and using some for herself. She could have had a presentation in school but she could also plan to use them. Whatever the reason, I suggest saying something like the following:

PARENT: *Whatever the reason you have them, if you are thinking about being sexually active or if you already are, then it's time to see a gynecologist and get a check-up. If you're responsible enough to be sexually active, then there should be no problem going to the doctor. Let's sit down and go over what I feel you need to know about sexual responsibility.*

PRIVACY

And how did you happen on those condoms, anyway? With all of this sex in the air, you may have a strong temptation to look for evidence. I strongly suggest that you resist the temptation to look in her room. If you think she's sexually active, talk to her. Don't violate her privacy. She'll be so angry and feel so violated that she'll either completely shut down and refuse to tell you what is going on, or feel justified in doing many stupid things later. You must respect your daughter's privacy so she feels she can trust you. Then you should be able to find out whatever you need to know.

The worst thing would be to go to her room and look. She doesn't trust you enough that you won't freak out. Ask her or get someone else to talk to her. If worse comes to worst and she won't tell you or

someone else, ask her best friend. If she has a boyfriend that's forc-
ing her, not using condoms, etcetera, her friend will know and be
worried about her.   Chandra, 16

IF YOU CATCH HER HAVING SEX

This has to rank up there with the most horribly uncomfortable experiences you can have as a parent. After you get over your shock and/or
embarrassment, leave the room and let them dress in private. Meanwhile,
calm down and breathe deeply. While you're waiting for the partner to
leave, prepare your thoughts.

Immediately sit down and talk with her. If either of you are too uncomfortable, bring in the ally. An effective response depends on the rules
you've already established with her. If you have forbidden boys to be in
her bedroom, she broke a rule, but focus first on the sex part. If this is the
first time you're finding out she's sexually active, you've got to give yourself some space to relax and come to grips with the idea.

PARENT: *Okay, that was completely embarrassing. When I get over the
shock—when I'm 102—I'll look back on this and laugh (smile). First,
I want to apologize for coming into your room without knocking, but
that doesn't obscure the fact that you have broken a rule that is important to me and one that I believed I had your agreement on. We are in
this together, and we have to trust each other. Your violation of this rule
means that I can't trust you and/or you don't respect my rule.*

*In addition, now that I know you're having sex, you must get a pelvic
exam and get information and make decisions about STDs and contraception. Now let's talk about what I need you to understand about
sexually responsible decision-making.*

Has she been to a gynecologist for a pelvic exam? If not, she needs to go
ASAP. This is a great thing the ally can do with her. I went with my sister
to her first exam. She was nervous, but I told her what would happen.
When she came out of the exam, she walked into the waiting room and
announced to me—and the ten women waiting for their appointments—
"Well, I guess *that* makes me a woman!" We both laughed, and then we

went out to lunch. Bonding moments are what and when you make them.

6. Help Your Daughter Recognize an Abusive Relationship

Of course, you want your daughter to have positive experiences with the people she dates, and no parent expects that their daughter will be involved in an abusive relationship. But if you know four girls (your daughter and three of her friends), you know a girl who has been or will be in an abusive relationship. How will you know, and how can you get her the help that she needs?

Girls don't get involved in abusive relationships out of the blue. They're vulnerable when certain ingredients combine. Those ingredients include values that communicate that it's critical to have a relationship for self-validation and self-worth, a community or ethnic group that does not admit that family violence could occur, seeing verbal and/or physical abuse in the family, and a peer social system that measures social status based on a boyfriend.

What Is Abuse?

First, let's define abuse, and the reasons why it can be so difficult to address. At its core is a relationship where one person verbally, emotionally, financially, and physically (but not always), dominates, intimidates, and controls another. Abuse is at once terrifyingly simple and complex. "Why doesn't she leave?" people ask. Because she loves him and it's impossible to fall out of love overnight, even when the person who loves you treats you like dirt. Because she has been so brought down that she has lost any confidence that she can make any decision. Because her clique thinks he's a great "catch," why, she's lucky to be with him. And because even the most abusive relationships have good moments. Abusers can make you feel like the most special person in the world. And if you love someone, you want to believe him. You see no other option, so you hope for the best.

Have you ever gone to a party and stayed later than you wanted to because a friend, spouse, boyfriend, or girlfriend wanted to stay? Ever gotten into a car with someone who drank enough wine at dinner that you knew he shouldn't be behind the wheel and you had no business being a passenger? I've done both. If you've stayed at that party or gotten into that car, you did so because you didn't want to offend someone, go against someone else's needs, or openly acknowledge that someone was doing something dangerous and irresponsible. Now imagine that if you did stand your ground, people would ridicule you or talk about you behind your back. If it's so hard to stand up to someone in these situations, imagine how hard it is for someone dealing with abuse.

Girls are particularly vulnerable to abusive relationships simply because they are who they are—teens. They think in extremes and in the short term (next year may as well be the next century) are prone to narcissism and drama, and have little experience with which to compare the relationship.

Why Wouldn't She Tell You?

Notwithstanding some of the jokes I've made about girls not wanting to talk to their parents, it's hard to imagine why your daughter wouldn't want to tell you if she's in an abusive relationship. Look at it from her point of view:

- She wants her privacy: Abusive relationships are maintained by creating a sacrosanct sphere around the couple.
- She thrives on melodrama: She feels things intensely and in extremes. She could be in love for the first time. An abusive relationship can feel like a drug. She needs the fix. The lows are very low but the highs are amazing. She can feel like the most loved person in the world. The drama reinforces the feeling that she's in a mature, adult relationship and it's them against the world.
- She feels special: She feels as if she's the only one who understands her boyfriend. She's the special "anointed" one. Abusive relationships exploit a girl's need to take care of and save someone.
- She's afraid you'll punish her: If she tells you, you won't let her date anyone else. She cherishes her independence, so she'll resist going to people she sees as an authority. She could easily feel,

rightly or wrongly, that if she seeks help, her newly gained independence will be taken away or her future relationships will be controlled.

- She's afraid of disappointing you: She's ashamed and feels as if she let you down. You may like him, and if she tells you, you won't like him. Or you tried to warn her, and she didn't listen.
- She's afraid she'll lose her status: Most likely she attends the same school and shares the same friends as her abuser. She could easily perceive her social status as dependent on her relationship with him.
- She's stubborn and feels invincible: She won't admit to anyone (sometimes including herself) that she's in over her head; she can tough it out.
- She's inexperienced: She could believe that his jealousy and controlling behavior are expected and normal aspects of relationships and has little to compare them to. She could see both as proof of his love (that's why what she sees modeled in her home is so important!).
- She feels helpless: She feels the abuser has complete power over her, so nothing will make it better.
- She's afraid she'll hurt others: He could threaten to hurt people, animals, or things she cares for.

What Does Abuse Look Like?

- She apologizes for his behavior (either to herself and/or others).
- She's stressed out. She's hypervigilant and overreacts to minor incidents because she's living under extreme tension. Reacting to this kind of constant stress may cause her to explode or become hysterical over things she can give herself "permission" to get upset about. Like lashing out at you.
- She gives up things or people that are important to her, such as after-school activities or friends.
- She has difficulty making decisions on her own, from the clothes she wears to what classes she wants to take. Abusers are very effective at making her feel that any decision she makes is stupid and a

- Six in every ten women who are victims of homicide were murdered by someone they knew. Domestic violence is the leading cause of injury to women between the ages of fifteen and forty-four.
- One of every three abused children becomes an adult abuser or victim.
- Women are more often victims of domestic violence than of burglary, muggings, or other physical crimes combined (The Commonwealth Fund, 1993).
- More than 90 percent of the injuries in dating violence occur to the woman in the relationship (*Domestic Violence Facts: Report by the Office of Women's Health* [Washington, D.C.: Department of Health and Human Services, 1997]).
- Not all perpetrators of violence are "macho" or fit the "bully" stereotype. Some are loud and aggressive while others are passive; some are social and some are loners.

mistake, so she becomes paralyzed. She has to check with him for every decision, such as if she can go somewhere.
- She changes her appearance or behavior because he asked her to.
- She comes home with injuries that she cannot explain, or whose explanation is inconsistent with the nature of the injury.
- She believes jealous, controlling behavior is an expression of love.
- She tries to be the "perfect" girlfriend and seems frightened of her abuser's reaction if she isn't.

How should you talk to your daughter if you think she's being abused?

Do
- Ask about the relationship.
- Maintain open and respectful communication.
- Help her recognize controlling behaviors in the relationship.
- Use all resources at your disposal including counseling, school, and the legal system.

- Plan for her safety.
- Call your local domestic violence agency for help.
- Assure her confidentiality. If you need to tell someone else, ask her permission first. If you need to tell the police or other authorities, tell her first and then jointly agree about who she wants to talk to. Make a plan with her so she feels safe and in control.
- Appreciate that she believes that sometimes the relationship is good for her and that the two may feel that they're in love with each other. She may feel that she can't survive without her abuser.
- Ask, "What can I do to help you?"
- Tell her that you're sorry she feels bad, but you know that you can't understand how she's feeling (teens *hate* it when adults pretend they know what teens are feeling, unless they have their own story to prove they do).
- Ask questions to help her recognize that her relationship is abusive.
- Support her courage for asking for help and respect her limits. You're helping her establish boundaries with others, including yourself. For example, if she wants to remain in an abusive relationship, don't tell her that her decision is wrong, but do tell her that you're worried for her safety and help her see the danger she's placing herself in if she returns to the relationship. Explain to her how you would intervene if you felt she was in immediate physical danger.
- Help her recognize that the explanations and excuses for his violence don't justify his behavior.
- Help her see that her feelings are valid. The abuser does not have the right to dismiss her feelings or recollection of events.

Don't

- Present her with ultimatums. Don't make her feel that she has to choose between you and her abuser.
- Assume she wants to leave or that you know what's best for her. If you make decisions for her, you reinforce that she can't make decisions for herself.
- Ask what she did to "provoke him." This type of question reinforces her feelings of self-blame.

- Talk to her and the abuser together.
- Take secondhand information.
- Pressure her into making decisions.
- Threaten or physically attack the abuser. Not only is this danger-
  ous, but it will likely make her side with the abuser.

How to Spot a Potential Abuser

- He acts pathetic to exploit a victim's sympathy and guilt.
- He's abusive toward others, especially small children or animals.
- He lashes out, calls her names, or demeans her.
- He causes fear through intimidating statements and actions.
- He calls her persistently.
- He shows up without warning at home, at her classes, or at her
  after-school job.
- He follows her.
- He tries to enlist family and friends in attempts to maintain the
  relationship.
- He's possessive to the point of controlling her behavior.
- He's often much older.
- He fights with others "over" the intimate partner.
- He has public displays of anger or ridicule toward women.
- He feels entitled—the community's rules do not apply to him.
- He has a Jekyll and Hyde personality. He's charming in public and
  mean and degrading in private.

You'll never have a more important opportunity to practice your listening
skills. Remind your daughter that she has more courage and resilience
than she knows, and that no matter what, you're there for her.

YOU'LL ALL GET THROUGH THIS

In preparing yourself for the worst, it's easy to forget that watching your
daughter learn to navigate more adult relationships can be fulfilling for
you both. Remember, dads, this can be your time to shine. You can role-
model positive, honest, caring, loving relationships with men. If she
comes up against a guy who is treating her poorly, she'll know by your

example that it's not right and she doesn't have to take it. Moms, you are important role models, too. Show her by your own actions how to have loving relationships based on mutual respect and equality. All of this can be overwhelming, but you can be an involved parent who guides your daughter toward respectful, responsible relationships that will give her joy.

Parties

Sex, Drugs, and Rock 'n' Roll

Two senior Queen Bees, Anna and Greer, have taken Nikki, a tenth grader, under their wing. Nikki's parents are going away for the weekend, leaving Nikki alone in the house for the first time. Anna and Greer convince Nikki to have a party that Saturday night and invite all their friends, including Derek, Anna's forever on-again, off-again boyfriend, and Colin, Derek's friend, on whom Nikki has a huge crush.

On Friday, Nikki is excited and nervous to get her parents out of the house, but she tries to be casual about it. It seems to take her parents forever to leave on Saturday morning, but around 11:00 A.M. they finally hit the road.

Saturday, 7:00 P.M.: Nikki, Anna, and Greer get the house ready while they experiment with various drinks from Nikki's parents' liquor cabinet. Since Greer has the best fake ID, she gets the keg. Greer and Anna show Nikki how to make Jell-O shots and punch with Everclear so people won't taste the alcohol. Nikki puts bowls of Doritos throughout the house.

7:30: The girls get dressed, put on music, and continue drinking.

8:30: A few close friends of Anna and Greer show up to get the party started. They gossip, predict who will get together or humiliate themselves, and continue drinking. Anna is a little worried about Derek. He was evasive the day before when she casually asked him if he'd be coming.

9:00: Other kids start to arrive. Nikki is now over her nerves and berates herself for her previous doubts that this party was a good idea. What was she so worried about? Anna and Greer are such good friends; she feels she's gotten so close to them recently. Things are going great! And hey, the doorbell's ringing again. More people are coming! Nikki isn't sure she recognizes the group of guys with bulky paper bags under their arms, but they greet Anna and Greer like family. She lets them in.

Say good-bye to the mailed invitations, party favors, and the early boy-girl parties where your biggest worry is whether anyone plays spin-the-bottle or pairs off in the closet. Parties for older girls combine all the issues and dynamics I've discussed so far in this book. When parties go well, they're a great escape from parents, homework, exams, and all the other common teen stressors. When they don't go well, it's anyone's guess how they'll end—with a visit from your friendly squad car, to arrests for underage drinking or drug use, to an experience with a boy who can threaten your daughter's health and well-being.

For your daughter, going to a party can be like traveling to another planet in another galaxy. Instead of breathing air, she's breathing a combination of peer pressure, adrenaline, self-doubt, and insecurity. She'll take whatever survival measures necessary because going to a planet filled with fun and excitement is such an adventure. When she returns to Earth, she gets to recount her experiences with her fellow travelers and the unfortunate people who were left behind.

WHAT YOU MUST KNOW

- Girls find out about parties from friends, flyers handed out around school, word of mouth, and e-mail.
- When parents go out of town, the temptation to have a party can be overwhelming.
- Girls love having a reputation for having a high tolerance to alcohol. They love drinking each other under the table proving it.
- The preparty is a sacred ritual where girls eat, drink, gossip, and discuss strategy and goals for the evening.

- The postparty next-day phone call is also a sacred ritual where girls discuss who got together with whom, who humiliated themselves, who got totally drunk and/or high, and any other gossip.
- Reputations are made and broken at parties. If a girl hooks up with a guy, she may be happy that her status increased, but if she went too far, she may be upset with herself—or find herself lower on the social totem pole.
- Many teens drink and drive.

Our parents drink three glasses at dinner and then drive home. So why should we do any different?   Natalie, 17

- Parties don't have to be at houses. They can be in parking lots, fields, anywhere kids can be "alone."

Let's spend a night at the Party from Hell (at least, from the parents' point of view). Of course, not all girls party as I'll describe below. Some go through high school never partying. Some start early (eighth grade) and stop by tenth. Some pick it up late and some party their way through. The only thing I want you to be careful of is assuming that your daughter hasn't or isn't partying—that will get you both in trouble.

Back to the party . . .

Saturday 7:00: Derek has invited Ally, a shy ninth grader, to Nikki's party. Ally doesn't know Nikki, and this will be her first high school party. Ally can't believe Derek asked her. When she asked Derek if she could bring a friend, he said sure, but jokingly (she thinks) said her friend had to be hot. Ally's pretty sure her parents wouldn't approve of her going to the party. So she lied and told them she'd be going to the movies with Bianca and sleeping over at her house.

    Ally and Bianca are really excited about going to the party. No one else in their grade is invited, and they want to look good, not like pathetic freshmen trying too hard to be cool. Before the party, they carefully prepare what they'll wear. They hang out at Ally's house, play music, look at magazines, and try on their outfits. Ally wears a skirt of Bianca's that Bianca has always said would look really good on Ally, and Bianca wears a dress she bought for the occasion.

8:30: Ally's dad drives them to "the movie." Ally kisses her dad good-bye, thanks him for the ride, and gets out of the car. As they walk away, Ally's dad thinks how lucky he is that he's got such a great kid who's steering away from all the stuff he did in high school.

8:35: Ally calls Derek from the movie, and he picks them up with his friend Colin. They drive to Nikki's house while Derek talks to Colin about a lot of people Bianca and Ally don't know but have heard about and seem very cool.

9:00: They arrive at Nikki's house. When they walk through the door, Derek and Colin are greeted by a group of guys with affectionate yells and grunts. Derek laughs, grunts back, puts his arm around Ally, and asks one of the guys where the beer is. The guy points to the back, and as they walk to the kitchen, Ally and Bianca pass by people they've only previously seen in the school hallway. Ally thinks she hears one of the guys say, "Bait" under his breath as she walks by.

9:05: Derek and Colin hit the keg. Derek asks Ally if she wants a beer. She's conflicted. She sort of wants the beer, but she also thinks people who get drunk are lame. As she's deciding what to do, she realizes that a group of girls are standing by the sink and one in particular is looking her over from head to toe as if she has no right to breathe in the same room with her. Derek pretends not to notice the tension, or maybe he's truly oblivious. Derek introduces Ally and Bianca to Anna and Greer. Derek says, "Hey, what's up, Anna. . . . What's your name . . . Nikki? Great party." He puts his arm around Ally, whispers something in her ear, and laughs as they walk out of the room. Prompting the following conversation.

GREER: *That's pathetic! He's just doing it to rub it in your face! It's so obvious! She's a freshman.*

NIKKI: *Who is she? I've never seen her before and did you see what she was wearing? . . . Not **too** desperate . . .*

GREER: *I think she's a freshman. Derek so clearly invited her so he can use her. Anna, I'm so glad you're over him, because he's so not worth it. He's such a loser.*

ANNA: *Yeah, I can't believe he would bring an ignorant freshman here to hook up with.*

9:10: Anna starts to drink a lot of punch. While she's drinking, she thinks, "How could he do this to me? Do I mean nothing to him? Is she prettier than me? Thinner than me?"

Got it? *Parties are drama!* When I poll girls at Empower, here's a short list of what they tell me goes on:

- Playing drinking games (card games, strip poker, quarters, beer pong)
- Having shot competitions (who can drink the most the fastest)
- Having or watching fights, either verbal skirmishes or physical brawls
- Gossiping
- Watching movies
- Performing acts of vandalism, such as trashing the house, TP-ing other houses, or smashing mailboxes
- Making out
- Hanging out, chilling out
- Dancing and listening to music
- Getting high

Some kids trash houses just for the fun of it or because they're angry and want to destroy something. At least if there's a parent there, there's a little more control. I walked into a bathroom and there was a guy smashing figurines. On New Year's I was at a party and watched a girl who weighs a hundred pounds and had never drunk before drink five shots of vodka in fifteen minutes. Her eyes rolled back into her head, she fell on the ground, and she was twitching. It was scary and we had no idea what to do. Someone eventually took her to the hospital.
— Emma, 15

ALCOHOL AND DRUGS

Alcohol and drugs are a fact of life in adolescent culture. Chances are good your daughter has tried or will try alcohol and/or drugs. If she does them regularly, another bonding experience she'll have with her friends is taking care of each other when they're drunk or high. Parties are where Fruit Cup Girl in the guise of Beer Cup Girl comes out in force. It isn't an absolute certainty that your daughter will get drunk or high when she goes to a party. It just shouldn't come as a surprise to you if she does.

> *When I go to a party, I circle around the house a couple of times to see who's there and who I want to hang with. If I see a hot guy and he's drinking beer, I try to avoid going up to him because I know it'll be really hard to say no. Half the time I'm successful.* Lynn, 16

> *When you're at a party, the real girl comes out. A lot of girls say, "I don't need drugs. I don't drink beer." Then you see someone you like and they're really cute and this is one of the few times when you can really talk, so you'll do it [drink or do drugs]. I mean you'll do really stupid stuff.* Nia, 18

> *Getting drunk at parties is definitely an escape. It's a chance for girls to be totally different people. They go from being soft-spoken and quiet to laughing, outgoing, and crawling all over the guys.*
> Jake, 16

> *When a girl gets drunk at a party, guys look at her like it's a golden opportunity. She's vulnerable.* Matt, 17

> *No matter how "good" your daughter is, she'll drink and do drugs. This doesn't make her a bad kid.* Kathy, 15

> *Drugs aren't a good thing, but they're an accepted part of teenage culture. It's easier for me to get heroin than alcohol because they've cracked down so much on fake ID's.* Nikki, 15

> *If you want to hook up, you get wasted first. Girls use partying as an excuse for getting with guys. They need an excuse. When people talk about them at school, they have an excuse.* Nia, 18

I ask girls in my Empower classes to tell me which drugs are readily available to them. Of course, availability will depend on what part of the country you live in, but the list could be as extensive as the one below:

Easily Available Drugs

Alcohol
Marijuana (pot, grass, weed, Mary J, reefer, dope, buds, cheeba, ganja)
Ecstasy (X, smerf, oriole)
Acid (LSD, L)
Ketamine (K, Special K)
Methamphetamine/Methamphetamine hydrochloride (speed, meth, chalk, crystal meth, crystal, jib, ice, glass)
Hash
Mushrooms ('shrooms)
Nyquil/Robitussin
Nitrous oxide (whippets)
Valium
Xanax
Codeine
Vicodin
Percocet
Ritalin/Adderall

The last six are prescription drugs. Your daughter can get any one of these drugs by:

Stealing prescriptions from parents who are doctors.
Selling or giving away pills from her own prescription to other people.
Selling or giving away pills from a sibling's prescription.

Let's go back to Nikki's:

11:00: The party is a success; the house is filled with people Nikki barely knows, and the whole place is really trashed. Nikki is just sober enough to know that she wants some of the people to leave, but she isn't sure how to make them go. Anna and Greer are so drunk they're useless. Anna has had ten Jell-O shots and has now decided that she has to talk to Derek. Greer is annoyed with Anna because she is "crawling back to Derek again."

Ally is at a table in the kitchen having a great time with Derek and his friends playing drinking games. Derek keeps telling her how good she is. She's not sure where Bianca is, but the last time she saw her, she was dancing with Colin in the living room. Meanwhile, Bianca is getting a little worried about Ally, but doesn't know how to bring it up and get her away from Derek.

12:00: Anna is so drunk she can barely stand, but she's determined to find Derek so they can talk. Nikki is miserable. She just went into her parents' room and found two random people in their bed. Ally is now sitting on Derek's lap, still playing drinking games. Anna walks into the kitchen.

ANNA: Derek, can I talk to you for a minute. It's important. . . .
DEREK: Can it wait? I'm sort of busy right now. [He smiles at the other guys around the table.]
ANNA: No, it's really important.

Anna and Derek go outside for half an hour. They talk intensely. Anna falls apart crying and Derek tells her that he still cares a lot for her, but wants to be able to do his own thing. He thought they agreed to this the last time they talked. He suggests doing something next weekend, after his game. When they come back inside, it's clear that Anna has been crying and Derek gives an impatient look to his friends. Anna goes back to Greer to dissect the conversation with Derek, while he goes back to Ally, who feels uneasy that Derek talked to Anna in private, but is flattered that he still wants to hang with her.

DEREK: Hey Ally, you want to dance for a little while?
ALLY: Sure, that'd be cool.

Once they're out of the kitchen, Derek asks Ally if she'll go upstairs so they can talk privately. They go to a bedroom; he closes the door,

locks it ("so we can be alone"), and sits on the bed with her. He con-
fides in Ally that he used to go out with Anna, that she's still in love
with him and won't let it alone. He likes Anna as a friend, but she just
needs to move on. He's trying to let her down nicely, but she just won't
drop it. He's really glad Ally is here. He reaches out to stroke her
cheek, and his elbow grazes her breast. Then he kisses her.

Downstairs, Anna is in tears. Greer tells her they should leave this
lame party and check out the one at Michael's. Nikki is desperate; the
whole party is out of control. It would be almost a relief if the police
busted them. Bianca is having such a good time dancing with
Colin—he's talking about going out next weekend—that she's com-
pletely lost track of Ally. She's probably fine.

Maybe Ally will be fine. There is a small chance that Derek and Ally will talk and that's it. But it's far more likely that Ally will be vulnerable to Derek's sexual overtures and will get in over her head. She feels special because Derek is confiding in her (and in her mind, someone only does that when you trust the person and are close to them). She's drunk, so she's not thinking clearly. Derek may have genuinely wanted to confide in her, but it's also a way to get Ally alone. He knows that telling Ally that another, older, cooler girl covets him makes him seem more desirable and makes her feel special. Now Ally is part of the drama—with a senior, no less—and it feels good.

When a girl feels close to a boy she's attracted to, she may want to do something sexual with him. And she's far more likely to silence her own concerns and boundaries because she's convinced that this person cares for her, and being drunk or high makes it hard to think straight. If she pushes him away, he'll think she's a tease or a baby. If she calls for help, she could get him in trouble—she isn't sure that's what she wants—and make herself the center of gossip in the process. In that situation, girls will almost always do what the other person wants, including having sex against their will.

WHY IT'S SO HARD TO SAY NO

Date rapes usually occur in situations like Ally's. Ally is intimidated by Derek because he's older, more popular, and has higher social status.

Derek personifies maturity to Ally, and she's flattered that he would even recognize her, let alone be attracted to her. Her insecurity makes her feel obligated to him. She feels that she knows him well, even though it's only been one night. When they go upstairs, she wants to go. She wants to be alone with him. She most likely wants to do something sexual with him (although she probably hasn't thought it through, including where she wants it to stop), so she willingly sits down on the bed. She doesn't get worried when he locks the door. Derek kisses her and it feels great.

This is how most date rapes begin. The girl wants to be there but may not want to have sex and be too intimidated to say so. She may worry that if she asks the boy to stop, he won't like her. Her good friend is distracted, and the other girls think she's a tramp, so they're not likely to check up on her either. Sometimes really bad things happen at parties. Any combination of drugs, alcohol, cliques, social intimidation, and in-the-box behavior can lead to rape or coerced sex, whether or not the perpetrator(s) knows it's coerced.

In general, I'm not a big proponent of statistics, because often they scare people and they can be easily manipulated to "prove" what you want. But here are some statistics that have consistently shown to be true: The vast majority of rapes occur when girls are between the ages of eleven and eighteen; the rapist is someone they know and is of the same race and socioeconomic background. In other words, sexual violence is rarely perpetrated by a crazed stranger who jumps out of the bushes. It is much more likely to happen at parties. Teens trust each other. At parties, it's common for a girl to meet someone she doesn't know well but feels she does because he goes to the same or nearby school, and/or has friends in common.

Why are girls easy targets?

- Girls think they know (and therefore trust) people they shouldn't. For example, most girls assume they can trust someone with whom they have friends in common.
- Girls often have poor personal boundaries; they'll sacrifice their best interests to please others.
- Cultural messages that teach girls to be nice and polite make it difficult to reject someone.

- They're inexperienced.
- They want to think the best of a situation.
- Like all teens, they feel invincible.
- Parties put them in new, unfamiliar places. (Think of the places you go when you go out to socialize: a friend's house for dinner, a restaurant. Now think of where she is when she goes out: a friend of a friend's house, another school for a dance or game.)
- They're curious; they want to try new things.
- They lack confidence.
- They want to be popular.

It's not easy to get up from the bed, unlock the door, and walk out. Most boys, of course, aren't predators. But there are boys in these situations who either know how the girl feels and take advantage of her insecurity and inexperience, or don't question themselves about how intimidating they can be. The girl can end up ignoring her own boundaries about what she does and doesn't want to do. In the worst case, a boy who feels the pressure to be "in the box," combined with the desire to have sex, can be unintentionally or intentionally blind and deaf to the subtle, or sometimes very obvious signs that he is raping her (she's not moving, she has tears in her eyes, she says no).

I hear versions of this story constantly. A girl walks up to me before class, eyes down, and whispers that she wants to talk to me after class. Later, she'll tell me, often with tears welling in her eyes, "Last Saturday night, I went to this party . . . and I sort of hooked up with this guy. He seemed so nice and cute and I don't really know what happened. . . ."

Many older girls only make the younger ones more vulnerable. Even though they probably made the same mistakes when they were her age, many junior and senior girls believe that a younger girl deserves to make her own mistakes. Older girls justify their behavior by saying, "What was she doing all over him like that? What did she expect? She should know better. Freshmen know they're fresh meat for senior guys." These same girls spread around their version of events at school the next day, so this fourteen-year-old girl has not only just been coerced into sex but also labeled a slut in the process.

*If you are a guy and you can figure this stuff out, you can play girls off
each other. All a guy needs to do is tell her she's pretty. Sometimes I
wish I were a guy, because it isn't hard.*   Katy, 15

CHECKING YOUR BAGGAGE

- When you were a teen did you drink, do drugs? Was it fun? Did you use it as an escape? Escape from what?
- Have you ever been drunk and/or high and done something (either as a teen or adult) you wouldn't have if you'd been sober? Did you ever have or go to a party without your parent's permission?
- What are the ways you run away and escape from problems? Why?

WHAT YOU CAN DO

When most parents think about what can happen to their daughters at parties, their first instinct is to put their Rapunzels up in the tower and throw away the key. But parties are a part of life. If the tower isn't a viable option, your best bet is to help your daughter enjoy herself responsibly at the parties she throws and those she attends. That means she has to take certain steps to make sure she's safe, think clearly about her boundaries ahead of time, and understand what situations will compromise those promises to herself.

If She's Giving the Party

And you thought the boy-girl invitation issue was a tough one. If your daughter wants to host a party when she's older, don't veto the idea out of hand. Certainly there are downsides: it's your house that could get trashed; it's your house the police will visit if the volume on the stereo is up too high; and in some parts of the country, it's you who will be held accountable if guests break the law on your premises or after leaving your premises. On the plus side, letting your daughter host the party gives you a chance to supervise her and model how a party should go.

The rules of engagement begin the same way as in Chapter 5, although the stakes are higher for older girls. Sit down with your daughter before and write down guidelines for both of you. For example, you can insist that there's no drinking or drugs; that admission is by invitation only (i.e., she can't let in anyone she doesn't know, even if it's a "friend of a friend"—she can blame you if her friends complain), and that the number of people invited not exceed a predetermined limit. You can insist that you must be on the premises during the party. She can ask that you stay upstairs unless she needs your help and/or you're concerned the party is getting out of hand. You may want to discuss what that means, because your definitions could be different. You think having a hundred people in your home is too much, while she thinks that's a definition of a successful party. Clarify under what circumstances you will interrupt the party (too loud, evidence of alcohol or drugs, too late) and the actions you will take (escorting guests out personally, calling parents). Go over her personal degree of accountability, including rules for reimbursement of costs and clean-up. Remind her once again that you'll act as the "eternal out"—her guests have to stick to the rules "because Mom and Dad said so, and they'd kill me if we broke them."

If you're harboring any notion of becoming a Hip Parent (see Chapter 2) and buying beer or other alcohol for the party, remember that not only is it illegal (and you could held accountable for repercussions), it's unwise. Buying beer not only means condoning underage drinking but more importantly the abuse of alcohol. If you buy beer, you also send the message to your daughter and her friends that it's more important to you to be liked than to impose rules. They'll walk all over you. You're a parent, not an older friend with an ID.

> *Compromise will work a hell of a lot better than getting in a screaming match. She can be grounded later. Understand where she's coming from and that parties are an integral part of teenage culture. Promise not to come downstairs with Rice Krispie treats and Tang.*
>
> Katrina, 16

BUSTED: THE UNPLANNED PARTY

It's not fun to contemplate, but your daughter might take advantage of your plans to go out of town to throw a party at your house. The best way to prevent this is not only to have a clear conversation about why you won't allow this (which should focus largely on safety issues), but to have a trusted friend or relative stay at the house with your daughter. Yes, she'll complain that you don't trust her and are treating her like a baby, but your house and child will be safe.

Signs She's Planning a Party

- Several people you don't know call the house the night before you're planning to leave.
- You have the feeling that your daughter is rushing you out of the house.
- You find a large amount of Doritos or other junk food in her closet (but that could also mean she's bingeing).
- She's nervous and superficially nice around you.
- She's a little too helpful around the house or with anything you need to do to get ready for the trip.

Signs There's Been a Party at Your House

- There are fresh carpet stains and scuff marks on the walls.
- Empty food cabinets and/or refrigerator.
- Mysterious items of clothing found about the house.
- The outside of your house is littered with cigarette butts.
- The house is cleaner than when you left it; the carpets are so recently vacuumed that you can see the vacuum marks and the trash cans in the rooms are all empty.
- Your daughter tells you she had a couple of friends over, then jokes about having a party (to distract you from the fact that she really did have one).
- There is not one roll of toilet paper anywhere in the house.
- She's really nice to you.
- When you ask her what she did over the weekend, her answers are very specific.

Usually when our parents ask us how we are or about what we did, we say "Fine" and "Nothing." But if we had a party, we talk to our friends so we all agree about what we did. So if we talk to the parent

about the movie we went to and how much we liked it, we had a
party.   Lynn, 16

What do you do if you make plans to be out of town and learn your daughter is about to have a party? It depends on when you find out. If you find out twenty-four hours or more before, cancel your plans if possible and stay home. (If you leave, she may have the party anyway because she'll feel she has nothing to lose.) If you can't stay in town, leave her with a relative or family friend or have an ally who has a strong backbone stay at the house (otherwise, she may have the party anyway).

If you find out the day of the party, monitor the phone (have a cordless phone in your hand at all times so you can pick it up at the first ring) and the door from 7:00 to 12:00 P.M. so you can assure guests that the party is off. If you want to punish her more than you already have (public embarrassment can be a great preventor of future party planning), you can ground her and cut off her communication. If you can't cancel your plans, have a friend or relative go over to your house and monitor the phone and door. Around 8:00 P.M. turn off all lights in the house. If you have to, limit it to one light upstairs. Do whatever's necessary to make the house look deserted.

If you find out when you're away, you'll appreciate why I said earlier that there's nothing wrong with your children having a healthy dose of fear. The kind of fear that stops your daughter in her tracks from doing something really stupid, irresponsible, and/or dangerous because she thinks "If my mom finds out I was at this party until four A.M. instead of baby-sitting like I told her, I'm dead." Or "I'll be so busted if I invite twenty people over to my house and take my mom's money so I can buy a keg of beer." If you're told she's having the party while you're away, have the friend or relative go over to the house and break it up. Punish her when you return.

If you've caught her sneaking out to go or come back from a party, waiting in the dark and watching her quietly sneak back into her room is always fun, and you definitely have the surprise factor on your side when you flip on the lights. Listen patiently as she attempts to correctly get out the logistics of the excuse she tried to memorize on her way home. After you do that, use the same strategies I outlined in Chapter 2 in the sneaking section.

RUNAWAY

The confrontation between you and your daughter can quickly escalate
to the point where she threatens to run away.

> *Be aware that teenagers are immediately defensive when they're
> caught. Your daughter will be infuriated because she'll lose face with
> her peers. She'll say stupid, reactionary things. When my parents
> found out I was going to have a party, they canceled their trip and
> stayed home. They grounded me and ruined my party. I am usually a
> pretty responsible kid, but that made me crazy. I left home with a cou-
> ple of friends and didn't come back until four days later. I didn't call.
> I just let them worry themselves sick about my whereabouts for a
> while.*   Katie, 16

Girls manipulate their parents' love and fear for their safety by threatening to run away. When she's older (especially if she can drive or has
friends that do), she can make good on the threat. If she's serious, her
threat puts you in an extremely difficult position (which she won't appreciate now but will apologize for years later). If you don't back down,
she'll run off, and you won't know where she is. If you give in, she'll stay,
but you'll have no credibility. Either you come across as an easily manipulated pushover, or you let her stay among the wolves. What should
you do?

Call her bluff, but do it strategically. If you think her friends are generally trustworthy, let her go. When she leaves, call the friends' parents
and tell them what is going on (don't be embarrassed; they'll probably be
as sympathetic in the situation as you would be). Ask them to keep their
eyes and ears open for your daughter's whereabouts. Ask them to call you
and keep you informed.

If you don't trust her friends, you can't stop her from leaving anyway.
But before she leaves, tell her the following:

PARENT: *I want you to know the following things: I know I can't stop you
from leaving. I love you and I am going to be really worried about you
until you are back here or somewhere else safe. Instead of going with X,
will you go over to Aunt Helen's? [If she turns you down] Know that the*

punishment still stands, you will be held accountable for your actions, but I love you and I don't want you to go.

LANDMINE!

Don't say "behavior" when you're talking about accountability, say "actions." "Behavior," like "watch your tone of voice," makes girls crazy.

TALK TO YOUR DAUGHTER ABOUT ALCOHOL AND DRUGS

One of my primary goals in writing this book is to help parents appreciate how the issues facing girls are interrelated. The decision-making skills your daughter needs are the same no matter what she's making the decision about, whether it's deciding to smoke cigarettes or pot, drink, or have sex. Your role as a parent is to communicate your values and ethics on the subject, help your daughter clarify her own, and teach her how to communicate her boundaries to others and act on her principles.

Your strategy for talking about alcohol, drugs, and sex should follow the same principles:

1. Recognize that they surround your daughter.
2. Talk with (not to) her regularly.
3. Be clear about your rules and expectations.
4. Be consistent (your actions must match what you're telling her).
5. Leave an open door for later conversations.
6. Don't be shocked and take it personally when she doesn't follow your rules.
7. Be clear about consequences and follow through.
8. Don't be in denial!

TALK ABOUT PEER PRESSURE

Peer pressure—where there're groups of people pressuring you to do something—doesn't happen anymore. It's not like they say,

A MOMENT FOR FULL DISCLOSURE

If you drank or did drugs in high school (and let's be honest, maybe junior high, too), you may feel on shaky (read hypocritical) ground telling your daughter about the evils of intoxication. You want to teach her that alcohol and drugs are bad and unhealthy, but you've done them and (hopefully) survived intact. Intoxicants surround all of us. Many of us anesthetize ourselves daily. You may have used occasionally, experimented, or struggled with an addiction. You may be overcoming an addiction right now. So the question is, should you tell your daughter about the alcohol and drugs you did when you were her age?

My one rule is: Don't lie. When she's younger (before she's thirteen), if you can't switch the topic, distract her, or run away, I would tell her how drinking made you very sick (surely you have unpleasant yet nostalgic memories of overindulging once or twice). When she's older, you have to talk to her about it. Tell her what you think about it. Why did you do it? What were the costs? Have you watched people you care about struggle with addiction? How did it change your relationship with that person? If you did drugs, talk about the dangerous situations you found yourself in or the experiences of people you know. Did you ever get drunk or high with "friends" you didn't really know or trust? If you struggle with an addiction right now, I would talk to a therapist and/or counselor first and organize what you want to say.

"Everyone's doing it, so come on." People are normally cool with your decision to not drink or do drugs. The only time when you will do it is when you want to fit in with an elite group or you want to impress a guy.   Sydney, 15

I love working with teens. They're totally capable of saying and believing two contradictory statements, as Sydney's remarks indicate. Sydney's mistaken; peer pressure is alive and well today. If their experience doesn't happen exactly like what they saw on a Public Service Announcement, then teens often deny its validity. What else is peer pressure but people you perceive to be cool or above you convincing you to do something you don't want to do?

Peer pressure today is just more subtle and internalized. Kids doing drugs or drinking are not going to say to someone "If you want to be our friend or be cool, you have to drink." Or "Come on and do it. All the cool people are." Instead, it's much more sophisticated. Drugs and alcohol are so much a part of teen culture that the motivation to drink and do drugs comes from an internal pressure to belong, not someone standing over you with a joint forcing you to smoke.

Getting on My Soap Box . . . Why I Hate "Just Say No"

In the late eighties, Nancy Reagan, surrounded by a diverse group of earnest young people, touted this slogan as part of a public awareness campaign to help kids resist peer pressure. I found the most offensive aspect of this campaign, besides its patronizing tone, was its refusal to see how multifaceted teen culture is and therefore how hard it is for teens to "Just Say No." I was in high school when the campaign came out, and I remember how it was immediately ridiculed—something to say right before you drank or got high. Teens still make fun of it to this day.

Unfortunately, mutations of "Just Say No" have always and continue to exist because most adults want to educate teens about sex, drugs, and alcohol primarily to make themselves feel better, not to provide the real information teens need. These programs are the best funded because they are fuzzy, warm, and safe. They touch the surface of these issues so they aren't controversial, and therefore they get lots of money. However, slogans like "Just say no" reaffirm teens' belief that adults are hopelessly and deliberately out of touch. For the same reason, the most ineffective thing to tell your daughter about sex, drugs, or alcohol is "Just walk away," "If you respect yourself, don't do it." I guarantee that your daughter knows plenty of teens who respect themselves *and* regularly have sex and use alcohol and/or drugs.

Zero-tolerance strategies also won't work because they smack of the hypocrisy that teens disdain. Your daughter lives in a world where sexual imagery, drugs, and alcohol are around every corner. Parents tend to focus on drugs, drinking, and sex separately, but your daughter uses the same skills to make decisions about all of them. While refusing may be the decision you want her to make, it's a process that she must go through, not an all-or-nothing proposition, and you don't have ultimate control about the outcome. How you help her make decisions must reflect the world she lives in, where advertising and peer pressure surround her. Here's what I say to kids; the first part really surprises them and gets them listening more seriously:

ME: *I'm not going to tell you not to drink or do drugs. I know that alcohol and drugs are easy to get and I'm pretty sure that many people you know and like are drinking and getting high. I will tell you that almost every date rape I've been told about includes alcohol. But I know it's your choice. I will tell you that I don't want you to drink or do drugs for the following reasons. When you're drunk or high, it's harder to make the responsible choices that can keep you safe. The facts are that bad things happen to really smart people when they drink and use drugs. I'm worried that someone will take advantage of you when you're drunk or high. I'm also really worried about you getting into a car with someone who's drunk or high. But I can't control what you do. When you're away from me, I've got to hope that you'll make choices that will keep you safe and out of trouble.*

There are other steps your daughter can take to increase her safety:

- She should always go to a party with a friend who will watch her back and vice versa. They should also have a signal that they can use to tell each other when they need help, as I'll discuss below.
- Many schools have parents and kids sign pledges that if a kid finds herself in a compromising situation at a party, she will call her mom and dad to pick her up, no questions asked. Consider making this pledge with your daughter.
- Many schools also have safe rides — students who promise to drive other students home. Tell her she can use these rides if she feels uncomfortable asking you.

Time for Another Sex Talk

When your daughter was younger, talking to her about sex was focused on the basics—the mechanics and the emotional ethical foundation for when it's appropriate. Now you need to build on the foundation of all your earlier discussions and expand the discussion to decision-making—how will she make the choice?

Knowing Her Boundaries

Go back to the party at the moment when Ally goes upstairs with Derek. As she's walking upstairs is the time for her to talk to Derek. But first she needs to know how she feels about the situation, and that, to say the least, can be very difficult for anyone. Ask your daughter to ask herself:

- How well do I have to know someone before I do something sexual with them?
- How do I define knowing someone well? (Meeting a friend of a friend at a party doesn't qualify.)
- What do I feel comfortable doing with someone sexually?
- What do I not want to do?
- How can I communicate that to the person I am with?
- What would make it more difficult for me to say what I want and don't want?

Obviously, it'll be really uncomfortable for your daughter to share her answers to these questions with you, let alone have a discussion, but you need to give her the starting point to establish her boundaries and then a person she can discuss it with. Again, her ally will be really important here.

A common problem girls have is that many worry that if they say something about their limits too early, it assumes that their date wants to have sex when in fact he may not have thought about sex at all. Please tell your daughters that they can be safe in making the assumption that their date does want to do something sexual (not necessarily have intercourse but they're on the road). If she thinks through all the possibilities, she can be clearer about where she wants to draw the boundaries, and she doesn't have to assume that every boy is a predator to take precautions to protect herself. She needs to remind herself that drinking or doing drugs will make it harder to do that.

As I've mentioned, girls don't like admitting it, but most are really bad at saying "no" clearly. They can sit in my class and tell me confidently that they have the right to say "no" whenever they want. But when they're actually in the situation, they tell me afterward, things are different. They don't want to offend the boy, they don't want to hurt his feelings, they don't want to admit to themselves that this guy may want to have sex. As a result, a girl often will say "no" while she's still kissing him and he may understandably be confused by the mixed message and keep going. She may say "Can't we wait" or "Maybe we should check on Rachel, I think she's throwing up in the bathroom" or "I'm not sure this is a good idea." None of these statements clearly communicate "I don't want to have sex." She must learn to say what she means: "No, I don't want to have sex." "No, you have to stop trying to persuade me to have sex." If she has been clear about this and he isn't stopping, as a last resort you can tell her to say, "If we have sex now, I will consider this rape."

I think it's worthwhile to tell you that boys in my classes tell me they want girls to be clear. They don't like having to guess what she wants to do or doesn't. And when we tell boys that we teach the girls to say "If we have sex now, I will consider this rape," they really get it.

SAFETY IN NUMBERS

Overall, the best strategy for your daughter's safety at a party is to have good friends who will look out for her and vice versa. She needs the buddy system now more than ever. She needs to strategize with one or two close friends before the party about how they will look out for each other. Do they need a signal that says "Bail me out"? If your daughter pairs off with a date to a secluded part of the house, does she have an agreement in place that a friend will come looking for her in five minutes to make sure everything's okay? It needs to be absolutely clear that no matter what, their sacrosanct bond is to watch out for each other.

If your daughter were in Bianca's place, what could she do? Your daughter sees a good friend who's really drunk going into a bedroom with a guy. Your daughter is sure her friend wouldn't be doing this if she were sober. Here is an effective intervention strategy: Your daughter should go up to her friend in the bedroom or wherever they've retreated and say, "I really need to talk to you privately. It's really important." If she gets any resistance from her friend or the guy says "Hey, everything's cool," she can say, "I'm having female problems, I need you right now!" Or she can say that the police have arrived. Lying can be a very good tool to get safe.

DATE RAPE DRUGS

In the last few years the media have reported an increase of drug-induced rapes. A flavorless drug is put into the victim's drink without her knowledge. Later, she passes out and is raped. The most well-known drug used for this purpose is Rohypnol, or "Roofies." The drug's effects include drowsiness, nausea, lack of muscle coordination, impaired memory, loss of memory, and dizziness. Roofie use is more often reported at college than in high school, but it's good to be aware. Your daughter can avoid this danger by following this commonsense advice:

- Don't leave drinks unattended.
- Don't accept open containers at parties.
- Watch the person pour your drink.
- Always go to parties with someone who will look out for you (the buddy system).

THE UNTHINKABLE: IF SHE'S BEEN RAPED

There's probably no other situation where you want to be there for your daughter as much as this one. If she's raped, the first people she'll want to tell are her friends, and the last people she'll want to tell are her parents. There are two reasons for not telling you, neither one of which reflects on you as a bad parent. She doesn't want to disappoint you, and she's afraid of your response. Listen to a seventeen-year-old girl who was raped at the end of a summer arts program.

After it was over, I put my clothes on and ran to my friends. But I didn't tell them. I put on my happy face because it was the end of the

*program. The next day my parents picked me up for a two-week vaca-
tion. I thought about it all the time but I didn't want to tell them. I
thought I'd be less than perfect in their eyes. I also didn't want to go
through telling people over and over again like the police or a counselor.*

*When school started, I smiled all day so much that it hurt. After
school, I'd go home so depressed. I would take five showers a day
and I was always fearful and watching the doors. I told my friends. I
did everything I could to avoid my parents. The counselor told my
parents and my mom was great. Then I felt really bad and hated
myself that I assumed she wouldn't be. Now I know I'm lucky. I'm in
this group of girls who've been raped and my parents have been the
best. The other parents of the girls in my group have told them they
were sluts or ignored them completely.*   Tess, 17

Think of all the ways pleasing other people hurts girls. Tess needed to
reach out to the people who could support her best—her parents—yet
she was the least likely to tell them because she didn't want to be "less
than perfect in their eyes." Guilt and shame stop girls from speaking out
about violence and getting the support from the people who love them.

As a general rule, if you suspect your daughter is keeping something
from you, tell her:

PARENT: *I'm not sure what is hurting you right now but my gut tells me that
something is wrong. I respect your privacy, but I want you to know that
you don't have to go through bad times by yourself, and sometimes
there are problems that are too big for anyone to handle alone. If something bad has happened or happens in the future, I'm here. I won't
judge you or think you're a bad person. I'm here for you and love you
no matter what. If you want to, I can help you think through what
you're feeling, but I won't force you to do anything you don't want to.
Just know that it's safe to come to me and I love you.*

- 22 to 29 percent of all forcible rapes against girls occur when they are eleven and younger
- 32 percent of all forcible rapes against girls occur when they are between the ages of eleven and seventeen
- The Guttmacher Institute reports intercourse was involuntary and nonconsensual for 74 percent of girls who had intercourse under age fourteen and 60 percent under age fifteen
- Over 20 percent of women report both physical and/or sexual abuse before age eighteen
- 27.4 percent of women under eighteen report sexual abuse alone while 18.5 percent report physical abuse
- Most common physical and sexual abusers are boyfriends at 29.3 percent
- Most common physical abusers are fathers/stepfathers (23 percent)
- In 55 percent of reported rapes, victims knew their rapist. Only 53 percent of all attempted or completed rapes were reported to police. Reporting the rape was found to be dependent on the relationship between the victim and the offender.

WARNING SIGNS

When girls are in trouble for a variety of reasons, the warning signs often look the same.

- Sleeplessness or constantly sleeping
- Not eating or overeating (often people who have been victims of sexual violence eat to create a physical wall between them and the world)
- Highly controlled behavior
- Extreme restlessness

The scariest thing is that, like Tess, the need to please is so strong in many girls that it gives them the capacity to put on a smile when they are dying inside. Tess was able to be on a vacation with her parents for two weeks and not say a word. Remember, her reluctance to tell you doesn't mean you've failed her in some way. Once you do find out, if you focus on supporting her, she'll realize that you really are her safe harbor.

If She Tells You

The first thing to say is "I'm so sorry that happened to you"—*always*. Don't start badgering her with questions about when, how, who, or what she wants to do about it.

YOU: *I'm so sorry that happened to you. I love you and it takes so much courage to tell me. Do you want to talk about it?*
YOUR DAUGHTER: *I'm not really comfortable telling you.*
YOU: *Well, if you aren't comfortable telling me, can we get you to someone you do feel comfortable talking to?*

When parents (especially dads) find out their daughter has been raped, their first reaction is often to want to kill the person who did this to her and then take their daughter to the police to report the rape. Imagine how difficult it is, then, when your daughter begs you to forget about it and refuses to go to the police. Unfortunately, it's normal that when a girl tells the people who love her that she has been raped, there's an immediate conflict. If she has been raped by someone in her community (school, church, neighborhood, etc.), don't be surprised if she is extremely reluctant to go to the police. She desperately wants things to go back to normal so she can forget it happened, whereas you want something to be done and justice served. No matter how you feel, this is her decision to make.

When I talk to girls who have been recently raped, I tell them that I would like them to report it. I tell them that people who rape don't do it one time. They will continue to rape until they are held accountable. By reporting the rape, she'll be punishing the rapist and standing up for other girls and doing her part to make sure it doesn't happen again. I tell her that I will be with her every step of the way and that it takes great courage. She gets to make the decisions, including taking her time to make them. Take it one step at a time. One day at a time.

If Someone Else Tells You

PARENT: *Your coach called today and told me something I'm really worried about. She told me someone hurt you. Do you want to tell me about it? You know that no matter what, I love you and will respect what and when you want to tell me. I just want to you to know that I'm here for you.*

I strongly suggest getting your daughter to a therapist, preferably one who specializes in helping girls who have been victims of sexual violence. For more information, please refer to the "Getting Help" chapter for ways to get her the help she needs.

"What Was She Thinking?"

It's horrible enough if your daughter's been violated. She might also have to contend with the condemnation of her peers. A common reaction that people have (including girls) is to blame the victim for something she did that "caused" the rape to occur. Girls are often their own harshest critics. It's common in Empower classes for some girls to say "There isn't enough love in the world for me to put up with a boy who hits me and if he does, I'm gone," or "Any girl who goes upstairs with a boy knows what he wants . . . what was she thinking? She deserves what she gets. No one can be that stupid."

Why this shocking lack of empathy? Girls say these things because it makes them feel that what happened to the girl who was raped or abused by a boyfriend won't happen to them. If they can pinpoint something that the girl did and blame her for it, then they can trick themselves into believing that if they don't do that exact same thing, bad things can't happen to them. Ironically, many of my "toughest, hardest" students who are most adamant about other girls' stupidity have been in abusive relationships and/or been raped. It seems contradictory but it isn't. These girls are putting up a front—and for good reason. If they admitted to their anger, frustration, grief, sadness, and shame, what resources would be there for them? Unfortunately, not many. The world isn't a safe and just place for girls, and they know it. The tough-girl front works well for getting by day to day, but often girls are so preoccupied proving to themselves that they are in control that they unwittingly walk right into the line of fire over and over again.

Remember, the reality is your daughter may tell her friends first. If she tells you first, and then wants to tell her friends, think through with her who she tells and when. She should obviously tell people who won't turn it into their drama (although their personal reactions to it are understandable) or gossip. Suggest to her that she request how they can help her through this difficult time. For example: "I have something to tell you that's really difficult to talk about. Last week at the party, I was raped by Frank. This is so hard for me and I really need you by my side right now. If I don't want to go to parties and just sit home in my pajamas and eat cookie dough, please do that with me. I just want you to be there for me and support me."

If they aren't supportive, then she could say: "As my friend, I need you to be there for me and I'm not feeling that you are. When you question me, I feel doubted and that I have to justify myself. You're my friend, but I need you to be here for me. If that's too hard, I can't hang out with you right now because I need to take care of myself."

In Sum

I worry a lot about the girls I teach. I worry that they will drink too much, use drugs, and not be around people who will or can help them if they need it. I worry that your daughter will meet someone she's really attracted to, who pays attention to her, and tells her she's pretty, and she'll have sex with him when she wasn't sure she wanted to but didn't know what to do. I worry about the things she'll see and experience that will make her feel less than and not good enough. I worry about the car she'll get into going home and the person driving that car.

Even though I'm not their parent, I want to make the girls in my classes promise me that they won't do anything contrary to what I teach. But I know they will at some point. Freaking out and jumping up and down won't work for me, and it really won't work for you.

I realize I may have scared the hell out of you about the perils of letting your teenage daughter go to parties. But remember, the tower isn't an option. Sooner or later, you've got to let her go into the world and test-drive her independence. Whether it's a high school party, or later college, travel, or the working world, she'll be out there without your protection, but always with your voice in your ear. She'll be ready if she can recognize when she is in over her head and has friends who will take care of her. And

1. She understands why other girls may turn on her and doesn't let their interactions with her make her feel insecure.

2. She knows her own boundaries about drinking, doing drugs, and having sex and is able to communicate them clearly to others.

3. She knows that if she makes a mistake, she can go to you or another adult you both trust for guidance.

4. She trusts her gut.

5. She recognizes her escape routes. When she's at a party, she sees where the nearest available door is.

6. If she breaks a family rule, she knows she will be held accountable but that you'll still stand by her.

YOU GOT THROUGH IT!

That was probably the most difficult chapter to get through, and you're done. I hope you now see the connection between girls' relationships with each other, their need to please, and their interactions with boys. I know it's painful to contemplate that your daughter could experience the type of pain we've talked about here. It's difficult to stomach that there are people in this world who will not cherish or respect her. As I say to my students: I want you to recognize danger on the horizon, not when it's hitting you in the face. With your help, she will.

Getting Help

So far in this book, I've concentrated on how you or your ally can help your daughter. However, there may come a time when your daughter will need to get professional help from a therapist or other mental health professional, so you should be prepared to see the signs if she does and get her to the help she needs.

One of the most significant advances we've made in the last several decades is to take away much of the stigma of seeking help from mental health professionals. We also have a language for violence that we didn't have even a generation ago. One of the reasons why it was so hard for me to talk about my abusive relationship in high school was that I, along with the rest of my community, wasn't educated about dating violence. I had no words to define what was happening. Now many girls in my situation do.

If your daughter is a victim of any kind of violence, you both will go through a process of recovery. Your love for her can make it very difficult for you to allow her to make her own decisions as she muddles through her recovery. And recovery is messy for everyone involved. If you find out from someone else, much later and after the fact, that your daughter needed professional help, you may feel hurt that she didn't feel comfortable telling you. Remember, girls don't tell their parents for one of two reasons: It's not safe to tell them because their reaction will make her feel worse, and they don't want to disappoint them.

People always ask if my parents knew that my relationship in high school was abusive. No, they didn't. I didn't tell them until I was twenty-four and was about to publish my first book, *Defending Ourselves*. Even then I was reluctant, but I didn't want them finding out from a friend instead of me.

So why didn't I tell them as a teen? Even though I was extremely private, I had a relatively good relationship with my parents. Like many of the girls I've interviewed, I felt that my parents liked me and liked being with me, but I didn't tell them because I didn't want them to be disappointed in me. For better or worse, I saw my boyfriend as a permanent fixture of my life throughout high school, and I didn't want my parents to hate him. I felt that I should be able to take care of any problem that came my way. I could barely admit it to myself; I certainly had no idea how to talk about what was happening. The only thing I knew was that I was embarrassed, and I didn't want anyone to know. I felt as if I were walking around all day with a secret that could be revealed at any moment. By my senior year, I was so sick from keeping it inside that I desperately wanted someone to find out—as long as I didn't have to say anything.

But my parents were still helpful—even though they didn't know it at the time.

My mother always told me that I, like anyone, could and would make many mistakes throughout the course of my life and that I would survive. If I made bad decisions, I could always fix them. Even though she says she didn't, I think she intuited something was wrong. One day, at the airport, while we waited to pick up my father, she said, "I don't know what's going on with you, but I know something is. Everyone makes mistakes. You're very private, but if you ever want to talk, I'm here." She opened a door, albeit just a crack, and I soon walked through it to get help. I was deeply ashamed that I had "let" the relationship get so out of my control. But her words let me see that there was a possibility of leaving the relationship behind me.

My reactions and reasons for not getting help were very common. It doesn't matter if the problem is an eating disorder, molestation, drugs, drinking, abuse, rape, depression, anxiety, or any combination. Girls feel ashamed, damaged, and unfixable, and they may not know anyone around them who has gone through similar experiences. I often say that abusers' insurance policy is the silence of their victims. People don't speak out and yet there's hardly a person around any of us who hasn't been touched by some kind of violence. The same is true of mental illness, which touches so many of us, yet the stigma is still there.

Like anyone, your daughter could easily have problems that are too big to bear by herself, let alone solve. Likewise, even if you're the world's perfect parent, your daughter could go through experiences where one, if not both of you, needs to look outside for help.

Make sure your daughter knows that it's not shameful or weak to ask for help. It's courageous to admit when you're in over your head. People kill themselves trying to look like they have it together when they're falling apart inside. Unfortunately, many parents themselves are reluctant to ask for help. Why? There's no easy answer. Sometimes the answer is that parents see their daughter's successes and failures as a reflection on themselves. Sometimes parents don't want others to know their family business. Sometimes looking at such problems is too painful.

For better or worse, being a parent gives you endless opportunities to admit and get over your own baggage. It's your responsibility, duty, and obligation to face your own demons and put them to rest as best as you're able so you can provide the love, guidance, and nurturing your daughter needs.

There are five reasons why girls don't go to their parents for help. It could be any one or combination of these:

- By the time she admits to herself that she needs help, she's in way over her head.
- She's afraid you'll deny that she's in trouble.
- She doesn't want to change the image you have of her.
- You've been known to freak out when she's come to you with other problems.
- In your home, family problems (including your daughter's) are private. The family doesn't need the help of outsiders to take care of its own.

"Allison" is one of my favorite girls. She's funny, intelligent, beautiful, and charismatic. She also suffers from anxiety and depression. Until recently, I had no idea. I knew middle school was painful for her—it was one of the reasons she got involved in Empower in the first place, but she was so good at keeping up her image that I didn't see her struggling.

Allison is a constant achiever. She was accepted early into an Ivy League school, has been on varsity sports teams since ninth grade, and her academic and extracurricular awards are endless. After three years of volunteering at Empower, this spring she told me she couldn't volunteer anymore. I was dumbfounded and angry. I immediately jumped to the conclusion that she was suffering from "senioritis" and was blowing everything off now that she'd been accepted into college. Where was her commitment? She just couldn't walk away from her responsibilities. Then she told me she had been depressed for years. She had even attempted suicide in eighth grade.

What has been her worst obstacle in getting help? That her parents didn't want her telling anyone. They wanted her to "keep it in the family." A few days later, we went out to lunch, and she shared with me that for years she had been working as hard as she could to be what everyone else wanted her to be. Her identity was so caught up in her accomplishments that she feels as if she's nothing without them. She kept a notebook under her bed with every award she'd received since eighth grade, and when she was depressed, she took it out and looked at all her awards. Allison asked me,

> Why are we so special that we have to pretend that we don't have problems? When my older sister had an eating disorder, the doctors wanted to hospitalize her. My parents refused. They thought they could take care of her at home. I overheard my parents discussing that if they did put her in the hospital they could always tell people that she had mono. My sister was down to eighty-five pounds and they didn't want to get her help because they were too ashamed.
>
> When I was first depressed, they took me to a psychiatrist that I actually liked. He told my parents that they were going to have to do some "reparenting." We never went back. Next I went to a therapist my mom knew. When my mom picked me up, they would talk about things, including their kids. There was no way I trusted her. Now I go to a psychiatrist who just sits there and I don't tell him what's really going on with me. Why should I? At least I'm on antidepressants now and they're really helping me.

Maybe you're reading this and thinking, What's wrong with Allison's parents? Can't they see what they are doing to their daughter? Watch out. Hubris will make you blind.

Allison comes from a "traditional" family. A mom and dad who live together in the suburbs, go to church, and are active members of the community. I know Allison's parents. They're caring, loving people. There's no question in my mind that they love their daughter and want what's best for her. Through her years volunteering at Empower, Allison's father commuted hours out of his way to drop her off and pick her up at my office. He is warm, caring, and clearly proud of her. So why in the world are they so scared to let Allison talk about her problems? Is it really more important what their neighbors think than getting help for their daughter?

Parents make miserably foolish decisions in the "best interest" of their daughter and the family. Because it's so hard for parents to reflect on their own parenting, it's easier to close ranks around the family and blame other people.

Keep the door open. Ask your daughter, "You seem upset. Is there anything I can help you with?" Keep asking gently if your gut tells you she's troubled but not ready to open up to you about it.

No matter how much you love your daughter, you won't parent her well if you let your issues interfere with getting her the help she needs. She needs to learn from you that when she makes a mistake, she'll learn from it and move on. That she isn't damaged and unfixable if she did something foolish or wrong. This doesn't mean you have to share your most intimate family problems with everyone you see. But don't tell your daughter to lie about her problem, pretend it's not there, and it'll go away. If she has to leave school early once a week to see a therapist, help her come up with what she feels comfortable telling people, but don't tell her to keep it a secret. If you do any of these things, you're sending the message that she should be ashamed. As long as she feels shame, she can't heal her wounds. Respect that she's her own person and you are her guide.

WHO NEEDS HELP

Every one of following signs could describe a normal teen, but if you're seeing a big difference over a relatively short time period, the actions indicate that they're coping mechanisms for dealing with whatever is bothering her.

Signs She Needs Professional Help
- Isolation and withdrawing
- Eating too little and/or too much (because she's anxious)
- Intense mood swings

Additional Signs She May Have Experienced Sexual Violence
- She takes showers all the time
- She keeps constantly busy
- She covers her body with huge clothes
- She's fearful in a way she wasn't before
- She doesn't want to be left alone

Additional Signs She May Have an Eating Disorder
- Infrequent or absent menstrual periods
- Denial of the seriousness of the current body weight
- Excessive exercise; misuse of laxatives, diuretics, or other medications; purging; and fasting

Additional Signs She May Suffer from Depression and/or Anxiety*
- Sleeping too much or too little
- Persistent physical symptoms that don't respond to medical treatment (headaches, digestive problems, chronic pain)
- Difficulty concentrating, remembering, or making decisions
- Thoughts of death and/or suicide
- Feelings of guilt, worthlessness, hopelessness, pessimism

*National Institute of Mental Health, see Website NIMH.nih.gov.

CHOOSING A COUNSELOR

I have had both good and bad experiences with counselors, but for the most part I think they're contrived. In seventh/eighth grade, going to the counselor with dilemmas was the cool thing to do. I was in there at least three times a week with problems — made up or blown out of proportion or real. It's good to know there's someone who will be there for you and make no judgments, but ultimately, finding real people like friends and family who support you unconditionally is far more satisfying. Brooke, 18

My doctor suggested I go, so I went to a psychiatrist. He just stared at me and asked why I was angry at my father. There was no way I would tell that man anything about me. Karen, 16

I can't tell you how many times girls finally get up the courage to go to a therapist, don't like the person, are turned off by the whole thing, and refuse to consider another. But if you can find a good therapist, she can be a great resource for your daughter. It's not always easy to find a good one. You probably don't want to have to shop around, but you must. If your daughter needs to see a therapist, you're going to be spending a lot of money, so let's make it worth your while.

Prepare three to five questions to ask the therapist over the phone. Ask your daughter to prepare her own questions. Here are a few I ask:

- How would she describe her style? Does she like to listen and sit back? Will she give her opinion?
- How does she see her role as mediator between parent and child? For example, at what point would she notify you of something about your child? Don't ask this question to hear that the therapist will tell you when and if your daughter's in imminent danger. You're looking for a tharapist who *won't* tell you things about your daughter. The best adolescent therapists have a clear understanding of their boundaries between themselves, the parent, and child.
- What are her areas of specialization? Find someone who specializes

in teens and the particular issue(s) your daughter has (e.g., eating disorders, rape, abusive relationships).

- Why does she work with teens? What does she find most rewarding? What does she find most challenging?

LANDMINE!

Be very careful when you pick your daughter up at the therapist, because she's watching you and the therapist like a hawk. She wants to know that you care, but if she's taking it seriously, she's creating a safe, private space for her to wrestle with her problems. Don't pounce on her with questions. Give her that space!

Here's an example of a mother and therapist doing an effective job. As a result, the girl, a recent rape survivor, is getting the help she needs.

> My mom called three [therapists] and said choose one. She told me I didn't have to talk, but she needed to know she tried to do something to help me. When I went to the psychiatrist, she didn't force me to speak about it. I talked about friends and other things in my life. All the other adults forced me to talk about it [the rape] but she waited until I wanted to bring it up.   Alexa, 16

If your child needs a therapist, it doesn't mean you've failed as a parent. If you can get her the help she needs, you're definitely doing the right thing.

Grace Notes: Before You Go

Now you know Girl World. I know it can be hard to read about what goes on there. But I hope you've also been able to see how you can not only make your daughter's teen years more bearable for both of you, but nurture her confidence and independence.

As I've stressed throughout this book, the best way to help your daughter is to get inside her world and figure out how to communicate with her more effectively. I know it's hard to spend time together when you're operating in parallel universes. I asked some of the girls I work with how they most like to spend time with their parents. Of course, all the activities listed below could be right up there with a visit to the periodontist if things are really tough between the two of you, but try a few and see if you can open the door.

Things She Won't Hate Doing with You

- Shopping
- Cooking
- Going to museums and movies
- Talking about school/college plans (dreams and aspirations—not applications!)
- Getting ice cream late at night
- Going out for nice dinners
- Going shopping for things to decorate the house

I like doing things with my parents, especially because I'll be leaving for college in the fall. I no longer feel dorky spending time with them. I'm much more socially confident so it doesn't matter anymore.

Joanna, 18

And what do the girls wish you'd do more of—and less of? Again, some suggestions from my completely unscientific survey:

Things She Wishes Her Parents Did

- "Dropped me off at places on time"
- "Talked to me more about what I'm passionate about"
- "Taught me more about my culture"
- "Asked me what's going on with school or work"
- "Asked to meet my friends"
- "Let go of stereotypes they were raised with even more than they have"
- "Had more real conversations with me"
- "Let me have the freedom to make more choices"
- "Told me when they're proud of me"
- "Stopped worrying about my messy room"
- "Was more patient with me"
- "Paid more attention to their own lives and given up less for me"

And what do they think you're still a little clueless about?

What Daughters Wish Their Parents Knew

- "Unconstructive criticism from parents who are supposed to support you unconditionally is a *bad* thing."
- "We like your suggestions, but it's hard to admit it."
- "We really want to make you proud of us."
- "There are things that we can't/won't tell you, but sometimes you have to trust us."
- "Picking me up on time is a big deal."
- "When I need to be left alone, my bedroom door is shut. This means I really need to be left alone. Your interference will only make me more irritated."

- "Sibling loyalty can be stronger than parental loyalty. I might not tell you something my siblings don't want you to know."
- "Sometimes we just want to vent, but that doesn't mean we want you to interfere."
- "I want freedom but we can still be close. I'm my own person. Don't limit my abilities or who I am, let me follow my intuition and be supportive."

As a parting note, I've asked some girls to share the messages they'd most like to leave with parents:

Don't try to understand your daughter's every thought; just show her that her feelings are valid and are not wrong. When you need to listen, listen. When you need to talk, talk. And most importantly, treat her with the respect you'd like to be treated with, even if she doesn't do the same. After all, this is probably the hardest time in her life and no matter what she says, she does need you.   Julie, 17

Communication is the biggest part to making your relationship with your daughter the best it can be. Teenagers love to know that their parents are really interested in what is going on in their lives. The most important thing to remember is not to pressure your child into talking and being open if they don't feel comfortable doing so. Keep the lines open and always be on the lookout so you know when something is bothering her. Showing your love and concern can do wonders for a teen's self-esteem.   Nia, 18

Just be there for me. Don't judge. Don't tell me how to make it better. Just tell me you love me.   Dia, 15

Know that I love you and want to make you proud of me.
                    Michelle, 15

Even when I'm fighting with you, sometimes I know you're right, but I don't want to admit it.   Kia, 16

You really do make a difference and I really do listen.   Sara, 16

Movie List

I have compiled a list of movies that will help you to familiarize yourself with Girl World. See as many as you can from the "Must Sees" and then I suggest watching three from the other lists. I'm sure I've overlooked some, and by the time this book is out, there'll be more, so feel free to add!

MUST SEES

16 Candles
The Breakfast Club
Boys Don't Cry
The Color Purple
The Craft
Drop Dead Gorgeous
Fight Club
Girl, Interrupted
Girls Town
Heathers

Higher Learning
It's Elementary (an excellent documentary
    on teaching tolerance)
The Joy Luck Club
Love and Basketball
Ma Vie en Rose
My Girl
Tank Girl
Welcome to the Dollhouse

FUN MOVIES

Quality runs from pretty boring and ridiculous to fun to watch, but all are good for Girl World analysis. Ask your daughter what matches up with her experience.

Bridget Jones' Diary
Can't Hardly Wait
Center Stage
Charlie's Angels
Clueless
It Could Happen to You
Josie and the Pussycats
A League of Their Own

Legally Blonde
Love Jones
Never Been Kissed
Runaway Bride
Save the Last Dance
She's All That
Ten Things I Hate About You
Waiting to Exhale

EXAMPLES THAT WE HAVE FARTHER TO GO

Many of these movies make me cringe or want to throw in the towel. Pay close attention to the images that are presented that perpetuate "Act Like a Woman" and "Act Like a Man" boxes and the worst of Girl World. You might want to watch a few with your daughter and ask her questions about the worldview in these movies.

Cruel Intentions
Entrapment
Head Over Heels
Heartbreakers
Jawbreaker

The Medicine Man
Pretty Woman
Stealing Beauty
Varsity Blues
Wild Things

IT'S NOT JUST HER GENERATION

Even though the impact of the media is more powerful today than it was when you were a teen, the movies you most likely watched were just as bad. I've named just a few:

Basic Instinct
Fatal Attraction (and almost any movie
     Michael Douglas and Anne Archer
     have ever been in)

9½ weeks (so obvious)
Three Men and a Baby (looks like it's not,
     but watch it again)

Resources

FICTION

Here are some books that offer important insights into girls' adolescence and young adulthood, prejudice, parent-child relationships, and the mother-daughter bond.

Almost a Woman by Esmeralda Santiago, Vintage Books, 1999.
> A memoir about a Puerto Rican immigrant coming of age in New York City and her struggle to establish an identity in her large family.

Bastard Out of Carolina by Dorothy Allison, Plume, 1993.
> An illegitimate girl comes of age in 1950s South Carolina fighting the label "trash" and the violent and sexual advances of her stepfather. The main message of the book is that people may be born into undesirable lives, but they can still be whoever they want to be.

The Bell Jar by Sylvia Plath, Harper Perennial Library, 2000.
> This novel tells the story of a gifted young woman's mental breakdown beginning during a summer internship as a junior editor at a magazine in New York City in the early 1950s.

Beloved by Toni Morrison, NAL, 1998.
> Set shortly after the Civil War in rural Ohio, this story revolves around Sethe, a runaway slave haunted by the baby daughter she murdered in order to keep her from a life of slavery.

The Bluest Eye by Toni Morrison, Dutton/Plume, 2000.
> Eleven-year-old Pecola Breedlove, a black girl growing up in 1940s America, prays for her eyes to turn blue so that she will be beautiful. It brings into question the American ideal of beauty and how it affects people who don't conform to that standard.

The Color Purple by Alice Walker, Pocket Books, reissued 1996.
> A novel about a woman's struggle to escape the abusive treatment by the men in her life.

Crooked Little Heart by Anne Lamott, Doubleday, 1998.
> A story of a girl going through the rite of passage from girlhood to adolescence. There are great descriptions of the torn loyalties girls feel between friends, parents, and within themselves.

The Divine Secrets of the Ya Ya Sisterhood by Rebecca Wells, HarperCollins, 1997.
> This book is about mother-daughter relationships and friendships and the special quality of unconditional love that exists between women who have shared all of their lives' best and worst events.

The Handmaid's Tale by Margaret Atwood, Anchor Books, 1998.
> This novel is set near the end of the twentieth century in a United States that has been transformed into a theocracy governed by a strict interpretation of the Bible, where women have very limited roles as wives, maids, "aunts," prostitutes, or handmaids (surrogate mothers).

The House on Mango Street by Sandra Cisneros, Vintage Books, 1991.
> A story about a young girl growing up in the Hispanic quarter of Chicago, where she discovers the fetters of class and gender, the specter of racial enmity, and the mysteries of sexuality—and manages to rise above them.

How the Garcia Girls Lost Their Accents by Julia Alvarez, Dutton Signet, 1992.
> This is a story of four sisters who must adjust to life in America after having to leave their lives of privilege and wealth in the Dominican Republic. They deal with issues of identity, racism, and adapting to American culture.

The Joy Luck Club by Amy Tan, Ivy Books, 1994.
> This book is about four Chinese-born mothers and their American-born daughters and the conflicts that arise as they learn to live in America. This novel demonstrates the complexities of mother-daughter relationships.

My Antonia by Willa Cather, Bantam Classics, reprint edition 1994.
> Set in Nebraska in the late nineteenth century, the story centers on Antonia, the daughter of an immigrant family, and her and her family's struggles with a foreign land and frontier life and the restraints women experienced at the time.

She's Come Undone by Wally Lamb, Pocket Books, 1998.
> Dolores, the main character, learns as she moves from adolescence into adulthood that it's not what a person looks like that matters, but how he or she makes you feel about yourself.

Spider Woman's Granddaughters by Paula Gunn Allen, Fawcett Book Group, 1990.
> A collection of traditional tales, biographical writings, and contemporary short stories by the most accomplished Native American women writing today.

Stones from the River by Ursula Hegi, Simon & Schuster, 1997.
> This book is a fictional work about the Holocaust from the German perspective. The main character, Trudi, is a dwarf living in Nazi Germany and longs to be a normal person.

Their Eyes Were Watching God by Zora Neale Hurston, HarperCollins, 1998.
> A story about Janie Crawford, a beautiful, proud, independent black woman coming of age in early-twentieth-century America who always lives life on her own terms despite the many challenges she experiences.

Time of the Butterflies by Julia Alvarez, Dutton/Plume, reprint edition 1995.
> This novel is set in the Dominican Republic in 1960 and tells the story of the Mirabal sisters, three young wives and mothers who are assassinated after visiting their jailed husbands.

NONFICTION

Girl Power Guides

Am I the Last Virgin?, edited by Tara Roberts, Simon & Schuster, 1997.
> Written for African-American teens but I think its audience is wider. Girls love this book.

Brave New Girls: Creative Ideas to Help Girls be Confident, Healthy, and Happy by Jeanette Goldberg, Fairview Press, 1997.
> Book is for younger girls but has good exercises to get girls thinking.

Changing Bodies, Changing Lives, revised edition, by Ruth Bell and other coauthors of *Our Bodies, Ourselves* together with members of the Teen Book Project. Three Rivers Press, 1998.

Nonjudgmental information about sex, love, friendship, and how the body works, filled with the voices, poems, and cartoons of hundreds of teenagers.

Deal with It! A Whole New Approach to Your Body, Brain, and Life as a Gurl by Esther Drill, Heather McDonald, and Rebecca Odes, Pocket Books, 1999.

Excellent graphics girls can relate to. This book is filled with important information about virginity, hair removal, friends, relationships, anxiety, periods, and other things girls want to know. I can't think of a topic they didn't cover.

Don't Give It Away by Ilyana Vanzant, Fireside Publications, June 1999.

Reviews of this book are glowing! There are workbook exercises to record dreams, thoughts, and ways to get through difficult life experiences. Filled with personal affirmations and strategies for self-empowerment.

Friendship from the New Moon Books, Girls Editorial Board, Crown, 1999.

This fun and honest book is filled with real girls' reflections of what it means to be a friend, with all the ups and downs and lots of helpful girl-to-girl advice. Daughters' newsletter provides parents of girls with the information, guidance, and support they need to raise strong, self-confident daughters. Promotes understanding and foresight as well as taking action; includes great resources and the experiences and wisdom of other parents. I recommend any of New Moon's publications for parents, teachers, and girls.

Girls Know Best: Advice for Girls From Girls on Just about Everything, compiled by Michelle Roehm, Beyond Words, 1997.

For the under-fifteen crowd but has funny descriptions of teachers, natural beauty recipes for skin and hair that are fun, creative, and focus on health instead of the media images, guides for divorce and depression.

My Gender Workbook, by Kate Bornstein, New York: Routledge, 1998.

The Period Book: Everything You Don't Want to Ask (but Need to Know) by Karen Gravelle and Jennifer Gravelle, Walker Publishing, 1996.

The author worked with her fifteen-year-old niece to provide a practical, down-to-earth book about menstruation. Great for girls about to start or starting their periods.

Real Girl, Real World: Tools for Finding Your True Self by Heather Gray and Samantha Phillips, Seal Press, 1998.

Great overview for girls about all the issues from beauty, sexuality, sexual behavior, and sexual assault. It has great resources in every chapter.

Reviving Ophelia: Saving the Selves of Adolescent Girls by Mary Pipher, Ballantine, 1994.

Girls' stories from the "front lines of adolescence." Good book for parents to gain insight into girls' common difficult experiences.

Taking Charge of My Mind and Body: A Girls' Guide to Outsmarting Alcohol, Drug, Smoking, and Eating Problems by Gladys Folkers, M.A., and Jeanne Engelmann, Free Spirit Publishing, 1997.

Probably acceptable for girls up to fifteen. Older girls will blow it off.

Reflections on Girl World

Odd Girl Out: The Hidden Culture of Girls' Aggression by Rachel Simmons, Harcourt Brace, 2001.

This book explores the phenomenon of indirect aggression and bullying between girls. It argues that the culture has refused to define many of these behaviors as formal acts of aggression, instead calling them "rites of passage" that are undeserving of formal strategies to deal with them. The book relies on the stories of girls, parents, and adult women to map out the range of ways girls can inflict pain on their peers.

Ophelia Speaks by Sara Shandler, Harper Perennial, 2000.

A collection of girls' stories about self-esteem, body image, friendships, and violence. Girls love this book!

Ophelia's Mom by Nina Shandler, Crown Books, 2001.

Mothers of adolescent girls speak out in their own words about *their* world.

Promiscuities by Naomi Wolf, Fawcett Books, 1998.

Details the dynamics of girls' sexuality, reputations, and self-esteem.

School Girls: Young Women, Self-Esteem, and the Confidence Gap by Peggy Ornstein, Anchor, 1995.

Based on the American Association of University Women's studies on girls' self-esteem and behavior in the classroom. Ornstein profiles six girls to reflect and comment on girls' overall experiences.

See Jane Win: The Rimm Report on How 1000 Girls Became Successful Women by Dr. Silvia Rimm, Three Rivers Press, 1999.

Great advice on how to assess the "health" of your daughter's environment. Gives concrete advice on more effective parenting.

Slut! Growing Up Female with a Bad Reputation by Leora Tanenbaum, Seven Stories Press, 1999.

Bordering on academic, this book details how the "slut" reputation controls women's and girls' behavior.

Physical Safety

Dating Violence: Young Women in Danger by Barrie Levy, M.S.W., Seal Press, 1993, 1997.

A teen guide to leaving abusive relationships.

Defending Ourselves: A Guide to Prevention, Self-Defense, Recovery from Rape by Rosalind Wiseman, Farrar Straus Giroux, 1995.

Gaeta, Lisa. *IMPACT Personal Safety: Women's Basics Course Workbook.* Tarzana, Calif.: IMPACT, 1993.

Getting Free: You Can End Abuse and Take Back Your Life by Ginny NiCarthy, Seal Press, 1997.

The Gift of Fear by Gavin de Becker, Little Brown & Co., 1997.

Provides excellent strategies for trusting fear and gut instincts to distinguish between real and perceived threats and a detailed description of perpetrators.

Heartbreak and Roses: Real Life Stories of Troubled Love by Janet Bode and Stan Mack, Franklin Watts, 2000.

In Love and Danger by Barrie Levy, Seal Press, 1998.

One of the first books to detail teen abusive relationships. Includes stories and concrete advice.

Protecting the Gift: Keeping Children and Teenagers Safe (and Parents Sane) by Gavin de Becker, The Dial Press, 1999.

The follow-up to *The Gift of Fear* and a parent's guide to keeping children safe and guiding them to develop their own skills and strategies.

Rape Aggression Defense Systems (Student Manual). Norfolk, Va.: R.A.D. Systems, Inc., 1993.

Surviving the Silence: Black Women's Stories of Rape by Charlotte Pierce-Baker, W.W. Norton & Co., 2000.

Tesoro, Mary. *Options for Avoiding Assault: A Guide to Assertiveness, Boundaries and De-Escalation for Violent Confrontations.* San Luis Obispo, Calif.: MMSLO, 1993.

Third Wave Feminism

Listen Up: Voices from the Next Feminist Generation by Barbara Findlen, Seal Press, 2001.

Manifesta by Jennifer Baumgardner and Amy Richards, Farrar Straus Giroux, 2000.
> An easy read that analyzes the history of feminism in the United States and its impact on today's generation of young women. This is a great discussion book.

To Be Real: Telling the Truth and Changing the Face of Feminism by Rebecca Walker, Anchor Books, 1995.

Body Image

Boston Women's Health Book Collective. *Our Bodies, Ourselves for the New Century: A Book by and for Women.* New York: Simon & Schuster, 1998.

Brumberg, Joan Jacobs. *The Body Project: An Intimate History of American Girls.* New York: Random House, 1997.

Claude-Pierre, Peggy. *The Secret Language of Eating Disorders.* New York: Vintage Books, 1999.

Gross, Michael. *Model: The Ugly Business of Beautiful Women.* New York: William Morrow, 1995.

Hirschmann, Jane R., and Carol H. Munter. *When Women Stop Hating Their Bodies: Freeing Yourself from Food and Weight Obsession.* New York: Fawcett Books, 1997.

Orbach, Susie. *Fat Is a Feminist Issue.* New York: Berkley Books, 1994.

Roth, Geneen. *When Food Is Love: Exploring the Relationship Between Eating and Intimacy.* New York: Plume, 1992.

Wolf, Naomi. *The Beauty Myth: How Images of Beauty Are Used Against Women.* New York: Anchor, 1992.

CURRICULUM RESOURCES

Gender, Adolescence, and Schooling

American Association of University Women. *How Schools Shortchange Girls: The AAUW Report.* Washington, D.C.: American Association of University Women Educational Foundation, 1992.

———. *Hostile Hallways: The AAUW Survey on Sexual Harassment in America's Schools.* Washington, D.C.: American Association of University Women Educational Foundation, 1993.

———. *Gender Gaps: Where Schools Still Fail Our Children.* Washington, D.C.: American Association of University Women Educational Foundation, 1999.

———. *Voices of a Generation: Teenage Girls on Sex, School, and Self.* Washington, D.C.: American Association of University Women Educational Foundation, 1999.

Bell, Ruth, *Changing Bodies, Changing Lives: A Book for Teens on Sex and Relationships.* New York: Three Rivers Press, 1998.

Curhan, Jared R., ed. *Teachers Manual: Young Negotiators.* Cambridge, Mass.: Consensus Building Institute, Inc., 1995.

Davidson, Ellen. *Open Minds to Equality: A Sourcebook for Learning Activities to Affirm Diversity and Promote Equity,* 2nd ed. Needham Heights, Mass.: Allyn and Bacon, 1998.

Hill, Marie S., and Frank W. Hill. *Creating Safe Schools: What Principals Can Do.* Thousand Oaks, Calif.: Corwin Press, Inc., 1994.

Karp, Cheryl L., Traci L. Butler, and Sage C. Bergstrom. *Activity Manual for Adolescents*. Thousand Oaks, Calif.: Sage Publications, 1998.

McLaughlin, Karen A., and Kelly J. Brilliant. *Healing the Hate: A National Bias Crime Prevention Curriculum for Middle Schools*. Newton, Mass.: Education Development Center, Inc., 1997.

Meeks, Linda, Randy Page, and Philip Heit. *Violence Prevention: Totally Awesome Teaching Strategies for Safe and Drug-Free Schools*. Blacklick, Ohio: Heit Publishing Co., 1995.

Orenstein, Peggy. *School Girls: Young Women, Self-Esteem, and the Confidence Gap*. New York: Doubleday, 1994.

Sadker, Myra, and David Sadker. *Failing at Fairness: How America's Schools Cheat Girls*. New York: Charles Scribner's Sons, 1994.

Thorne, Barrie. *Gender Play: Girls and Boys in School*. New Brunswick, N.J.: Rutgers University Press, 1993.

Gender, Race, and Adolescence

Apter, T. E., and Ruthellen Josselson. *Best Friends: The Pleasures and Perils of Girls' and Women's Friendships*. New York: Crown Publishing Group, 1999.

Brown, Lyn Mikel. *Raising Their Voices: The Politics of Girls' Anger*. Cambridge, Mass.: Harvard University Press, 1998.

Brown, Lyn Mikel, and Carol Gilligan. *Meeting at the Crossroads: Women's Psychology and Girls' Development*. Cambridge, Mass.: Harvard University Press, 1992.

Carlip, Hillary. *Girl Power: Young Women Speak Out*. New York: Warner Books, 1995.

Harper, Patricia, Gladys B. Baxley, and Linda Y. Fisher. *The Status of Black Adolescent Females in the District of Columbia*. Washington, D.C.: DC Community Prevention Partnership Inc., 1999.

Hersch, Patricia. *A Tribe Apart: A Journey into the Heart of American Adolescence*. New York: Ballantine Books, 1999.

Hooks, Bell. *All About Love: New Visions*. New York: William Morrow, 2000.

Leadbeater, Bonnie J., and Niobe Way. *Urban Girls: Resisting Stereotypes, Creating Identities*. New York: New York University Press, 1996.

Phillips, Lynn. *The Girls Report: What We Know and Need to Know About Growing Up Female*. New York: National Council for Research on Women, 1998.

Taylor, Jill McLean, Carol Gilligan, and Amy Sullivan. *Between Voice and Silence: Women and Girls, Race and Relationship*. Cambridge, Mass.: Harvard University Press, 1995.

Tracy, Laura. *The Secret Between Us: Competition Among Women*. Boston: Little, Brown, 1991.

Way, Niobe. *Everyday Courage: The Lives and Stories of Urban Teenagers*. New York: New York University Press, 1998.

Sex and Sexuality

Artz, Sibylle. *Sex, Power, and the Violent School Girl*. New York: Columbia Teachers College Press, 1999.

Bass, E., and K. Kaufman. *Free Your Mind: The Book for Gay, Lesbian, and Bisexual Youth and Their Allies*. New York: Harper Perennial, 1996.

Heron, A. *One Teenager in Ten: Writings by Lesbian and Gay Youth*. Boston: Alyson Publications, 1983.

Kirby, Douglas. *No Easy Answers: Research Findings on Programs to Reduce Teen Pregnancy*. Washington, D.C.: National Campaign to Prevent Teen Pregnancy, 1997.

Maynard, Rebecca A., ed. *Kids Having Kids: Special Report on the Costs of Adolescent Child-bearing.* New York: Robin Hood Foundation, 1996.

Roberts, Tara. *Am I the Last Virgin? and Other Tales About Black Female Sexuality.* New York: Simon & Schuster, 1997.

Schoen, Cathy, Karen Davis, and Karen Scott Collins. *The Commonwealth Fund Survey of the Health of Adolescent Girls.* New York: Commonwealth Fund Commission on Women's Health, 1997.

Thompson, Sharon. *Going All the Way: Teenage Girls' Tales of Sex, Romance, and Pregnancy.* New York: Hill and Wang, 1995.

Sexual Harassment and Homophobia

Anti-Gay/Lesbian Violence in the United States: Local and National Trends, Analysis, and Incident Summaries. New York: Gay and Lesbian Anti-Violence Project, 1994.

Blumfield, W. J., ed. *Homophobia: How We All Pay the Price.* Boston: Beacon Press, 1992.

Friend, Richard A. "Choices, Not Closets: Heterosexism and Homophobia in Schools." In *Beyond Silenced Voices: Class, Race, and Gender in United States Schools.*, edited by Lois Weis and Michelle Fine. Albany: State University of New York Press, 1993.

Friends of Project 10. *Project 10 Handbook: Addressing Lesbian and Gay Issues in Our Schools.* Los Angeles: Friends of Project 10.

Larkin, J. *Sexual Harassment: High School Girls Speak Out.* Toronto: Second Story Press, 1994.

Pharr, S. *Homophobia: A Weapon of Sexism.* Inverness, Calif.: Chardon Press, 1988.

Stein, N., and L. Sjostrom. *Flirting or Hurting? A Guide on Student-to-Student Sexual Harassment in Schools.* Wellesley, Mass.: Wellesley College Center for Research on Women, 1994.

Stein, N. D., N. Marshall, and L. Tropp. *Secrets in Public: Sexual Harassment in Our Schools.* Wellesley, Mass.: Wellesley College Center for Research on Women, 1993.

Abusive Relationships

American Psychological Association. *Violence and Youth.* Washington, D.C.: American Psychological Association, 1993.

Buchwald, E., P. Fletcher, and M. Roth. *Transforming a Rape Culture.* Minneapolis, Minn.: Milkweed Editions, 1993.

Denfeld, Rene. *Kill the Body the Head Will Fall: A Closer Look at Women, Violence and Aggression.* New York: Warner Books, 1997.

Enns, Greg, and Jan Black. *It's Not Okay Anymore: Your Personal Guide to Ending Abuse, Taking Charge & Loving Yourself.* Salem, Oreg.: Hannibat House, Inc., 1996.

Everyday Violence: How Women and Men Experience Sexual and Physical Danger. Pandora Press, 1990.

Expect Respect: A Support Group Curriculum for Preventing Teenage Dating Violence and Promoting Healthy Relationships. Austin, Tex.: Safe Place, 1995.

Fairstein, Linda A. *Sexual Violence: Our War Against Rape.* New York: William Morrow and Co, Inc., 1993.

Ferrato, Donna. *Living with the Enemy.* New York: Arpeture Foundation, 1991.

Francisco, Patricia Weaver. *Telling: A Memoir of Rape and Recovery.* New York: Cliff Street Books, 1999.

Johnson, Kathryn M. *If You Are Raped: What Every Woman Needs to Know.* Homes Beach, Fla.: Learning Publishing, Inc., 1985.

Jones, Ann. *Women Who Kill: Battered Women That Killed in Self-Defense*. New York: Ballantine Books, 1980.

Gordon, Margaret T., and Stephanie Riger. *The Female Fear: The Social Cost of Rape*. Chicago: University of Illinois Press, 1991.

Hanmar, Jalna, and Mary Maynard, eds. *Women, Violence and Social Control*. Atlantic Highlands, N.J.: Humanities Press International Inc., 1987.

Hester, Marianne, Liz Kelly, and Jill Radford. *Women, Violence and Male Power*. Philadelphia: Open University Press, 1996.

Kelly, Liz. *Surviving Sexual Violence*. Minneapolis: University of Minnesota Press, 1988.

Ledray, Linda E. *Recovering from Rape*. New York: Henry Holt and Co., Inc., 1986.

Lees, Sue. *Ruling Passions: Sexual Violence, Reputation and the Law*. Philadelphia: Open University Press, 1997.

McCaughey, Martha. *Real Knockouts: The Physical Feminism of Women's Self-Defense*. New York: New York University Press, 1997.

Michael, Lee. *I Started to Say "I Love You" but Your Fist Got in the Way and Other Love Poems!* Kingston, NY: Quinn Publishing, 1994.

Nelson, Joan M. *Self-Defense: Steps to Success*. Champaign, Ill.: Leisure Press, 1991.

Odem, Mary E., and Jody Clay-Warner. *Confronting Rape and Sexual Assault*. Wilmington, Del.: Scholarly Resources, Inc., 1998.

Preventing Violence Against Women: Not Just a Women's Issue. Washington, D.C.: National Crime Prevention Council, 1995.

Prothrow-Stith, Deborah, with Michaele Weissman. *Deadly Consequences: How Violence Is Destroying Our Teenage Population and a Plan to Begin Solving the Problem*. New York: Harper Perennial, 1991.

Raine, Nancy V. *After Silence: Rape and My Journey Back*. New York: Three Rivers Press, 1998.

Reality of Women and Guns. Washington, D.C.: Violence Policy Center, 1994.

Sanday, Peggy Reeves. *Fraternity Gang Rape: Sex, Brotherhood, and Privilege on Campus*. New York: New York University Press, 1990.

The Silent Witness National Initiative Report on Domestic Homicide Reduction in the United States. Minneapolis, Minn.: The Silent Witness National Initiative, 2000.

Sousa, Carole, Lundy Bancroft, and Ted German. *Preventing Teen Dating Violence: A Three-Session Curriculum for Teaching Adolescents*. Cambridge, Mass.: Dating Violence Intervention Project.

Stalking and Domestic Violence: The 3rd Annual Report to Congress Under the Violence Against Women Act. Washington, D.C.: U.S. Department of Justice, 1998.

Stanko, Elizabeth. *Intimate Intrusions: Women's Experience of Male Violence*. Boston: Routledge, 1985.

Vachss, Alice. *Sex Crimes: 10 Years on the Front Lines Prosecuting Rapists and Confronting Their Collaborators*. New York: Random House, 1993.

Violence Against Women. Washington, D.C.: District of Columbia Commission on Violence Against Women, 1998.

Warshaw, Robin. *I Never Called It Rape*. New York: Harper and Row, 1988.

Wolfe, L. R., and J. Tucker. *Victims No More: Girls Fight Back Against Male Violence*. Washington, D.C.: Center for Women Policy Studies, 1997.

Women in Criminal Justice: A Twenty Year Update. Rockville, Md.: National Criminal Justice Reference Service, 1998.

Women's Self-Defense: A Complete Guide to Assault Prevention. Los Angeles: Commission on Assaults Against Women, 1987.

Empowering Boys

Boyd-Franklin, Nancy, A. J. Franklin, and Pamela Toussaint. *Boys into Men: Raising Our African American Teenage Sons*. New York: Dutton, 2000.

Creighton, Allan, and Paul Kivel. *Helping Teens Stop Violence: A Practical Guide for Counselors, Educators and Parents*. Alameda, Calif.: Hunter House, 1992.

Garbarino, James. *Lost Boys: Why Our Sons Turn Violent and How We Can Save Them*. New York: Free Press, 1999.

Gurian, Michael. *A Fine Young Man*. New York: Putnam, 1999.

Hersch, Patricia. *A Tribe Apart: A Journey into the Heart of American Adolescence*. New York: Ballantine Books, 1999.

Katz, Jackson. "More than a few good men: strategies for inspiring boys and young men to be allies in anti-sexist education." Working paper series, Wellesley, MA. Wellesley Center for Research on Women, 1998. (Jackson Katz has also done an excellent video, "Tough Guise: Violence, Media, and the Crisis of Masculinity." Media Education Network, 2000.)

Kimmel, Michael, *Manhood in America: A Cultural History*. New York: Free Press, 1996.

Kindlon, Daniel, and Michael Thompson. *Raising Cain: Protecting the Emotional Life of Boys*. New York: Ballantine Books, 1999.

Kivel, Paul. *Boys Will Be Men: Raising Our Sons for Courage, Caring and Community*. Canada: New Society Publishers, 1999.

Kivel, Paul. *Growing Up Male: Identifying Violence in My Life* (Workbook). Center City, Minn.: Hazelden Educational Materials, 1993.

———. *Men's Work* (Facilitator's Guide). Center City, Minn.: Hazelden Educational Materials, 1993.

Kivel, Paul, and Allan Creighton. *Making the Peace: A Fifteen-Session Violence Prevention Curriculum for Young People*. Oakland, Calif.: Hunter House Publishers.

McCall, Nathan. *Makes Me Wanna Holler: A Young Black Man in America*. New York: Vintage Books, 1994.

Pollack, William. *Real Boys: Rescuing Our Sons from the Myths of Boyhood*. New York: Random House, 1998.

Pollack, William, and Todd Shuster. *Real Boys' Voices*. New York: Random House, 2000.

Real, Terrence. *I Don't Want to Talk About It: Overcoming the Secret Legacy of Male Depression*. New York: Fireside, 1997.

Way, Niobe. *Everyday Courage: The Lives and Stories of Urban Teenagers*. New York: New York University Press, 1998.

Good Organizations and Their Websites

Unfortunately, I am sure I will not know to include many worthwhile organizations. For the most up-to-date list, contact the Empower Program website at www.empowerprogram.org.

Advocates for Youth
1025 Vermont Avenue NW, Suite 200
Washington, DC 20005
Phone: 202-347-5700
www.advocatesforyouth.org

Alan Guttmacher Institute
NEW YORK
120 Wall Street, 21st Floor
New York, NY 10005
Phone: 212-248-1111
www.alanguttmacher.org

WASHINGTON, D.C.
1120 Connecticut Avenue NW, Suite 460
Washington, DC 20036
Phone: 202-296-4012
www.agi-usa.org

American Association of University Women
1111 Sixteenth Street NW
Washington, DC 20036
Phone: 800-326-AAUW
www.aauw.org

Break the Cycle
P.O. Box 64996
Los Angeles, CA 90064
Phone: 310-286-3366 or 888-988-TEEN
www.break-the-cycle.org

Coalition for Positive Sexuality
3712 North Broadway, Suite 191
Chicago, IL 60613
Phone: 773-604-1654
www.cps@positive.org

Communities Against Violence Network (CAVNET)
www.cavnet2.org

Corporate Alliance to End Partner Violence
2416 East Washington, Suite E
Bloomington, IL 61704
Phone: 309-664-0747
www.caepv.org

Dads and Daughters
P.O. Box 3458
Duluth, MN 55803
218-722-3942
www.dadsanddaughters.org

Family Violence Prevention Fund
383 Rhode Island Street, Suite 304
San Francisco, CA 94103-5133
Phone: 415-252-8900
www.fund@fvpf.org

Feminist Majority Foundation
1600 Wilson Boulevard, Suite 801
Arlington, VA 22209
www.feminist.org

Findthegood.org
The Colorado Bar Association
1900 Grant Street, 9th floor
Denver, CO 80203
303-824-4345
www.findthegood.org

**Gay, Lesbian, and Straight Education
    Network (GLSEN)**
122 West 26th Street, Suite 1100
New York, NY 10001
Phone: 212-727-0135
Fax: 212-727-0254
E-mail: GLSEN@glsen.org
www.glsen.org

Girl Scouts
420 Fifth Avenue
New York, NY 10018
Phone: 800-GSUSA-4-U
www.girlscouts.org

Girls Incorporated
120 Wall Street
New York, NY 10005
www.girlsinc.org

Gurl.com
1440 Broadway, 21st Floor
New York, NY 10018
www.gurl.com

JacksonKatz.com
Mentors in Violence Prevention Center for
    the Study of Sport in Society
716 Columbus Avenue, Suite 161
Boston, MA 02120
Phone: 617-373-4025
www.sportinsociety.org/mvp.html

Ms. Foundation
120 Wall Street, 33rd Floor
New York, NY 10005
Phone: 212-742-2300
www.ms.foundation.org

National Center for Victims of Crimes
www.nvc.org

**National Coalition Against Domestic
    Violence**
1532 16th Street NW
Washington, DC 20036
Phone: 202-745-1211
Fax: 202-745-0088
www.ncadv.org

**National Partnership for Women and
    Families**
1875 Connecticut Avenue NW, Suite 650
Washington, DC 20009
Phone: 202-986-2600
Fax: 202-986-2539
www.nationalpartnership.org

**New Moon: A Magazine for Girls and
    Their Dreams**
P.O. Box 3620
Duluth, MN 55803
Phone: 800-381-4743
www.newmoon.org

PROJECT 10
www.project10.org

Riotgrrl.com
www.riotgrrl.com

Sexuality Information and Education Council
130 West 42nd Street, Suite 350
New York, NY 10036-7802
Phone: 212-819-9770
www.siecus.org

Sexual Minority Youth Assistance League (SMYAL)
410 7th Street SE
Washington, DC 20003-2707
Phone: 202-546-5940
www.smyal.org

Silent Witness National Initiative
20 Second Street NE, Suite 1101
Minneapolis, MN 55413
Phone: 612-623-0999
www.silentwitness.net

Stalkingvictims.com
P.O. Box 400
Arnold, CA 95222
www.stalkingvictims.com

Third Wave Foundation
116 East 16th Street, 7th Floor
New York, NY 10003
www.thirdwavefoundation.org
Phone: 212-388-1898
Fax: 212-982-3321

Index

Abusive relationships, 10–13, 177, 235, 242, 254, 269–274, 302, 305–306
  defining, 269–270
  recognizing, 269
  resources on, 325
  spotting potential abusers, 274
  statistics on, 272
  talking about, 272–274
Academic accomplishments, hiding, 32, 114, 115
Acid, 282
Acting ghetto, 90, 93
Actual Happy Person, 129
Advocates for Youth, 328
African-American girls, 87–94, 106
Alan Guttmacher Institute, 328
Alcohol, 51, 211, 276–284, 292–294, 298
  talking about, 292–293
Aloof/Distant Guy, 180, 181
American Association of University Women, 179, 328
Anorexia, 85, 105
Apologies, 141, 148–150, 161, 162
Appearance (*see* Beauty Pageant)
Asian-American girls, 87–88
Athletes, 39, 79, 114, 115, 126

Bad boyfriends, 259, 264–265
Bad teasing, 116, 118–120

Bad words, 117
Banker, 25, 29–30, 33, 47, 209
Barbie, 80
Beauty Myth, The (Wolf), 105
Beauty pageant, 75–110
  body hair, 96, 106–107
  body image, 80–81
  breasts, 82–84, 102
  clothing, 28, 75–77, 96–101
  definitions of femininity, 77–79, 87, 177
  markers, 82, 91, 96, 107
  obsession with appearance, 76–81, 86–87
  racist standards of, 87–94
  teen magazines, 78–81
  weight, 84–85, 103–106
Beer Cup Girl, 211, 281
Benign Neglect Parent, 51–52
Berry, Halle, 88, 89
Best Friend Parent, 50, 51
Best-friend relationships, 162–166
Big Girl/Tomboy, 126
Bill of Rights
  Daughter's (*see* Daughter's Bill of Rights)
  Parental, 55–56, 97
Birth control, 253, 254, 266–267
Bitch, use of word, 116, 117
Blowing each other off, 166–171, 241–242, 260, 261
Body hair, 106–107

Body image, 80–81
    resources on, 321
Boring stories, 63
Boyfriend Stealer, 127–128
Boyfriend stealing, 242–243
Boy-girl relationships, 201–233 (see also
    Abusive relationships)
    bad boyfriends, 259, 264–265
    Bill of Rights, 216–218
    boyfriend stealing, 242–243
    breakups, 212–213, 232–233, 262
    communication in, 186–188, 244–247,
        260–262
    crushes, 204–205, 207
    dances, 206
    dating, 203–204, 231, 236–239, 260, 261
    fathers and, 218–219
    fighting over boys, 211–212
    flirting versus sexual harassment, 247–253
    Fruit Cup Girl, 209–211
    going out, 236, 239
    hooking up, 236, 238
    matchmaking, 205–209, 240–241
    obsessions, 205
    oral sex, 256–258
    parties (see Parties)
    pleasing boys, 243–244, 246–247, 255
    positive relationships, 259–260
    running in packs, 230
    sex education, 219–220
    sexual, 253–259, 261, 265–268, 284,
        296–297
    talking about, 214–220
Boy personality profiles
    Aloof/Distant Guy, 180, 181
    Desperate Annoying Guy, 181
    Geek, 181
    Good-Boy Jock, 182
    Misunderstood Guy, 180, 181
    Mr. Unattainable, 182
    Nice Guy, 180–181
    Player Guy, 181, 182
    Thug/Bad Boy, 180, 181
Boys Don't Cry (movie), 225
Boy World, 175–200 (see also Boy-girl
    relationships)
    cliques, 183–185
    definition of masculinity, 176–179,
        188–190, 192, 195
    homophobia and, 187, 189–191
    honor codes, 191–192, 194
    personality profiles (see Boy personality
        profiles)
    questions about girls, 186–188

    thoughts about girls, 185–186
    violence, 179, 189–196, 226–227
Break the Cycle, 326
Breakups, 212–213, 232–234, 262
Breasts, 82–84, 102
Bulimia, 105

Caller ID, 66
Call waiting, 207
Carrie (movie), 120
Cell phones, 67–68
Check-in time, 230
Cliques, 18–48 (see also Beauty pageant;
    Power plays)
    boy, 183–185
    definition of, 19
    gossiping and, 111–113, 121–124,
        135–150
    parental, 55
    positions in, 24–36
    power of, 13, 23
    reputations and (see Reputations)
    rules of, 37
    as self-reinforcing, 40
    talking about, 46–48
    teasing and (see Teasing)
Clothing, 28, 75–77, 96–101
Coalition for Positive Sexuality, 236
Codeine, 282
Coming out, 225–226
Communication, 14, 49–74
    about dress, 75–77, 96–101
    affirmations, 61, 97
    allies and, 62
    boring stories, 63
    in boy-girl relationships, 186–188,
        244–247, 260–262
    get-togethers, 57–60
    listening, 59–60, 63
    lying and sneaking, 63–71
    opening up lines of, 56–59
    problem solving and, 61–62
    reconnaissance strategies, 67–68
    silence and, 62
    using slang, 61
Communities Against Violence Network
    (CAVNET), 328
Condoms, 253, 266–267
Conference call capacity, 207
Contraception, 253, 254, 266–267
Corporate Alliance to End Partner Violence,
    328
Counselors, choice of, 311–312
Crowe, Russell, 197

Cruise, Tom, 197
Crushes, 204–205, 207
Curriculum resources, 323–327

Dads and Daughters, 329
Dances, 206
Date rape, 177, 242, 284–286, 295, 298–303
Dating, 203–204, 231, 236–239, 260, 261
Daughter's Bill of Rights
    with Boyfriends, 216–218
    with Friends, 159, 169, 172, 173
    with Parents, 56
Defending Ourselves (Wiseman), 306
Depression, 310
Desperate Annoying Guy, 181
Diaries, reading, 68
Divided loyalties, 156–162
Don't-Ask, Don't-Tell Parent, 53
Dress (*see* Clothing)
Dressing room privacy, 104
Drugs, 211, 280, 281, 292–294
    availability of, 282
    talking about, 292–293

Eating disorders, 85, 105–106, 310
Ecstasy, 282
E-mail
    privileges, 71, 72
    reading, 68
Evil popularity, 23–24, 114

Family Violence Prevention Fund, 329
Fathers, 5–6, 72, 98, 218–219
Femininity, definitions of, 77–79, 87, 177
Feminism, 78, 83, 188, 196, 323
Feminist Majority Foundation, 329
Fiction resources, 319–320
Fighting over boys, 211–212
Findthegood.org, 329
Fine Young Man, A (Gurian), 191
Flirting versus sexual harassment, 247–253
Floater, 25, 30–31, 47
Flunkie, in boy cliques, 184
Fruit Cup Girl, 209–211, 228, 281

Gang rape, 189
Gay, Lesbian, and Straight Education
    Network (GLSEN), 329
Gay Student Alliances (GSA), 227
Gay students, 128–129, 221–228
Geek, 181
Gender identity, 222
Gender stereotypes, 176, 177
Get Real (movie), 225

Get Wit's (G.W.'s), in boy cliques, 184–185
Girl Scouts, 329
Girls Incorporated, 329
Girl World (*see* Beauty pageant; Boy-girl
    relationships; Cliques; Power plays;
    Reputations)
Going out, 236, 239
Good-Boy Jock, 182
Good liars, 64–65
Good popularity, 23–24, 114
Good teasing, 116–117
Gossiping, 111–113, 121–124
    dealing with, 135–150
    parental, 122, 135
Group dynamics (*see* Cliques; Power plays)
Gurian, Michael, 191, 192
Gurl.com, 329

Hairstyles, 92–93, 96, 98
Halloween, 100–101
Hamm, Mia, 79
Hash, 282
Hazing, 193, 194
Heroin, 281
Heterosexism, 222
Hip Parent, 51, 288
HIV (human immunodeficiency virus),
    257
Homophobia, 40, 128, 179, 187, 189–191,
    222–224, 226–227
    resources on, 325
Homosexuality, 221–228
Honor codes, 191–192, 194
Hooking up, 236, 238

Image (*see* Reputations)
Imaginary audience syndrome, 122–123
*Incredible Story of Two Girls Falling in Love,
    The* (movie), 225
Indian girls, 89
In-Your-Face Angry Girl, 125–126

JacksonKatz.com, 329
Jock, 126–127
Journal of the American Medical Association,
    13
Junk food, 104–105
"Just Say No" campaign, 294

Katz, Jackson, 190
Ketamine, 282
Killing Us Softly (video), 105
Kindlon, Daniel, 176
Knowles, Beyonce, 88

Leader, in boy cliques, 183
Lesbian/Butch/Dike, 128–129
Lesbians, 221–228
LGBTQ (lesbian, gay, bisexual, transgendered, and questioning), 222
Listening, 59–60, 63
Lock-Her-in-a-Closet Parent, 50
Loner, 126
Lopez, Jennifer, 88, 89
Loving Hard-Ass Parent, 54
Lying, 63–71

Madonna philosophy, 84
Magazines, 78–81
Makeup, 96–97
Maps, of school, 40–45
Marijuana, 185, 282
Markers, 82, 91, 96, 107
Masculinity, definition of, 176–179, 188–190, 192, 195
Matchmaking, 205–209, 240–241
Ma Vie en Rose (movie), 225
Media influences, 7, 10, 80–82, 103
Messenger (see Pleaser/Wannabe/Messenger)
Metal detectors, 195–196
Methamphetamine, 282
Mr. Unattainable, 182
Misunderstood Guy, 180, 181
Movies, 120, 225, 317–318
Ms. Foundation, 329
Mushrooms, 282
Music, 126

National Center for Victims of Crimes, 329
National Coalition Against Domestic Violence, 329
National Partnership for Women and Families, 329
New Moon: A Magazine for Girls and Their Dreams, 329
Nice Guy, 180–181
Nitrous oxide, 282
No-Excuses Parent, 52
Nonfiction resources, 320–323
No-Privacy Parent, 52–53
Nyquil/Robitussin, 282

Obsessions, 205
Occult, 126
Oral sex, 256–258
Organizations, 328–330
Overbearing Parent, 53

Parental Bill of Rights, 55–56, 97
Parenting styles, 49–54
    Benign Neglect Parent, 51–52
    Best Friend Parent, 50, 51
    Don't-Ask, Don't Tell Parent, 53
    Hip Parent, 51
    Lock-Her-in-a-Closet Parent, 50
    Loving Hard-Ass Parent, 54
    No-Excuses Parent, 52
    No-Privacy Parent, 52–53
    Overbearing Parent, 53
    Private Parent, 52
    Pushover Parent, 51
    Worried Parent, 53
Parties, 28, 51, 228–230, 276–298
    date rape and, 284–286, 295, 298–303
    drugs and alcohol at, 276–284, 292–294, 298
    safety in numbers, 297–298
    uninvited to, 153–156
    unplanned, 288–290
Peer pressure, talking about, 292–294
Pelvic exams, 268
Percocet, 282
Perfect Girl, 127
PFLAG, 225
Phone privileges, 71, 72
Physical development, 82–84, 102
Piercing, 77, 96
Pipher, Mary, 122
Player Guy, 181, 182
Pleaser/Wannabe/Messenger, 25, 28, 29, 33–34, 47
    gossiping and teasing and, 119, 136
    matchmaking and, 209
    parties and, 154, 156
Pollack, William, 176–178
Popularity, 20–23 (see also Cliques)
    good versus evil, 23–24, 114
Positive relationships, 259–260
Power plays, 151–174
    best-friend relationships, 162–166
    blowing each other off, 166–171
    dealing with, 171–174
    divided loyalties and tag-alongs, 156–162
    uninvited to parties, 153–156
Pregnancy, 253–254, 257
Principals, talking to, 146
Privacy, 4–5, 267–268
Private Parent, 52
Problem solving, 61–62
Professional help, 302, 305–312
PROJECT 10, 329
Puberty, 82–84, 102–103

Punishment, 71, 72
Pushover Parent, 51

Queen Bee, 25–27, 47, 81, 82, 91 (see also Cliques)
  dating and, 238, 240
  gossiping and teasing and, 119, 135–136, 138–147
  matchmaking and, 208–209
  parties and, 154, 155
Quiet, Morose Girl/Loner, 126

Racism, 40, 87–94, 196
Raising Cain: Protecting the Emotional Life of Boys (Kindlon and Thompson), 176
Rape, 177, 242, 284–286, 295, 298–303
  resources on, 322
Reagan, Nancy, 294
Real Boys: Rescuing Our Sons from the Myths of Boyhood (Pollack), 176
Real Boys' Voices (Pollack), 177–178
Reconnaissance strategies, 67–68
Rejection, 212–213, 232–233, 262
Relationships (see Abusive relationships; Best-friend relationships; Boy-girl relationships)
Reputations, 39, 112, 124–134
  Actual Happy Person, 129
  Boyfriend Stealer, 127–128
  In-Your-Face Angry Girl, 125–126
  Jock, 126–127
  Lesbian/Butch/Dike, 128–129
  Perfect Girl, 127
  Quiet, Morose Girl/Loner, 126
  Slut, 129–134
  Social Climber, 127
  Square, 129
  Teacher's Pet, 127
  Tease, 128
Resources
  curriculum, 321–325
  feminist reading, 321–322
  fiction, 319–320
  nonfiction, 320–323
Reviving Ophelia (Pipher), 122
Riotgrrl.com, 329
Ritalin/Adderall, 282
Rites of passage (see Power plays)
Rohypnol ("Roofies"), 298
Role models, 72–73
Running away, 291–292

Safe rides, 295
Safe School Initiative: An Interim Report on the Prevention of Targeted Violence in Schools, 195
School directory, 67
Self-esteem, 10, 20, 79, 80, 174
Sex education, 219–220
Sexism, 40, 93
Sexual harassment, 12
  flirting versus, 247–253
  resources on, 324–325
  responding to, 260, 263–264
Sexuality, 83–84, 129–133, 188
  resources on, 322
Sexuality Information and Education Council, 330
Sexually transmitted diseases (STDs), 253, 255, 257, 268
Sexual Minority Youth Assistance League (SMYAL), 330
Sexual orientation, 221–228
Sexual promiscuity, 39, 254
Sexual relationships, 253–259, 261, 265–268, 284, 296–297
Sexy clothing, 98–101, 130, 187
Shame, 52
Shaving, 96, 106–107
Sidekick, 25, 27–28, 47
  parties and, 155
  teasing and, 119
Silence, 62
Silent Witness National Initiative, 330
Slang, 61
Slut, use of word, 117
Slut reputation, 129–134
Sneaking, 290
  good sneaks, 66–67
  out of house, 71
Social Climber, 127
Square, 129
Stalkingvictims.com, 330

Tag-alongs, 156–162
Tannen, Deborah, 245
Target, 25, 33, 34–36, 48, 154
Teachers, talking to, 142–143, 145–146
Teacher's Pet, 127
Tease, 128
Teasing, 112, 113, 115–121
  bad, 116, 118–120
  Big Girl/Tomboy, 126
  dealing with, 135–150
  good, 116–117
  outside clique, 119–121
  unintentional bad, 116, 117–118
Teen magazines, 78–81

Telephone calls, 66, 207
Third Wave Foundation, 330
Thompson, Michael, 176
Thug, in boy cliques, 184
Thug/Bad Boy, 180, 181
Tomboy, 126
Torn Bystander, 25, 31–33, 47
Transsexual, 222
Transvestite, 222
Trust, 69–71

Unintentional bad teasing, 116, 117–118
Uninvited to parties, 153–156
United States Secret Service National Threat
    Assessment Center, 195
Unplanned parties, 288–290
Us-versus-the-world mentality, 19

Valium, 282
Vandalism, 280

Vicodin, 282
Victoria's Secret, 78, 79
Violence, 179, 189–196, 226–227
Virginity, definition of, 254–255

Wannabe (see Pleaser/Wannabe/Messenger)
Websites, 328–330
Weight, 84–85, 103–106
Wigger, 93
Williams, Andy, 196
Williams, Serena, 79
Williams, Venus, 79
Wolf, Naomi, 105
Worried Parent, 53

Xanax, 282

You Just Don't Understand (Tannen), 245

Zero-tolerance strategies, 195–196, 294

About the Author

ROSALIND WISEMAN is the cofounder and president of the Empower Program, a nonprofit organization that empowers youth to stop the culture of violence. Empower recognizes that children live within a culture where they are socialized to be perpetrators, bystanders, or targets of violence. Empower's revolutionary approach teaches boys and girls to transform their silence into effective action.

Ms. Wiseman has written several articles on violence against women and girls' self-esteem. She is the author of *Defending Ourselves: A Guide to Prevention, Self-Defense, and Recovery from Rape*, published by Farrar, Straus, and Giroux in 1995.

Ms. Wiseman speaks throughout the country at universities, corporations, schools, and associations, including the American Association of University Women, the Millennium Conference on Domestic Violence, National Organization for Women's Young Feminists Summit, the National Educational Association, the National Crime Prevention Conference, the Young Presidents Organization, the Congressional Youth Leadership Conference, the National Capital Girl Scout Council, the International Association of Chiefs of Police, and the National Football League.

She has been profiled on *The Oprah Show* and interviewed on national television and radio including *CBS Evening News with Dan Rather*, CNN, and National Public Radio affiliates throughout the country. She has been featured in *USA Today Weekend*, *Ms. Magazine*, *17 Magazine*, the *Washington Post*, and *Seventeen*, among others.